P9-DMY-718

To John from
John
July, 1981

The Religion
of the
Republic

The
Religion
of the Republic

Edited by ELWYN A. SMITH

FORTRESS PRESS

PHILADELPHIA

Library of Congress Catalog Card Number 70–130326

2600E70   Printed in the United States of America   1–49

Contents

Foreword

ELWYN A. SMITH

Religion, families of religions, denominations, and sects we know. Yet the student of American life is constantly reminded that amid the mixed waters of immigration, revivalism, and religious thought a mainstream struggles to disclose itself. Why have American religious groups never spawned sedition? Why have they been patriotic to the point of ethical delinquency? Why have they so uniformly praised the First Amendment to the Constitution?

American religious groups have usually shrunk from the notion of a common denominator—"cold water religion," Catholic Bishop John Hughes of New York called it—and no common faith has emerged by that route. But there is tantalizing evidence of general fidelity to . . . precisely what?

Will Herberg has called this object "the American way of life."[1] John E. Smylie has answered, "the nation itself."[2] Robert N. Bellah has suggested that the American faith may be read in national rituals which compose and express an "institutionalized civil religion."[3] Sidney E. Mead sees in Abraham Lincoln the premier theologian of the "religion of the republic."[4] Long familiar is John Dewey's "common faith," a conception with particular appeal in a sectarianized America: "the unification of the self through allegiance to inclusive ideal ends."[5]

1. Will Herberg, *Protestant, Catholic, Jew: An Essay in American Religious Sociology*, new rev. ed. (Garden City: Doubleday & Co., 1960 [paperback]).
2. John E. Smylie, "National Ethos and the Church," *Theology Today* 20 (1963): 313–14.
3. Robert N. Bellah, "Civil Religion in America," *Daedalus*, vol. 96, no. 1 (1967), pp. 1 ff.
4. Sidney E. Mead, "Abraham Lincoln's 'Last Best Hope of Earth': The American Dream of Destiny and Democracy," *Church History* 23 (1954): 3 ff.; and idem, " 'The Nation with the Soul of a Church,' " *Church History* 36 (1967): 262 ff.
5. John Dewey, *A Common Faith*, Terry Lectures (New Haven: Yale University Press, 1934), p. 33.

The public schools were considered from their origin a principal instrument for the moral elevation of the people; and George Washington warned in 1796 that it was perilous to separate morals from religion. The vehemence of the disputes that swirl around public education are largely to be explained by widespread agreement with Washington's judgment, which perhaps justifies the suggestion that the American public school system is the nation's equivalent to the European established church.

Here, then, is the subject and problem of this book: How is the *general* American phenomenon of religion to be described, analyzed, and evaluated?

The title we have selected, *The Religion of the Republic,* has at least the merit of directing attention to religious phenomena that bear upon the welfare of the republican society of the American people. There is scarcely an imported faith that has not felt the authoritative touch of "Americanization"; precisely what that term has meant must be determined by historical examination of the encounter of the several religious groups with American culture. If no "religion of the Republic" differentiated itself from surrounding society by the dramatic appearance of charismatic lawgivers, novel doctrines, an exotic ethos, a distinctive priesthood, and a new sacred literature—Mormonism provides such a model—something of the reverse occurred: religious meanings and values were attributed to the American Republic. For example, the Bible has repeatedly been declared to be its source of moral vigor, and all its presidents, save one, required to pay at least lip service to Protestant doctrine and rule. A few, caught in such tragic choices as dominated the later career of Abraham Lincoln, have drawn heavily on the religious resource tenaciously preserved in the Puritan tradition.

We leave the further exposition of the religion of the Republic to the authors of this book. How the phenomenon ought to be described, what it may mean—in short, how it ought to be named —all await more conclusive determination. This book is designed to inform and advance that inquiry.

1

The Status of
"Civil Religion" in America

JOHN F. WILSON

In 1967 Robert N. Bellah published an article which he titled "Civil Religion in America." Its thesis was summarized in the first sentence: "There actually exists alongside of and rather clearly differentiated from the churches an elaborate and well-institutionalized civil religion in America."[1] Bellah argued that this phenomenon must be understood sympathetically because it possesses "its own seriousness and integrity and requires the same care in understanding that any other religion does."[2] His article suggested what terms might be appropriate for such an analysis. In the present discussion, I am concerned to assess "civil religion" as a concept through which to clarify religious aspects of contemporary American culture.

Civil Religion in America? Bellah began his discussion with a reference to President John F. Kennedy's inaugural address (January 20, 1961) in which "God" was mentioned three times. He understands these references, in context, to be the "statement of a theme that lies very deep in the American tradition, namely, the obligation, both collective and individual, to carry out God's will on earth,"[3] and as such it clearly exemplifies "civil religion." American civil religion, Bellah believes, rises from primordial national events, e.g., the Declaration of Independence, as well as subsequent "words and

1. Robert N. Bellah, "Civil Religion in America," *Daedalus,* vol. 96, no. 1 (1967), p. 1.
2. Ibid.
3. Ibid., p. 5.

1

acts of the founding fathers," and he traces the manner in which they have been appropriated. Thus the Revolutionary era has been celebrated within American civil religion as the founding period of the cult. In a basic respect the tone and cast of these materials is Hebraic and suggestive of the Old Testament. New elements (seemingly more "Christian" in tone) derive from the national experience of civil war. Especially Lincoln is prominent as a Christ-figure, and associated with him have been the explicit "themes of death, sacrifice, and rebirth."[4] Bellah also believes that Memorial Day and Thanksgiving, together with other holidays which grew out of that era, provide for the celebration of a ritual national calendar. Of course much of American civil religion was ultimately derived from Christianity in a selective manner, but Bellah argues that when functioning as official symbol, ritual, and belief this material has been differentiated from traditional faith.

The foregoing represents, in Bellah's view, the basic content of American civil religion. A major section of his essay turns out to be a positive evaluation of these phenomena—as constitutive of a religion—against the many who have criticized or undervalued it. Especially he notes that American civil religion has not been anti-pathetic toward traditional religions. For this reason the nation has thus far managed to avoid the stresses of anticlericalism and militant secularism. Generally, though not always, civil religion has provided support for worthy domestic causes, although its contribution to international relationships has not been so positive because it has fostered a Manichean approach to other nations as they have sought to realize their proper aspirations. Bellah concludes that in the present era American civil religion is experiencing a "third time of trial." As he sees it the particular challenge is whether, as a system of symbols and beliefs, it can become part of, and contribute to, a "new civil religion of the world"—especially if a "transnational sovereignty" develops from the United Nations. "Since the American civil religion is not the worship of the American nation but an understanding of the American experience in the light of ultimate and universal reality . . . a world civil religion

4. Ibid., p. 10.

2

could be accepted [within it] as a fulfillment and not a denial of American civil religion." [5]

A final interesting aspect of Bellah's article is his expression of wonder that "something so obvious should have escaped serious analytical attention."[6] He concludes that a "peculiarly Western concept of 'religion' " as a differentiated and fully conscious activity (often defined in terms of explicit orthodoxy, i.e., correct belief) lies at the root of this obscurity. For this reason it has been more readily possible to apprehend within a non-Western culture the truth of the proposition that "every group has a religious dimension."[7] On this basis Bellah argues that religious elements are integral to the American social system. Indeed he seems to imply that, blessed with this insight, we may readily discover a "positive institutionalization" of civil religion in our national past and present.

Have the phenomena Bellah identified actually been overlooked? During the decades prior to the publishing of Bellah's article there had been a considerable literature directing extensive attention to various religious phenomena in American culture which, in one fashion or another, contribute to social unity. In passing he acknowledged some of these studies, and my brief remarks do not exhaust the topic. In this present context it will be useful to distinguish among three kinds of socially unifying religious phenomena which have been noted: rituals or ceremonies, beliefs, and institutions.

W. Lloyd Warner has imaginatively studied certain rituals or ceremonies which contribute religious sanction to American society as an entity. Much of this material was originally included in the Yankee City Series and has been re-presented in a paperback, *The Family of God.*[8] There the unifying topic is "sacred symbolism" in an emerging secular society. His classical analysis of Memorial Day celebrations, for instance, indicates one way in which specific symbolic expression is given to loyalty toward the Amer-

5. Ibid., p. 18.
6. Ibid., p. 19 n.
7. Ibid.
8. William Lloyd Warner, *The Family of God: A Symbolic Study of Christian Life in America* (New Haven: Yale University Press, 1961 [paperback]).

ican Republic.[9] Indeed, Warner proposed that a "national calendar" effectively marks off a "sacred year," which in part at least
serves the purpose of structuring American experience.[10] Obviously Memorial Day, the Fourth of July, Columbus Day, Veterans
Day explicitly fit this interpretation. The recognition accorded
Washington's Birthday as well as Lincoln's (and in the future,
perhaps, Martin Luther King's) illustrates the same pattern. Comment upon regional additions to or variations upon the national
calendar, e.g., Bunker Hill Day, could be elaborated at great length.
Indeed, with appropriate demythologization or interpretation it is
possible to discern a fundamentally America-affirming ceremony
latent within such events as Easter and Christmas.[11]

Following out these lines, it is not entirely farfetched to see in the
"imperial architecture" of the capital city the rudiments of a civic
cult. What is one to make of the "father of his country" when he is
commemorated by an outsize phallus dominating the landscape?
Could it be appropriate except to celebrate a nation whose reach
spans the continent and whose mission girdles the globe? The
Lincoln Memorial is surely to be perceived as a classic temple,
raised in commemoration of the charismatic leader and propitiating
sacrifice in the struggle to preserve the sacred American Union. If
the symbolism within the capital which is directed toward Washington and Lincoln respectively suggests the first and second persons of the Christian Godhead, it may not be entirely accidental
that the Kennedy memorial evokes the imagery usually associated
with the Holy Spirit; certainly the eternal flame and the open
burial plot permit this construction. Such references are not inappropriate, for that matter, in view of his "achievement" in effectively laying to rest the assumption that Roman Catholics would be
excluded from full participation in the highest reaches of national
political life. In this precise sense he was the agent of national

9. See also Warner's treatment of the theme in *American Life: Dream and
Reality* (Chicago: University of Chicago Press, 1962), chap. 1.
10. Warner, *The Family of God*, chap. 9.
11. See two articles by James H. Barnett which are suggestive: "Christmas
in American Culture," *Psychiatry*, vol. 9, no. 1 (1946); and "The Easter
Festival—A Study in Cultural Change," *American Sociological Review,* vol.
14, no. 1 (1949).

reconciliation, overcoming the dreadful legacy of four centuries of Protestant-Catholic strife born in the Old World and continued in the New.

Sacred cities are besieged, conventionally, by pilgrims, and Washington is not without its thronging visitors. Whether with the tired and blasé indifference of the middle classes, with the nervous and compulsive curiosity of the school trips, or with the frustrated anguish of the occasional "marches," the capital city is experienced as the central "Mecca" for pilgrimage on behalf of the American polity. As such it is also, naturally, the locus for the routine symbolization of continuity in the civil life. The pageantry of the inauguration ceremony, held only every fourth year, dominates this genre of events. But no less do the routines of Congress and the formalities of the Supreme Court serve as regular expressions of civil piety. When the fabric of the national life is rent, the sacred city is the focus of the attempt to reestablish the ordered cosmos. In our experience the death of President Kennedy illustrates the primordial impulse to invoke the symbols of social unity in a time of crisis. Less politically traumatic occurrences, however, also evoke responses which originate in many of the same sources of collective life: domestic crises, natural disasters, international uncertainties all occasion the display of the symbols of civil order at press conferences or other "events" contrived for maximum effectiveness.

Possibly the most interesting aspect of civil ceremonial is its extension throughout the land. On the one hand this takes the form of replication of national rituals within the states so that both federal and state authority are conjointly present in the experience of citizens. Whether in post office buildings, executive proclamations, or civil courts, ceremonial elements point toward the American polity which sustains the experience of order—*summum bonum* of the American faith. On the other hand it also takes the form of periodic visitations from national dignitaries, now vicariously available to everyone through the magic of the ubiquitous video tube. The circumscription which finally all but eliminated presidential appearances during the last years of the Johnson administration should not lead us to overlook how exceptional was that abridgment of function. For all the shortcomings of our provision for extended presidential primaries, followed by a drawn-out campaign, we should not fail to recognize that in symbolic terms the aspirants to the office are literally drawing strength from the people so that they may properly stand for them.

The religious phenomena of ceremonial or ritual here indicated (which might be elaborated at great length) stand in a context of "beliefs" which they summarize and communicate to the citizen. It is not possible within the scope of this discussion to give a systematic analysis of this "belief structure" of American religion. If not always sympathetically viewed, however, this component of American civic religion has not been ignored or overlooked. Will Herberg, in his writings, while ultimately critical of the "American Way of Life" for its theological shallowness, did not fail to recognize it as, in Robin Williams's phrase, a "common religion" of our society, or the embodiment of "central ultimate values" which Americans embrace to the point of failing to tolerate opposition to them. Indeed, Herberg characterized it as "at bottom, a spiritual structure, a structure of ideas and ideals, of aspirations, of values, of beliefs and standards."[12] He saw it as precisely the kind of common religion which Bellah took to be required by American society —because required by all societies. Its actual content was a sort of "secularized Puritanism" or generalized Protestantism, valuing positively "individual freedom, personal independence, human dignity, community responsibility, social and political democracy, sincerity, restraint in outward conduct, and thrift."[13] While the particular enumeration may sound a bit quaint, perhaps in part because derived from Dorothy Canfield Fisher's older analysis of the Vermont character, in substance these virtues do not seem to be contradicted by those currently espoused. "Doing one's own

12. Will Herberg, *Protestant, Catholic, Jew: An Essay in American Religious Sociology,* new rev. ed. (Garden City: Doubleday & Co., 1960 [paperback]), p. 75.
13. Ibid., p. 80. Robin Murphy Williams's discussion of common religion occurs in *American Society: A Sociological Interpretation* (New York: Alfred A. Knopf, 1951), chap. 9.

thing," for instance, or "community control" might be heard as renderings in a contemporary idiom of the first four listed above.

Herberg's discussion emphasized, of course, the manner in which this "common religion" had developed in a symbiotic relationship to the traditional religions of American society. Other authors have delineated less traditional aspects of the common religion in much more detail. Irvin G. Wyllie's *The Self-made Man in America*,[14] for example, dealt with the development of one element within the American faith. Louis Schneider and Sanford Dornbusch attempted to analyze American "inspirational books" written between 1875 and 1955. Thus *Popular Religion*[15] sought to fix a profile of the "religious values" subscribed to by the reading public, roughly since the Civil War. A rather different historical perspective underlay Donald Meyer's *The Positive Thinkers*.[16] Here the attempt was to suggest the sort of religious quest which expressed a pronounced strain of piety especially characteristic of our culture since the later nineteenth century. These phenomena should be regarded as basically individualistic versions of American religion. Together these various kinds of belief belong to what Herberg identified as common religion on the conceptual model he derived from Robin Williams.

A third relevant kind of religious phenomenon in contemporary American experience—one that contributes to social unity—is that of provision for institutional reinforcement. Symbolic rituals or ceremonies and the belief structure noted above are intimately connected with social institutions which embody, clarify, reinforce, and interpret them to groups as well as to individuals. This is to recognize that common religion has institutional expression. Accordingly the public school system certainly must be viewed as a powerful engine for reinforcement of common religion. Some years ago J. Paul Williams persistently argued that since a society presupposes

14. Irvin Gordon Wyllie, *The Self-made Man in America: The Myth of Rags to Riches* (New Brunswick: Rutgers University Press, 1954).
15. Louis Schneider and Sanford Maurice Dornbusch, *Popular Religion* (Chicago: University of Chicago Press, 1958).
16. Donald B. Meyer, *The Positive Thinkers: A Study of the American Quest for Health, Wealth, and Personal Power, from Mary Baker Eddy to Norman Vincent Peale* (Garden City: Doubleday & Co., 1965).

shared values, it is necessary for at least some of these values to be religiously supported and sustained.[17] In our case, of course, the values have been those of a democratic social order and the religious sanction has taken the form of faith in democracy. His further point was that while various private institutions within American society may support and affirm these values, "the state must be brought into the picture" as well.[18] Here he had in mind the instrumentality of the public school. Williams actually laid out this specific program as early as 1946 in *The New Education and Religion*.[19] The particulars of the program do not concern us as much as the historical conclusion arrived at by Sidney Mead in discussing it, viz., that adoption and implementation of the general proposals would be to create a "state church" on the historic model of religious establishments in European societies, in effect declaring that the American tradition of separation had been, socially considered, a failure.[20]

If Williams seemed to call for a manifest recognition of the values of the democratic ethos, the more subtle question is whether our school systems have not for some time been functional equivalents of a religious establishment. Certainly parochial as well as public schools have directly nurtured values central to the entire social order.[21] Even the recently proposed strategy of public financing for community-controlled schools for urban areas would not contradict this insight into essential characteristics of American primary and secondary education. Thus one might precisely argue that Williams was actually an advocate of what already was the

17. See J. Paul Williams's argument in *What Americans Believe and How They Worship* (New York: Harper & Bros., 1952), pp. 355 ff. (also: [New York, Harper & Row, 1962], pp. 477 ff.). Williams's phrases have been slightly reworded to make clear their relevance to the present discussion. I do not believe that their fundamental meaning has been changed. The position is close to Robin Williams's proposal that a common religion is requisite for every society.
18. Ibid., p. 371.
19. J. Paul Williams. *The New Education and Religion* (New York: Association Press, 1945), pp. 143 ff.
20. Sidney E. Mead, *The Lively Experiment: The Shaping of Christianity in America* (New York: Harper & Row, 1963), p. 69.
21. See, for example, Peter H. and Alice S. Rossi, "Some Effects of Parochial-School Education in America," *Daedalus*, vol. 90, no. 2 (1961), pp. 300–28.

case, though in a latent sense, viz., that the school systems are in fact the American religious establishment through their state symbolism, civic ceremonial, inculcated values, exemplified virtues, and explicit curricula.

With broader reference to beliefs and values, surely communications media play important roles. On this point Warner suggested that the influence of television and radio as socially formative institutions is subtle and deep-going in shaping American life.[22]

An additional institution within American society embodies in an especially pronounced manner the common values which define the horizons of life within our society—American death ceremonial and practice. Several years ago Jessica Mitford used her sharp tongue and ready wit to flail the industry.[23] While at the time public outrage seemed to be aroused, the casual observer must conclude that the storm has subsided and more recently business as usual has prevailed—except probably even better and more profitably. Of course the outrage was directed toward the poor taste, the excessive profit, and the psychological and theological poverty of the business. More interesting is the question whether in functional terms the institution does not represent the development of a religious institution unique to American culture, replete with symbolism, ceremonies, and functionaries, which provides the final rites of passage required by an affluent, urban, highly mobile social order. Adopting elements from traditional faiths, of course, cooperating uneasily with established churches, to be sure, but finally paying a kind of tribute to Americans in their deaths far more expressive of the common value of the society than the benedictions pronounced over them in any of the traditional rituals.

From the above discussion several conclusions may be drawn. First, significant attention has in fact been given during recent decades to phenomena such as Bellah identified with the substance of what he designated American civil religion. Second, while to be sure certain voices have been stridently hostile or critical of the

22. William Lloyd Warner, "Mass Media: A Social and Psychological Analysis," in *American Life*, pp. 247–73.
23. Jessica Mitford, *The American Way of Death* (New York: Simon & Schuster, 1963).

9

phenomena, others have been entirely open toward a conception of religion centered on American society, and indeed a few have explicitly advocated innovative social policies on the basis of that assumption. Third, insofar as any general conceptual model has possessed widespread currency, it has been the kind of analysis Robin Williams offered of the "common religion" or the "central ultimate values" of American society.

Thus it has been widely held that elements of piety primarily embodying American values rather than, e.g., Christian virtues, are prominent in contemporary American culture. Most precisely Bellah has raised the issue of whether these phenomena ought to be considered as peculiarly focused on civil order and thus constitutive of a specific religion rather than as representing loosely related elements of piety within the culture.

Should these phenomena be termed religious? Do these phenomena manifest characteristics which properly require their identification as religious phenomena? Are they really so complementary and coherent that they constitute a religious symbol system? To argue that there are some analogies or resemblances between these phenomena and others conventionally or historically designated as religious phenomena is to beg the real question: What are appropriate criteria for invoking that designation?

In an epilogue to *Religion and Progress in Modern Asia*,[24] Bellah clarifies his conception of the relationship between religion and the social order. There he proposes that religion be viewed as "a set of symbols" which "define in broadest terms the nature of reality."[25] Other images suggest Bellah's interpretation of the social function of religion. It may be said to act as a "cultural gyroscope," and it may be conceived of as a "cybernetic control mechanism" in both society and personality.[26] Thus he emphasizes the identity-giving function or role of "religious symbol systems." For Bellah "the

24. Robert N. Bellah, *Religion and Progress in Modern Asia* (New York: Free Press, 1965). This provides a fuller theoretical statement than is available in his *Tokugawa Religion* (Glencoe, Ill.: Free Press, 1957).
25. Bellah, *Religion and Progress*, p. 171. In *Tokugawa Religion* Bellah utilized a conception of "the central value system" (pp. 178 ff.) which seems to carry much the same meaning.
26. Bellah, *Religion and Progress*, p. 173.

central function of religion [is] to provide stable points of reference for human action."[27] Thus "a society is generally officially committed to a particular set of religious symbols shared usually by a majority of the groups and individuals in it, though not necessarily compulsory for all."[28]

Put in such terms it is difficult to discover any distinction between religion as the "horizon of social symbols" and religion as the "central cultural values of a society"—precisely the sort of position taken by Robin Williams and, following him, Will Herberg. But surely in proposing to adopt the "civil religion in America" Bellah had in mind something very much more precise and tangible; he seems to have meant to suggest an extensively delineated and institutionalized phenomenon. For the sake of clarity on this point it is important to recognize some elementary distinctions between conceptions of religion appropriate to preliterate, prehistoric, or primitive (used descriptively, not pejoratively) societies on the one hand, and literate, historic, or developed and differentiated societies on the other. In general it seems quite proper to recognize that in societies of the first type religious behavior and belief are scarcely distinguishable from espousal of the values basic to the society. But in differentiated societies, while there may be a residual identification of religion with the realm of social values, it is also the case that institutionalization of specifically religious beliefs and practices occurs. In brief, with respect to developed societies, *religion* as a term has at least two sorts of references—which are not necessarily commensurate: one of a nonspecific sort pointing to a residual realm of values; and another consisting of developed or institutionalized patterns of behavior and belief specifically marked off from other activities understood more properly as, e.g., social, political, economic, or aesthetic in character.

Thus, there is a kind of systematic ambiguity if not confusion in Bellah's combining a generalized definition of religion—congruent with the functional values of society—with the conception of a

27. Ibid., p. 176.
28. Ibid., p. 172.

specifically civil religion in America, by which one infers he means an explicit and institutional religion. For establishing the latter point he would need to demonstrate that the phenomena under consideration fulfill general conditions associated with the definition of historic religions. Thus it would be crucial to look for: (1) cultic aspects to the phenomena, i.e., provision for periodic (frequent) ceremony or ritual which provides definitive interpretation of it; (2) recognized leadership offices invested with effective authority; (3) explicitly defined means of participation in the religion (thus establishing the grounds of membership); (4) at least implicit delineation of beliefs—if not "correct belief"; (5) influence upon behavior at one or more levels and in a manifest way; (6) finally, and perhaps most important, a coherence of the above in order for the conception of religion to be applicable. Beliefs and behavior must have some manifest relationship to each other.[29]

Ceremonies or rituals centered on "America" certainly exist in our society, though not without variation according to region and cultural stratum. Leadership roles there are closely related to these cultic phenomena. "Citizenship" in many respects fulfills the condition that participants in the cult be explicitly identified. Beliefs and values coherent with the above—though they probably do not form a structure or orthodox set in the manner prescribed—undoubtedly exist and are viewed as binding upon all "Americans." Finally, behavior patterns related to the foregoing certainly are commonplace. There is no persuasive evidence, however, that the acknowledged phenomena sufficiently cohere to constitute a *religion* within a historic culture. The elements out of which full-blown common or civil religion could be shaped may be present, but they come together more in terms of diverse elements of piety juxtaposed in a "culture" than as a formal religion. Accordingly, I think, these phenomena are correctly perceived as "religious" in

29. If the objection is proposed that such a scheme presupposes that "historic" religion must be socially differentiated, that is my point. It is certainly the case in modern cultures that religious or quasi-religious elements may be encountered apart from a social "system." But under those circumstances they are not evidence for a religion as in "American civil religion." Bellah develops a rather elaborate scheme about general "stages" of religion in relationship to society. See Robert N. Bellah, "Religious Evolution," *American Sociological Review* 29 (1964): 358–74.

the first and generalized sense. Thus it is appropriate to identify them as elements of piety or religiosity if we require a precise designation. But they do not, by the same token, manifest the kind of interrelatedness, institutionalization, and coherence of expression which would warrant identifying them as positive evidence for a developed and differentiated religion in the second sense.

What, then, is the relevance of Rousseau's conception? Bellah derived the phrase *civil religion* from *The Social Contract*, and he observed that the idea was "part of the cultural climate of the late eighteenth century."[30] From the foregoing discussion, however, it ought to be clear that Bellah actually intended to develop a contemporary interpretation of civil religion rather different from Rousseau's, shaped out of his work with Asian societies. For this reason we might inquire into what Rousseau seems to have meant by the phrase in order to place Bellah's allegedly modern conception in critical perspective. The subject is discussed toward the end of *The Social Contract*.[31] Specifically, the rights of the sovereign over subjects, Rousseau believes, do not "exceed the limits of public expediency."[32] Thus the opinions of subjects are of concern to the sovereign only insofar as they "matter to the community." That "each citizen should have a religion" does matter to the community very much, since it "will make him love his duty."

> The dogmas of that religion concern the State and its members [however] only so far as they have reference to morality and to the duties . . . to others. Each man may have, over and above, what opinions he pleases, without it being the Sovereign's business to take cognizance of them . . . provided they are good citizens in his life.[33]

Rousseau concludes that the sovereign "should fix the articles" of "a purely civil profession of faith." These are not "exactly . . . religious dogmas, but . . . social sentiments without which a man

30. Bellah, "Civil Religion in America," p. 5.
31. Jean Jacques Rousseau, *The Social Contract*, chap. 8, "Civil Religion." For a recent discussion of Rousseau's conception of civil religion in the context of his understanding of religion, see R. Grimsley, *Rousseau and the Religious Quest* (New York: Oxford University Press, 1968), pp. 76–86.
32. Rousseau, *The Social Contract*, Everyman Edition (London, 1913), p. 120.
33. Ibid., p. 121.

cannot be a good citizen or a faithful subject." He goes on to enumerate certain "positive dogmas," viz., God, Providence, a life to come, justness of life, and the "sanctity of the social contract and the laws." To these Rousseau adds one negative dogma: he insists that intolerance be rejected.[34]

Quite clearly Rousseau recognized that the "civil religion" he identifies is not strictly comparable to traditional religions or conventional religiousness, but it is a kind of social sentiment serving a function equivalent to what (in European culture of the previous centuries) had been fulfilled by versions of Christianity—the maintenance of social stability. While Rousseau defined this social sentiment or civil religion in terms of ideational content, its critical contribution is to civic behavior.

Thus Rousseau understood civil religion in a way that was fundamentally different from Bellah's understanding. Three points may be offered to contrast these differing conceptions. First, the operative conception in *The Social Contract* is that of the "civic order," the primary goal being its maintenance, with religion understood to be an instrumentality toward this end. It is clear that Bellah, on the other hand, is working with more recent concepts of "society" and "personality." Thus the influence of Talcott Parsons upon his work is obvious, and less directly he is indebted to Max Weber and Ernst Troeltsch, although some of Durkheim's insights are also present. His conception of religion would seem to be commensurate in large measure with the recent proposals offered by Thomas Luckmann and Peter Berger.[35] There is more than a little ambiguity in attempting to assimilate to modern theories about the symbolic basis of all social order Rousseau's limited postulate of civil religion as a means to political order.

Second, Rousseau explicitly held that the only religious opinions held by citizens which might be "of concern to the Sovereign" were

34. Ibid.
35. Specifically, Peter L. Berger, *The Sacred Canopy: Elements of a Sociological Theory of Religion* (Garden City: Doubleday & Co., 1967 [paperback]); Peter L. Berger and Thomas Luckmann. *The Social Construction of Reality: A Treatise in the Sociology of Knowledge* (Garden City: Doubleday & Co., 1967 [paperback]); Thomas Luckmann, *The Invisible Religion* (New York: Macmillan Co., 1967).

those which affected the community through making "him [the citizen] love his duty." Implicitly, other religious professions and sentiments were not to be identified with civil religion. Rousseau seems to have been ready to allow a pluralism of actual faiths, provided their social effects were not divisive. This is rather different from Bellah's definition of religion as those sets of symbols which establish the reality actually experienced in a given culture. More than anything else, Rousseau's formulation suggests the Imperial Cult of ancient Rome which permitted, indeed encouraged, the coexistence of tolerating religions—the specific contents of which might be defined as transcendent or not, provided that their civic effects were not divisive. In this respect Rousseau's formulation has a very modern sound, thus contradicting first impressions. It appears to be congruent with urbanized polyglot culture (for which, indeed, Rome has probably been the closest thing to a historical anticipation), whereas, curiously, Bellah's formulation is more reminiscent of the role apparently played by religion, for instance, in the great despotic water cultures.[36]

Finally, Bellah views it as a Western error to identify religions with professions of belief.[37] In these terms, however, Rousseau is of all men most Western since he precisely identifies certain dogmas thought to entail desirable patterns of behavior as definitive of civil religion. In terms of his analysis, of course, Bellah himself is also culpable, since in order to support his proposal that there is an American civil religion he quotes almost exclusively from, and cites as his primary evidence, the rhetorical declarations made by presidents of the United States in their inaugural addresses or on other state occasions. Ironically, while Bellah is committed to a theory of civil religion very different from Rousseau's postulate that it creates civic solidarity, the kind of evidence on which he rests his case is far more appropriate to sustaining Rousseau's sort of theoretical construct! If we are expected to take seriously the proposal that there is an American civil religion (which seems not to be

---

36. See Karl A. Wittfogel's discussion of theocratic and hierocratic Hydraulic Regimes in *Oriental Despotism: A Comparative Study of Total Power* (New Haven: Yale University Press, 1957), pp. 87–100.
37. Bellah, "Civil Religion in America," p. 19 n.

required by the evidence), then we must be prepared to generate a coherent construct and to argue the case wholly in terms appropriate to it.

Of course, there are problems with Rousseau's position. After all, it represents a very "political" way of looking at things, for it directly reflects the ancient territorial principle that the uniformity of religion contributes in a fundamental manner to political unity. On purely instrumental grounds, viz., the stability of the state, religious homogeneity was advocated in *The Social Contract* since it served to ensure good citizenship. Typical of his time, Rousseau even noted that the sovereign "can banish from the State whoever does not believe [the articles] . . . not for impiety, but as an anti-social being."[38] The modern insight, of course, is that such an abstract and explicit model of the state corresponds to nothing in our actual experience any more than "orthodoxy" in religion today resembles its classical form. Bellah clearly shares this conviction from his own work on Asian societies, and he has emphasized that shared symbols and values, i.e., religion, make social orders possible. On the other hand, Bellah has failed to analyze what these symbols and values might be in the American case, and whether they may better be construed as functional equivalents for preliterate religion than as religious phenomena in a historic culture. To argue that in the present day x functions as an equivalent for prehistoric religions does not, of course, logically require us to pronounce it "religious" from the point of view of society. It might as well be argued that the function presently fulfilled by x ought more properly lead us to designate that function, for example, as the political aspect of historic religions. In this sense "functional equivalency" is a two-edged sword, which requires specification of the precise sense in which we deem something to be religious.

From this discussion there follows a seemingly absurd suggestion that Bellah's "modern" conception of religion as the common symbol-horizon of a social order in fact should be perceived as but a recent version of a very ancient interpretation of the subject. By

38. Rousseau, *The Social Contract,* p. 121.

contrast, Rousseau's understanding of civil religion—as a limited political device to secure loyalty on the part of citizens to a contingent social order—actually represents the attempt to break with the tyranny of that conception. This newer tradition of thought was probably derived from reflection upon the political requisites of urban life in antiquity and certainly it was associated with the political experience of the Roman Empire, which historically anticipated the religiously pluralistic, multifaceted urban social order currently identified as the emerging form of life in the present "modernizing" age. This truly modern viewpoint distinguished between the social function of religion as the "cement of society" and its substantive truth claims, irrelevant to the former purpose. In the case of Rousseau, he recognized that "civil religion" was purely an instrumental thing, and he did not hesitate to term it a "social sentiment" not to be confused with, for instance, theocratic religions which make rather distinctive truth claims.

What, then, is the status of civil religion in America? The pattern of thought developed by Rousseau was taken to a more radical conclusion in the formative years of the American political tradition. What has usually been referred to as the separation of church and state may be perceived more accurately to have been a formal disengagement of religious institutions from civil governments. Consequently civil sanction was deemed irrelevant for religious life no less than formal religious sanction was declared inappropriate to the political realm. Relationships between religious institutions and civil governments have continued to exist under this arrangement, but they have taken the forms of competition and rivalry as well as mutual support. On this basis, one would expect elements of civic piety to be very much present in modern urban American society, but also that they would not be accorded any formal status, as in a "civil religion."

With some peril one undertakes to offer interpretation of the specific provision concerning religion in the United States Constitution as amended. While the exclusion of a religious test for office (Article 6) seems to be unambiguous, the provision that Congress should not legislate regarding an establishment of religion or pro-

hibiting the free exercise of religion (First Amendment) is sufficiently equivocal to suggest that it was carefully contrived. For
whatever different reasons, it is clear that representatives of very
divergent viewpoints and opinions could agree that the federal
government should be permitted neither to create a formal establishment nor to abridge religious performance through legislation.[39] Jeffersonians who would have erected a "wall" between
church and state could agree on this with evangelical disestablish-
mentarians no less readily than with staunch defenders of particular
New England establishments. This resolution, in other words,
represented the only possible polity for a federal republic among
the separate colonies to become states. It was as acceptable to those
who would strenuously argue that a general Protestant Christianity
actually constituted an informal establishment (as effective in their
view as a real one), to those who steadfastly resisted the program-
matic consequences of such "republican Protestantism" when represented, for instance, in the Sunday mails issue of the 1820s.[40]

James Madison was profoundly correct in his assessment of what
had transpired in the founding period of the American political
tradition. Placing the American polity in historical perspective, he
identified it as "the prevailing opinion in Europe, England not ex-
cepted, . . . that Religion could not be preserved without the support of Government nor Government be supported without an
established religion." This "great and interesting subject" North
America brought "to a fair, and finally to a decisive test." By 1832
(when these words were written), Madison opined, sufficient evidence was in. It had been effectively demonstrated that religion
"does not need the support of Government and it will scarcely be
contended that Government has suffered by the exemption of Religion from its cognizance, or its pecuniary aid." He did admit that
"Religion left entirely to itself may run into extravagances injurious

39. See the discussion in Mark De Wolfe Howe, *The Garden and the
Wilderness: Religion and Government in American Constitutional History*
(Chicago: University of Chicago Press, 1965), chap. 1, where the author
explores characteristics of the federal system as related to religion.
40. See materials relating to this issue in John F. Wilson, ed., *Church and
State in American History* (Boston: D. C. Heath, & Co., 1965), chap. 4.
"The Era of Republican Protestantism."

both to religion and to social order," but he believed that the ascendency of "Reason" and the counterbalancing of contrary viewpoints were more effective checks than direct control or interference on the part of government. Finally, Madison candidly admitted that "it may not be easy, in every possible case, to trace the line of separation between rights of religion and the Civil authority with such distinctness as to avoid collisions and doubts on unessential points."[41]

> The tendency to a usurpation on one side or the other, or to a corrupting coalition or alliance between them, will be best guarded against by an entire abstinence of the Government from interference in any way whatever, beyond the necessity of preserving public order, and protecting each sect against trespasses on its legal rights by others.[42]

Madison's comments (expressed, to be sure, in the idiom of his age and directly reflective of his own experiences) both judiciously set the American experiment in proper historical perspective and correctly identify its central operative principle, which was precisely to abjure formal religious sanction for government no less than governmental sanction for religious institutions. By these terms "civil religion" was also excluded, if one actually means by that any more than the loyalty appropriately required from citizens, the social sentiments necessarily shared by coresidents in a commonwealth, or the patriotism expected of nationals.[43]

In closing it is appropriate to return explicitly to the question which gives title to this discussion: What is the status of civil religion in America? It has been argued that the answer must

---

41. Specifically and most to the point in a little-known letter to the Reverend Jasper Adams. It is preserved in *The Writings of James Madison*, ed. G. Hunt (1819–36), (New York: Haskell, 1910), 9:484–88. It is reproduced in my *Church and State in American History*, pp. 77–79.
42. Ibid.
43. See the article by Sidney E. Mead, "Neither Church nor State: Reflections on James Madison's 'Line of Separation,' " *Journal of Church and State*, vol. 10, no. 3 (1968), pp. 349–63. This article argues that the American polity dissolved the traditional categories of "church" and "state" into those of "religious bodies" and "institutionalized foci of civil authority." In these terms Mead argues the "complete inadequacy of Jefferson's simple concepts [which are] not applicable to the realities experienced in the United States" (p. 361). This general interpretation of the matter underlies my *Church and State in American History*.

be twofold. On the one hand, there is precisely no "provision," "place," or "position" for a formal civil religion within the American social order, anymore than the establishment of a traditional church can be imagined. On the other hand and contrariwise, elements of "civic piety" are, not surprisingly, prominent as phenomena on the American social scene. Far from constituting a paradox, provision for this coresidence of religious elements (including civic piety) and government(s), while yet being held formally distinct, is the essential "church-state postulate" of the American tradition. Doubtless well-meaning religiously disposed persons, be they traditional, conventional, or fanatic in their faiths, would wish it otherwise, each in his own fashion. Many who exercise the powers of government would undoubtedly feel more secure therein if an explicit civic cult existed to celebrate their authority, whatever the relationship between that cult and an established church. In this sense the American polity embodies the proposal that men should live their political lives in terms of political symbols which are desacralized. This arrangement is a direct challenge to the ancient overwhelming impulses toward social solidarity, often religiously expressed. These impulses originated in prehistoric communities of men and continue strong into the present, even among otherwise enlightened, indeed sophisticated, persons. Overcoming them would also seem to represent, however, a necessary precondition for modern man to construct the differentiated and pluralistic urban cultures which seem to offer the only hope for world humanity.

In these terms Bellah has raised up to view a fascinating topic. That certain symbols, ceremonies, and patterns of behavior within contemporary American society (as within any society past or present) are widely experienced by individuals and groups as religious is a proposition which is incontrovertible. But it is equally the case that in the United States these phenomena are not accorded the kind of status appropriate to a religion. Accordingly Bellah has not, it seems to me, adequately delineated at the theoretical level what we might mean by *American civil religion*. Neither has he made a compelling case that the relevant phenomena, which are widely recognized, become intelligible only in these terms. Indeed, he has not proposed criteria in terms of which such a determination might be attempted. Thus American civil religion remains problematic and very much subject to additional analysis. This discussion has argued, however, that such a program, if carried out in terms necessarily somewhat different from those Bellah adopts, would lead to conclusions in certain respects directly opposite to those proposed in the original article.

2

Is the Public School
Religious or Secular?

ROBERT MICHAELSEN

Sociologist Robert N. Bellah and historian Sidney E. Mead both argue with some force that there is an American religion which exists alongside the religion of the denominations.[1] They also maintain that the public school is a primary institution for the inculcation and practice of this American religion. I propose to explore this thesis regarding American religion and the public school by raising the question posed in my title in the context of the closing decades of the nineteenth century.

Bellah and Mead point out the inadequacy or even inaccuracy of the word *secular* in describing the American experience. Mead argues that what the First Amendment did was not to secularize civil authority but to desectarianize it. But to be nonsectarian or antisectarian was not to be nonreligious or antireligious. The founding fathers—especially Franklin and Jefferson—were antisectarian because they wished to plumb to what they regarded as the essential elements in every religion. The theology they sought to articulate was "cosmopolitan, inclusive, universal." [2] And Bellah maintains that what he calls civil religion has never been "anticler-

1. Robert N. Bellah, "Civil Religion in America," *Daedalus,* vol. 96, no. 1 (1967), pp. 1–21; Sidney E. Mead, *The Lively Experiment: The Shaping of Christianity in America* (New York: Harper & Row, 1963), esp. chaps. 4 and 5; idem, "The Post-Protestant Concept and America's Two Religions," *Religion in Life* 33 (1964): 191–204; and idem, "The 'Nation with the Soul of a Church,'" *Church History* 36 (1967): 262–83.
2. Mead, "The 'Nation with the Soul of a Church,'" pp. 269–70.

ical or militantly secular. . . . At its best [it] is a genuine apprehension of universal and transcendent reality."[3]

The effort to derive from the American experience that which is common in faith and morals and to offer this to postulant Americans is a major motif in the history of the public school in the United States. This was the guiding principle in the work of Horace Mann, who offered the residents of Massachusetts common religion (or "the religion of nature" or "of heaven") chiefly through reading from the Bible. And this remains the guiding principle of educators in their most sober and reflective mood—as expressed, for example, in the National Education Association statement on moral and spiritual values in the public schools, issued in 1951.[4] A generation ago Payson Smith summarized this history cogently: "For more than a century the people of the United States have shown a consistent determination to achieve two seemingly irreconcilable ends; one of them to keep sectarianism out of the public schools, and the other to keep religion in them."[5]

Americans have tended to assume that somewhere between the extremes of sectarianism (the specific religion of the sects or religious groups) and secularism (no religion at all) there is a middle ground marked "religion" or "religious." This middle ground might be understood to be common ground in two senses. (1) All could stand on it because it bordered on sectarian territory on one side and secular on the other. In this understanding the common religion resulted from the encounter of sectarian religion with the needs of the American world, and in the process some of the particulars of sectarian religion were modified or even dropped but religion was not entirely destroyed. (2) The middle ground might also be understood to be common in the sense of original or fundamental—that is, more primary than either sectarian religion or a

3. Bellah, "Civil Religion in America," pp. 12–13.
4. Educational Policies Commission of the National Education Association, *Moral and Spiritual Values in the Public Schools,* (Washington: NEA, 1951) The commission included James B. Conant and Dwight D. Eisenhower.
5. Payson Smith, "The Public Schools and Religious Education," in *Religion in the Post-War World,* ed. W. L. Sperry (Cambridge, Mass.: Harvard University Press, 1945), p. 32.

condition in which religion was completely absent. (As Mead points out, this was the view of Franklin and Jefferson.) Whichever the case might be, historically one can trace an almost constant endeavor—to change the figure—to precipitate a common substance out of the American mixture with the needs of the nation acting as a reagent. Whether this precipitate can be called religion or not depends upon one's habits of definition. It is clear, however, that Americans generally have fixed that word upon both church or denominational religion and something more—or less—than that.

After the Civil War the public school moved rapidly toward adolescence. It was a fast-growing institution and one that was impressionable and capable of being swayed by dramatic leadership. And men grappled mightily for the soul of this prize prospect. These evangelists ranged from those who sought to secularize the school completely to the dedicated religionists, some of whom sought to make the public school distinctively Protestant while others (the Roman Catholics) wanted to make the religious school public. In the end neither extreme succeeded; the public school became neither sectarian nor completely secularized. The men who had the greatest influence upon the direction of the public school were those who saw what Payson Smith pointed out a half-century later. They understood that to desectarianize was not to dereligionize. Those among them who were affiliated with one of the religious denominations realized that they must subordinate their sectarianism to the commonweal if they were to reach the common ground upon which the common school must stand. Those who where not so affiliated (e.g., Dewey) realized that they could not reach that common ground by a clearly marked antireligious route.

Perceptions of the actual situation in the public school varied in the late nineteenth century as they do now. The English observer Francis Adams concluded in 1875 that "the attempt to find a common religious ground cannot be said to have succeeded. The question for the present remains unsettled—but it is a growing opinion that the common school, to be preserved, must be placed upon a distinctly secular basis."[6] Little more than a decade later the distinguished church historian Philip Schaff pointed out that "the great majority of American schools are religious without being sectarian."[7] About this same time Wisconsin Justice Harlow South Orton, onetime Baptist preacher, argued that the common schools were "as completely *secular* as any other institutions of the state." These schools were "Godless," Orton asserted, in the sense that their purpose "must be exclusively secular."[8] But Orton's colleague on the Supreme Court of Wisconsin, Justice William Penn Lyon, maintained that it was perfectly legitimate for the common school to teach what all religious sects held in common—such as "the existence of a Supreme Being of infinite power and goodness . . . and the duty of all men to adore, obey, and love Him."[9] The determinative criterion for Lyon was nonsectarian, not secular. Still, in the same year in which these opinions were issued as part of a decision of the Wisconsin court (1890), Archbishop Ireland told the National Convention of the National Education Association that "there is and there can be no positive religious teaching where the principle of non-sectarianism rules."[10] Obviously such varied perceptions led to varied courses of action.

Under the title *The Secularization of American Education* Samuel W. Brown pointed out that it was practical necessities which had brought about the "secularization" of the common school.[11] Rapid growth in population, increasing religious diversity, and the enlarged role of the state in the educational process brought about

6. Francis Adams, *The Free School System of the United States* (London: Chapman & Hall, 1875), p. 6. Adams was secretary of the National Education League of England.
7. Philip Schaff, *Church and State in the United States* (New York: G. P. Putnam's Sons, 1883), p. 75.
8. Harlow South Orton, in the case of *Weiss* v. *District Board of Edgerton,* 76 *Wisconsin Reports* 177, 218–19 (1890). Weiss and his associates were Roman Catholics who successfully challenged the practice of reading from the King James Version of the Bible in the schools of Edgerton.
9. William Penn Lyon, in ibid., pp. 194–95.
10. John Ireland, "State Schools and Parish Schools: Is Union between Them Impossible?" in *Journal of the Proceedings and Addresses of the NEA,* vol. 29 (1890), pp. 179–85. (Ireland's address is reproduced in *Catholic Education in America: A Documentary History,* ed. Neil G. McCluskey, S.J. [New York: Teachers College, Columbia University, 1964], pp. 127–40.)
11. Samuel W. Brown, *The Secularization of American Education* ([orig. 1912] New York: Russell & Russell, 1967), pp. 1–4.

increasing centralization and uniformity in the common school. That uniformity, Brown assumed, was not religious; it was "secular."

Brown's analysis is often appealed to by historians of American education as an accurate summarization of nineteenth century developments. But his title is misleading. Church or denominational religion was not generally routed from the common school arena, nor did it engage in any full-scale retreat. Furthermore, even where religious diversity and court decisions tended to reduce the influence of church religion, irreligion or "secularism" scarcely secured the field. Actually the field came to be occupied mostly by the temporizers, the moderates who sought neither to advance nor to destroy church religion but to subordinate it to other ends. Whether these ends could be labeled secular depends again upon one's definition. One could as easily argue that they were religious— especially following Bellah and Mead. If neither *secular* nor *religious* would do then perhaps *civil* or *national* would. Hence Brown might more accurately have summarized trends in the nineteenth century under the title "The Civilization or Nationalization of American Education." If that were too prepossessing a title, then "The Desectarianization of American Education" might have been more descriptive.

Brown used *secularization* in a formal—almost legal—sense to refer to obviously religious or "sectarian" practices and control. Used in this sense, it is clear that American education did become increasingly "secularized" in the nineteenth century. Denominational religion, in its Protestant forms, almost universally discontinued direct operation of elementary and secondary schools. At the same time, increasing religious diversity posed a serious threat to the hegemony of the Protestant ethos in the common school. In cosmopolitan Cincinnati, for example, a coalition of lay Catholics, Jews, liberal religionists, and nonbelievers, working in and through the board of education, succeeded in 1869 in removing what were essentially Protestant practices from the public schools. Later in the century some lay Catholics in Wisconsin successfully challenged the practice of Bible reading in the public schools. In both of these cases the courts moved in the direction of secularization, in the sense in which Brown used that term. The Ohio Supreme Court, where the Cincinnati controversy was finally decided, denied that Christianity was "a part of the common law of this country. . . ." The notion of "legal Christianity" was found to be "a solecism, a contradiction of terms."[12] The Wisconsin court declared public school Bible reading to be a sectarian practice and hence prohibited by the Wisconsin Constitution.[13]

The Ohio and Wisconsin cases are significant, both for Brown's analysis and for ours. It would not be correct to conclude, however, either that they were typical of court decisions generally or even that they were clear instances of a fully secularized position. Brown himself dealt with a number of state supreme court decisions which were favorable to what he called "the religious ideal of education." Furthermore, as we have seen, while the Wisconsin court ruled out Bible reading, Justice Lyon, who wrote the decision of the court, left ample room for common religious teachings.

The Cincinnati case affords an especially rich illustration of the complexities of our question, and of a movement away from sectarianism which stopped short of secularism.[14] On a motion by one of its religiously unaffiliated members the Cincinnati Board of Education voted in 1869 (by a majority of 22 to 15) to discontinue Bible reading and hymn singing in the public schools of the city. The "true object and intent" of this motion, according to its mover, was "to allow the children of the parents of all sects and opinions, in matters of faith and worship, to enjoy alike the benefit of the Common School Fund."[15] Since some citizens—chiefly Roman Catholics—had objected to the traditional opening ex-

12. *Minor* v. *Board of Education of Cincinnati*, 23 *Ohio Reports*, 211, 238, 239 (1872).
13. *Weiss* v. *District Board of Edgerton*, 76 *Wisconsin Reports* 177 (1890).
14. I have dealt more fully with this case in "Common School, Common Religion? A Case Study in Church-State Relations, Cincinnati, 1869–70," *Church History* 38 (1969); 206–17.
15. *The Bible in the Public Schools, Containing Arguments before the Superior Court of Cincinnati in the Case of Minor v. Board of Education of Cincinnati (1870) with the Opinions of the Court and the Opinion on Appeal of the Supreme Court of Ohio* (orig. pub. 1870), with an introduction by Robert G. McCloskey (New York: Da Capo Press, 1967), pp. 6–7. Hereafter cited as *The Bible in the Public Schools (1967).*

ercises, it seemed to a majority of the board that the wisest course was to discontinue those practices.

The action of the Cincinnati board polarized that city and resulted in a courtroom encounter. Protestants generally were loud in opposition to the board's action. Many of them claimed that the Constitution of Ohio required religious teaching in the public schools. (That constitution acknowledged the importance of "religion, morality and knowledge" to the general welfare and called for the support of schools in this connection.) Most who held this position understood this teaching to be some form of common—as against sectarian—Protestantism or common Christianity. "The religion to be taught in the common schools," argued one of the attorneys in opposition to the board's action, "is not sectarianism ... but the eternal, immutable, and essential principles of the Bible, the religion taught by the great head of all religion."[16] One of the judges of the Cincinnati Superior Court acknowledged the force of this argument for common Christianity when he declared that the religion referred to in the Ohio Constitution was the "revealed religion ... made manifest in the Holy Scriptures."[17] Conveniently, in the minds of most opponents of the board, that "revealed religion" of the "Holy Scriptures" was identical with what some of the more subtle among them called variously "political religion," "public religion," "religion itself," and "universal religion."[18]

The Supreme Court of Ohio, as we have seen, rejected the claim that the Ohio Constitution established or even gave any special status to the Christian religion. Furthermore, the court concluded that under that constitution there was no such thing as "a religion of the state." All that was "comprehended in the word 'religion' " in the Ohio Constitution, and all that could "be the subject of human 'instructions,' must be included under the general terms 'knowledge.' " Hence nothing further was enjoined by the constitutional

16. Words of Rufus King, in ibid., p. 326.
17. Ibid., p. 379.
18. The first designation is Rufus King's, in ibid., p. 341. The other three were used often by the liberal clergyman and board member Amory Dwight Mayo, who vigorously opposed the removal of Bible reading from the schools. See Mayo, *Religion in the Common Schools: Three Lectures Delivered in the Fall of 1869* (Cincinnati: Robert Clarke & Co. 1869), pp. 4, 26, 46.

provision relative to "religion, morality, and knowledge" than the increase of knowledge.[19]

Some who supported the action of the Cincinnati board called for the complete secularization of the common school. Since "the state has no religion," Rabbi Isaac Mayer Wise pointed out, the public schools must be "secular."[20] J. B. Stallo, the freethinking philosopher and attorney for the board, was even more outspoken in supporting secularization. The state was not only secular, in his view, it was "as godless as a steam engine." Neither it nor its instruments, including the common school, had a religion, not even a "neutral, non-sectarian religion." In fact, Stallo argued, the state was so limited in function in the American system that it was not only prevented from teaching *"religious truth"* but it could not even *"inculcate morality as such."* [21]

Few board supporters went as far toward secularization as Stallo did, however.[22] Most of them supported common morality in the common school, and the ultimate sanction of that morality was more than secular. Judge Alphonso Taft used the lower-key word *neutral* in preference to the word *secular* in describing the state vis-à-vis religion. And the kind of neutrality that the religiously liberal Taft had in mind was a benevolent and even "Christian" neutrality, as suggested in his assertion that while the state could not "profess to be Christian," it could exercise "a truly Christian charity toward all."[23]

When under heavy fire for their action in discontinuing Bible

19. *Minor* v. *Board of Education of Cincinnati*, 23 *Ohio Reports* 211, 238 ff.
20. Isaac Mayer Wise, in *American Israelite*, October 8, 1869.
21. J. B. Stallo, "Our State Gospel and Its Clerical Proponents," a lecture reported in the Cincinnati *Commercial*, April 4, 1870, and published subsequently under the title *State Creeds and Their Modern Apostles* (Cincinnati, 1872). See also *The Bible in the Public Schools (1967)* p. 103. (Italics in the original.)
22. See, however, a pamphlet entitled *Arguments upon the Secularization of the Public Schools* (Cincinnati, 1870).
23. The argument of Alfonso Taft in dissent from the majority decision of the Cincinnati Superior Court, *The Bible in the Public Schools (1967)*, pp. 392, 415. The majority of the superior court permanently enjoined the board from carrying out its decision to exclude Bible reading from the schools. Taft dissented. His view was sustained by the Ohio Supreme Court on appeal of the case. Taft's opinion was cited by the Supreme Court of the U.S. in *Abington School District* v. *Schempp*, 374 U.S. 203, 214–15 (1963).

reading and hymn singing in the schools, the majority of the board of education justified themselves by appealing to the importance of common experience in the common school as a basis for common citizenship. Since these practices mitigated against this commonality—since, indeed, they had the practical effect of separating children "into opposing factions" and hence leaving them "to grow up in suspicion and distrust of each other"—it seemed better to discontinue them. This would then open the way for all the pupils to "grow up together in our schools and thus learn by daily intercourse to love and respect each other and to work in harmony for the common weal."[24] The language anticipates Dewey—from common experience to common faith and common citizenship. Whether one describes it as secular depends, of course, upon one's definition of the term. Like Dewey, one might discern religious undertones in such words (and values) as *love and respect, harmony*, and *common weal*.

Common experience in the common school seemed desirable—and to some even necessary—as a basis for common citizenship and common identity as Americans. It should be the aim "of every true American," one resolution in support of the board held, "to make the Public school a thorough and efficient means of Americanizing" the people. What this meant essentially was the achievement of "a homogenized nation" out of "the several peoples that reside in the United States."[25]

This kind of language anticipates that used later in Oregon and other states in favor of laws requiring all youngsters to attend public schools. This was necessary to Americanization—or so it was thought by some. But, like the melting pot idea, the notion of homogenization raised as many questions as it answered. What was to be the shape of the pot or the complexion of the homogenized end product? And was it really necessary to American identity that all differences be melted away or broken down? Such a notion smacked of a kind of religious nationalism.

Perhaps homogenization was not the best of notions; subordina-

24. Reported in the Cincinnati *Commercial,* March 31, 1870.
25. Reported in the Cincinnati *Enquirer,* September 27, 1869.

tion might have been better. Or so it seemed to Rabbi Max Lilienthal, one of the more perceptive participants in the Cincinnati controversy. He was, Lilienthal proudly proclaimed, "first an American, and then a Jew," and he hoped that others were first Americans and then Christians.[26] Certainly Thomas Jefferson would have approved of that sentiment.

No doubt some balked at Lilienthal's bold assertion. It was not easy for some Americans, especially Protestants, so to distinguish between sectarian and national identity. In reaction to the Cincinnati case the Dutch Reformed *Christian Intelligencer* warned against the dire effects of voting the reign of Jesus Christ "out of the public schools in the name of American liberty. Such a course could only result in handing the schools—and the nation—over to "Pope, Pagan, and Satan."[27] And the Episcopalian *American Churchman* wondered in alarm what would happen if it was generally proposed "in Cincinnati fashion, to expurgate English literature to suit German infidels, Frankfurt Jews, and Maynooth priests."[28] Since the Bible was "the palladium of our liberties," the Methodist State Convention of Massachusetts urged, removing it from "our public schools" would be nothing less than "a blow at the foundations of republicanism."[29]

But some Protestants were willing to subordinate their sectarian to their national identity, or at least to grant that their particular religious orientation was not essential in every detail to the welfare of the state. An "evangelical Protestant" argued in the *Advance,* leading journal of Western Congregationalism, that a basic distinction must be made between religion and morality. The former did not belong in the common school; morality, on the other hand, was essential to the very structure of society and hence must be taught there.[30] The *Herald,* a Presbyterian journal published in Utica, New York, admitted that "in a cosmopolitan sense" the

---

26. Reported in the Cincinnati *Commercial,* March 31, 1870.
27. Editorial the *Christian Intelligencer* (New York), December 30, 1869. Reprinted in *The Bible in the Public Schools: Opinions of Individuals and of the Press, and Judicial Decisions* (New York: J. W. Schermerborn Co., 1870), p. 98. Hereafter referred to as *The Bible in the Public Schools (1870).*
28. *The Bible in the Public Schools (1870),* p. 79.
29. Ibid., p. 115.
30. Ibid., pp. 76–77.

reading of a particular version of the Bible was "sectarian."[31] Catholics and Protestants should agree as citizens, argued the Reverend Samuel T. Spear in the Congregational *Independent,* "to omit the reading of any version of the Scriptures in our public schools." Supporting the "voluntary principle," Spear pointed out that it was "best for the state and best for religion" if the two were in no way "organically connected." He concluded by questioning the "practical wisdom" and "consistency as American citizens" of those Protestants who proposed "to fight this thing through to the bitter end." [32]

Acknowledging the existence of religious diversity in America, the Reverend Henry Ward Beecher was willing to give up what he called "technical religion" in the common schools. The essential elements in these schools were "intelligence," "fellowship and common feeling," and what Beecher called "Practical Christianity." By this last designation he meant essentially "morality and true virtue." While the state needed these in its citizens, Beecher argued, it was "not indispensable that . . . citizens should be Calvinists or Arminians, Protestants or Catholics, or even Christians of any sect." Hence the "free common school" should be "*unsectarian.*" But for Beecher, to be "unsectarian" was not to be completely secular or unreligious.[33]

Beecher's theological liberalism and relatively mild sense of Protestant identity and distinctiveness enabled him to respond with some irenicism to what he discerned as the needs of the nation. Some years after the Cincinnati controversy had subsided the Reverend Josiah Strong essayed a similar response, but with noticeably less irenicism than Beecher had managed. Strong spoke for an "undenominational religious teaching" which stood somewhere between the "perils" of "Romanism" and "Secularism." This "undenominational religion" was essential to the welfare of the state.

31. Ibid., p. 90.
32. Ibid., pp. 37 ff.
33. Ibid., pp. 3–14. This is a report of a sermon by Henry Ward Beecher on "The Common School as an Element of National Unity," preached on Thanksgiving Day, November 18, 1869, and printed in the New York *Christian Union,* December 4, 1869. This onetime resident of Cincinnati had one eye on developments in that city when he prepared this sermon.

"Popular morality" could not be secured apart from its sanctions. "Reverence for law" sprang "only from reverence for God." Hence this religion must be taught in the common school, Strong urged. And he summarized this nonsectarian religion under "the three great fundamental doctrines" which he found to be "common to all monotheistic religions," that is, *"the existence of God, the immortality of man and man's accountability."*[34]

Strong's views were far from being secular. Were they sectarian? While his "three great fundamental doctrines" were those of the eighteenth century Deists and hence were more—or less—than Protestant, it seems doubtful that many non-Protestant monotheists greeted Strong's suggestion with enthusiasm. Given the context in which he made these suggestions, this is especially evident. From the high ground of Anglo-Saxon Protestantism, Strong looked down upon the "perils" that threatened "our country," including "immigration," "Romanism," and "Mormonism." He declared that "the cleavage of population along religious lines" was "un-American." He fixed that same label on "Romanism" which, he maintained, represented an "alien civilization"—as evidenced, e.g., in the fact that it kept its children out of the American public school. And he remonstrated with Jews and agnostics for their "secularism."[35] To all such non-Protestants Strong's message must have seemed more than vaguely Protestant.

Strong was commissioned by the Congregational Home Missionary Society to do his book *Our Country* as a campaign document. In keeping with this purpose, his attitude toward the public schools bore a clear resemblance to missionary motivation. While the schools were not Protestant "because *distinctively* Protestant doctrines" were not taught in them, and while they were not to be used to convert people to any sectarian religion, they must be employed, Strong urged, to salvage that large percentage of the children who did not come under direct religious influence at home or

34. Josiah Strong, *Our Country,* chap. 6. First published in 1886. I have used the John Harvard Library edition, ed. Jurgen Herbst (Cambridge, Mass.: Harvard University Press, Belknap Press, 1963). Quotation on p. 98 (italics in original).
35. Ibid., pp. 93–96.

in Sunday school. (Strong estimated the number at one-half the total school population.) Without the public school these children would grow up godless, immoral, and un-American. With it, and its "undenominational religion" they might become decent citizens.[36]

Josiah Strong raised an umbrella under which he hoped all monotheists—"all Protestants, Catholics and Jews"—could stand as Americans. But his umbrella was colored a Protestant gray. That was probably enough to keep most Jews and Catholics from stepping under its protective covering. Strong did not even invite agnostics or atheists to join him. In their case "the necessities of the State"—i.e., the monotheistic teachings of "undenominational religion"—stood "above individual rights." [37]

In his discussion of "undenominational religion" Strong took note of Archbishop Ireland's contention that there could "be no positive religious teaching where the principle of non-sectarianism rules." He did so, however, only to refute the archbishop by quoting Daniel Webster to the effect that all Christians really held certain "great religious truths" in common and that these truths could be taught in the schools without perplexing the minds of children "with clashing doctrines and sectarian controversies."[38] But the refutation would scarcely have satisfied the archbishop and most of his Catholic brethren.

Roman Catholic response to our questions was ambivalent. To the naked eye of the participant observer the public school often looked quite Protestant. Hence the removal of Protestant practices was all to the good. But when exposed to the full effulgence of Roman Catholic teaching the public school seemed very secular. The Catholic *Tablet* of New York observed, following the action of the Cincinnati Board of Education in 1869, that if this had "been done with a view to reconciling Catholics to the common-school system, its purpose [would] not be realized." A secular school was worse

36. Ibid., pp. 95, 102.
37. Ibid., p. 98.
38. Ibid., pp. 105–6.

than a sectarian (Protestant) one. A few Protestant practices constituted "a far less evil than German infidelity."[39]

Whether Protestant *and* secular or Protestant *or* secular, the public school was not treated lovingly by most Roman Catholic spokesmen. In 1875 the Sacred Congregation of Propaganda, in response to a request from American bishops, described the public school system as "most dangerous and very much opposed to Catholicity." The American prelates were urged "to use every means in their power to keep the flocks committed to their care from all contact" with those schools.[40] In this same spirit Bishop McQuaid of Buffalo warned Rome in 1892 that in the public school children were exposed to a liberalism that bordered on "infidelity," to an atmosphere of "indifferentism," and to an "association with all classes, Protestants, Jews and infidels," which threatened "contamination" of the faithful.[41]

Some Catholic leaders, however, struggled valiantly against imposing odds to achieve some rapprochement with the majority of Americans who supported the public school system. They were well aware of the symbolic importance of that system to prevailing American notions of national identity and of the consequent effects of Catholic reservations about it. That "opposition against the system of national education which is attributed to us," Cardinal Gibbons wrote Pope Leo XIII in 1890, "more than any other thing, creates and maintains in the minds of the American people the conviction that the Catholic Church is opposed by principle to the institutions of the country, and that a sincere Catholic cannot be a loyal citizen of the United States."[42]

Cardinal Gibbons and some of his more liberal associates set out to disprove this prevailing American conviction. Their strategy in education consisted primarily of projecting a vision of a common endeavor in popular education for the good of all. They stressed

39. Editorial in the *Tablet* (New York), quoted in *The Bible in the Public Schools (1870)*, p. 54.
40. Quoted in *Catholic Education in America*, pp. 122–23.
41. Ibid., p. 163.
42. James Cardinal Gibbons to Pope Leo XIII, 1890, quoted by John Tracy Ellis in *The Life of James Cardinal Gibbons* (Milwaukee: Bruce Publishing Co., 1952), I: 664–65.

what a later generation was to call "moral and spiritual values," but they used the more specific language of historic religion. They were certain that all Americans could agree on the noble goal of producing faithful, loyal, and morally upright youngsters; the only question at issue was one of means. While these Catholic leaders were unwilling to give up religious schools as they understood them, they were avowedly dedicated to improving the quality of education in their own system. Furthermore, they sought means of developing closer relations with the public school system.[43]

Cardinal Gibbons and Bishop John J. Keane, rector of Catholic University, spoke in such terms to the annual convention of the National Education Association in Nashville in 1889. "To keep the social body within its orbit," the cardinal asserted, "the centripetal force of religion should counterbalance the centrifugal motion of free thought." Bishop Keane assured his audience that there was no incompatibility between being a Christian and being an American. Indeed, he argued, "the best Christian is sure to be the best American." One could count on "a good Christian" being "fully trustworthy and self-sacrificing and faithful as a citizen." It followed, then, Keane concluded, that the schools of America "ought to be the most truly Christian schools in the world."[44]

Gibbons and Keane spoke primarily in behalf of "denominational schools." A year later Archbishop Ireland dramatically caught the attention of his listeners and startled many of his fellow Catholics when he forthrightly declared before the meeting of the National Education Association in Saint Paul: "I am a friend and advocate of the state school. . . . The right of the state school to exist is . . . a matter beyond the stage of discussion." That school was not only necessary, but its work in "imparting secular instruction" was, the archbishop enthusiastically confessed, "our pride and glory. . . . Withered be the hand," then, that would be "raised in sign of its destruction."

43. See Robert D. Cross, *The Emergence of Liberal Catholicism in America* (Cambridge, Mass.: Harvard University Press, 1958), chap. 7.
44. James Gibbons and John J. Keane. "Should Americans Educate Their Children in Denominational Schools?" in *Journal of the Proceedings and Addresses of the NEA,* vol. 28 (1889), pp. 5, 9, 10.

While praising the "wondrous edifice" which Americans had raised in the "state schools," Archbishop Ireland was clearly critical of that system for not giving adequate religious instruction. To the argument that "the state school teaches morals," he replied: "Christians demand religion"; and not a vague, "non-sectarian" religion, not even "common Christianity," but the distinctive teachings of the various religious groups. To achieve this goal of adequate religious instruction Ireland suggested two alternatives: (1) permeate the regular, existing state school with the religion of the majority, "be it as Protestant as Protestantism can be" and "pay for the secular instruction given in denominational (chiefly Catholic) schools"; or (2) inaugurate a system in which parochial schools would become state schools between 9 A.M. and 3 P.M.[45]

The archbishop's speech, together with his own support of a cooperative arrangement between public and Catholic schools in Faribault and Stillwater, Minnesota, brought storms of protest from both Protestant and Catholic quarters. In the eyes of the former he did not go far enough in his support of the public schools. Futhermore, his Faribault-Stillwater Plan was greeted with the suspicion that it represented a capitulation to "Romanism." On the Catholic side Ireland's actions became the focal point of what Merle Curti described as "one of the most bitter and dramatic controversies in the history of the Catholic Church in America."[46] Ireland went much too far for conservative Catholics in his praise of the state school and in seeking rapprochement with it. In fact, neither the Protestant nor the Catholic community was ready for the irenic approaches of such Catholic leaders as Ireland, Gibbons, Keane, and Bishop John Lancaster Spalding of Peoria.[47] And the upshot of the controversies of the late nineteenth century was a

---

45. Ireland, "State Schools and Parish Schools," in *Catholic Education in America*, pp. 127–40.
46. Merle Eugene Curti, *The Social Ideas of American Educators* (New York: Charles Scribner's Sons, 1935), p. 352. On the controversy see also Cross, *The Emergence of Liberal Catholicism;* Thomas Timothy McAvoy, *The Americanist Heresy in Roman Catholicism, 1895–1900* (Notre Dame: University of Notre Dame Press, 1963); and Daniel F. Reilly, *The School Controversy, 1891–1893* (Washington: Catholic University of America Press, 1943).
47. On Spalding see Curti, *The Social Ideas of American Educators*, chap. 10.

widening of the gulf between the Roman Catholic church on one side and the public school and its supporters on the other. Apparently there was no common ground upon which Catholics and non-Catholics could stand together in support of some kind of common educational endeavor. Papal decisions embodied in the encyclicals on Americanism (1899) and Modernism (1907) indirectly supported those within the Catholic church who denied that such ground existed and who consequently took a hard line in opposition to the common school. And the institution was left to the Protestants—and to the "secularists."

Whether *secularist* was the correct designation or not, educational leaders of the period did devote great energy to developing a common school system devoid of obvious sectarian religious practices and teachings. One of the greatest of these, William Torrey Harris, advocated what he called secular instruction in certain fundamental subjects in the common school. These fundamentals were grammar, literature and art, mathematics, geography, and history. The list did not include religion. Harris, who was a believing Christian, argued that efforts to develop a common Christianity or any other form of nonsectarian religion either degenerated "into mere deism without a living providence" or else became specifically denominational. In the latter instance the school ceased to be a public and became a "parochial school."

Harris was willing to settle for a relatively modest role for the common school. The home and the church could provide for religious education. The common school could, then, through its program of "secular instruction" do the necessary task of common education, including the inculcation of common morals and the development of an appreciation for what might be called "spiritual values"—that is, the "aesthetic and intellectual aspirations of the culture."[48]

48. William Torrey Harris, "Religious Instruction in the Public Schools," *Independent* 55 (1903): 1841–43. See also William Torrey Harris, "Morality in the Schools," *The Christian Register*, January 31, 1889. On Harris see Curti, *The Social Ideas of American Educators*, chap. 9, and Neil G. McCluskey, S.J., *Public Schools and Moral Education; The Influence of Horace Mann, William Torrey Harris, and John Dewey* (New York: Columbia University Press, 1958).

Harris's idea of "secular instruction" was too antiseptic for the American people, just as his notion of "spiritual" was too archaic. A livelier option was needed, one that caught up the dynamic character of the American approach to the common school and the quasi-religious nature of American communal strivings. Such an option was offered by John Dewey. He assigned to the public school the preeminent role in educating, socializing, civilizing, nationalizing, and humanizing the American people. And he saw this role as essentially religious in nature.

In 1908 Dewey wrote an article titled "Religion and Our Schools" which is worth examining carefully for what it reveals both about the development of Dewey's views and about his sensitivity to the role of religion in the American scene.[49] There is in this article a foreshadowing of the distinction between *religion* and *religious* which Dewey made explicit in his Terry Lectures two decades later.[50] It will be recalled that Dewey used *religion* to refer to the traditional, historical, institutionalized phenomenon usually associated with that noun. *Religious,* the adjective, was attached by Dewey to a quality of human experience. The former was associated in his mind with a supernatural view, while *religious* referred to natural human experience giving rise to the highest in human striving. In his 1908 article Dewey addressed himself first to those who wished to have religion taught in the common school. Such a practice, Dewey warned, constituted an importation into the school of that which was both unnatural to vital human experience and divisive in its effects upon the community. As such, one could say that it was unreligious or even irreligious because it would divert the school from the truly religious task of humanizing and communalizing Americans. What was needed in America was "a fuller religious consciousness" which would not be based on the supernaturalistic teachings of traditional or church religion but would

49. John Dewey, "Religion and Our Schools," *Hibbert Journal,* July 1908. The article was reprinted in *Characters and Events: Popular Essays in Social and Political Philosophy,* ed. Joseph Ratner (New York: Henry Holt & Co., 1929), 2:504–16. Quotations are from this latter source.
50. John Dewey, *A Common Faith,* Terry Lectures (New Haven: Yale University Press, 1934).

be closely associated with "the state, the new science, and the new democracy."

The American tradition of separation of church and state had a twofold object, Dewey maintained: (1) it put the denominations on their own, giving none an unfair advantage over others; and, even more importantly, (2) it was necessary in assuring "the integrity of the state against all divisive ecclesiastical divisions." The United States, fortunately, "became a nation late enough in the history of the world to profit by the growth of that modern . . . thing—state consciousness." For its own well-being it could not allow institutional religion to detract unduly from this consciousness. Hence educators "rightly objected" to "sectarianism in the schools" because it "sapped . . . state consciousness . . . by the growth of social factions." The task of the school, on the contrary, was to bring together those of "different nationalities, traditions, and creeds," and to assimilate "them together upon the basis of what is common and public." In doing this they performed "an infinitely significant religious work"; they promoted the "social unity out of which in the end genuine religious unity must grow."

In his stress on communal values Dewey seemed to lend support to the prevailing nationalistic mood of the day. In fact, the logic of his position appears at times to point toward compulsory public school attendance. But Dewey was not so simpleminded as to assume that the desired "state consciousness" could be achieved through such legalistic devices. Furthermore, as is well known, he often found himself at odds with the superpatriots who sought to use the public schools as conduits for their particular notions and standards of "Americanism."

Homogenization is not a word that Dewey would have used to describe the desired state consciousness. It was not necessary that all people and groups be spun together into one unified entity. Dewey expressly disavowed "the concept of uniformity and unanimity in culture" and "the theory of the Melting Pot." Each group, he wrote in supporting Zionism, must have the opportunity "to cultivate its own distinctive individuality" so long as this did "not become dangerous to the welfare of other peoples and groups."[51] Hence Dewey called for the subordination of group interest to community welfare but not for the dissolution of ethnic and religious differences.

From the standpoint of some religionists Dewey required entirely too much subordination of traditional faith to "state consciousness" as he understood it. He drained the supernatural from his "religious consciousness" and consigned the churches to regions outside the public school. In this sense he was a secularist. But in actuality his conceptions of education and the public school were more religious than secular. [52] At its best, the learning process was akin to "getting religion," as Dewey put it. Learning involved "a personal experiencing and vital realisation," a "conversion of character into spirituality."[53] Education was a communal experience, both the exhibition and the achievement of that "spiritual community"[54] which Dewey understood democracy to be. Ideally every individual was free to participate in this communal experience, in forming and realizing social values. Finally, the common faith that emerged from common experience in the democratic community was not narrowly tribalistic or nationalistic. Dewey saw it as "implicitly the common faith of mankind."[55] Here, then, was a universal vision of the role of education and the public school.

Dewey stood firmly on American ground. He was nurtured on American confidence in education, and he detected and aided in the apotheosis of the public school. He was deeply rooted in the "American democratic faith." And he recognized and took advantage of that prevailing American propensity to steer the public school on a course somewhere between the Charybdis of sectarian domination and the Scylla of complete secularization. As a result

51. John Dewey, "The Principle of Nationality," *Menorah Journal* 2 (1917): 203–8; quotations are from pp. 205–6. See also "The School as a Means of Developing Social Consciousness and Social Ideas in Children," *Journal of Social Forces* 1 (1923): 515 for Dewey's adverse comments on the Oregon compulsory public school attendance legislation.
52. I agree with Christopher Dawson's assertion that Dewey "had a conception of education which was almost purely religious." See "Education and the State," *Commonweal* 65 (1957): 423–29.
53. Dewey, "Religion and Our Schools," pp. 511–12.
54. Dawson's terminology.
55. Dewey, *A Common Faith*, p. 87.

he fashioned a philosophy of education which exerted great influence in American educational circles and even among some religious leaders—chiefly those within the religious education movement in Protestantism in the early years of the twentieth century.

Still, for some Americans Dewey's course was close to the Scylla of secularism. They wanted more of religion, as traditionally understood. And they sought to get it by continuing or introducing in the schools such devices as Bible reading, prayer, and released time religious education. By midcentury thirty-seven states required, permitted, or condoned Bible reading.[56] Cooperation between churches and the public schools in offering released time religious education spread from a single program in Gary, Indiana, in 1914 in which 619 pupils participated to an estimated 2,200 communities involving an estimated 2,000,000 participants in the mid-1940s.[57] For other Americans, however, these programs represented too much of religion in the public school. And again, as in the latter part of the nineteenth century, these questions came to be debated and decided—provisionally, at least—in the courts.

In recent decades the U.S. Supreme Court has declared unconstitutional such obviously religious practices in the public schools as school-sponsored prayer, devotional Bible reading, and on-premises released time religious education.[58] One might conclude, as many have, that as a result of these decisions the court has moved the public school in a secular direction. But I would suggest that some of the same caution is warranted in describing the court's decisions as we have used in approaching a particular historical period. I suggest this caution for two reasons: (1) while ruling out certain religious practices, the court has been unwilling

56. Donald E. Boles, *The Bible, Religion and the Public Schools,* 2d ed. (Ames: Iowa State University Press, 1963), p. 53.
57. Quoted by Justice Frankfurter in *McCollum* v. *Board of Education,* 333 U.S. 203, 224–25, and n. 16 (1948).
58. *Engel* v. *Vitale,* 370 U.S. 421 (1962); *Abington School District* v. *Schempp,* 374 U.S. 203 (1963); and *McCollum* v. *Board of Education,* 333 U.S. 203 (1948).

to prohibit all public school attention to church religion;[59] and (2) in its own way the court has also given due attention to the phenomenon described by Mead as "the religion of the Republic" and by Bellah as "civil religion."[60] In so doing the court has articulated a position which is neither sectarian nor consistently secularistic.

Generally church or denominational religion has been denied a primary role in the American public school. At the same time, Americans have neither sought nor desired a public school atmosphere devoid of all religious influence. The American body politic has not been infected with a vigorous anticlericalism or antiecclesiasticism, nor has radical atheism flourished therein. The common good has appeared to require common commitments and aspirations which were conditioned but not dominated by church religion. In their very commonness they went beyond church religion, but still they displayed some of the qualities which men have associated with the elemental human phenomenon of religion. Hence one might speak of a common religion in America which is both influenced by and different from the religion of the denominations. I am inclined to think, however, that it might be more accurate to refer to a process of common religionizing than to imply that there is some hard and fast reality known as common religion. This process has involved interaction through time between men of various religious affiliations and ideas. It is a dynamic process which has necessarily been a part of the thrust toward American identity. And the common school has been the primary center in and around which this common religionizing has gone on.

The process of common religionizing has sometimes appeared to require subordination of religious particularities to the common good. Indeed, at times it has seemed to some to require even more than subordination—that is, a kind of homogenizing effect in which all differences would disappear in the one great nationalistic

---

59. *Zorach* v. *Clauson,* 343 U.S. 306 (1952); and passages in *Abington School District* v. *Schempp,* 374 U.S. 203 (1963) dealing with the study of religion.
60. The Jehovah's Witnesses' flag salute cases and the desegregation cases are especially significant in this regard. See also *Engel* v. *Vitale,* 370 U.S. 421, 433 ff.

faith and in its church, the public school. But at least two factors have militated against this monolithic effect: (1) the continuing vigor of church or denominational religion—as evidenced in such widely different examples as the amazing record of the Roman Catholic church in maintaining its own school system and the refusal of Jehovah's Witnesses to pledge allegiance to the flag; and (2) that very transcendent element which Bellah and Mead note in their discussions of common religion. A common religion which only sacralized the nation without bringing it under the judgment of a transnational referrent would not accord with the best in the heritage.

3

American Cultural Impacts
on Catholicism

THOMAS T. McAVOY

Outside of the Spanish descendants in the missions of the Southwest and a few French settlers whose decendants lived on within the United States, Roman Catholicism in the present United States began with the arrival of the English colony of Lord Calvert in Maryland in 1634.

In this earliest English Catholic group in Maryland there arose almost at the start the first of many discussions about what parts of European Catholicism should be incorporated into the Catholicism of the New World. The Jesuits claimed the rights of the clergy in Catholic lands and were opposed by the proprietor. The result was the first accommodation of Catholicism to the New World. In the story of Catholicism in Maryland after 1689 was contained also the fear of a non-Catholic majority which characterized American Catholicism during the next two centuries.

John Carroll, by special permission elected by his fellow priests, became the first bishop of Baltimore. One of his first functions as bishop was to convene a synod of the clergy of the diocese in Baltimore on November 7, 1791. Judging from the decrees of the first synod,[1] Catholicism in the United States followed in spirit the reforms of the Council of Trent, with special emphasis on the sacraments as the essentials of Catholic practice. The official version of the Scriptures was that of Douay. Where priests were available,

1. *Concilia Provincialia Baltimori Habita ab Anno 1829 usque ad Annum 1849,* 2d ed. (Baltimore, 1851), pp. 11–24.

the center of worship was the Mass, with the reception of Holy Communion at least once a year after the first Communion, which was to be delayed until the youngster had some maturity. The prayers mentioned in this first synod were the common prayers such as the Pater, the Ave, and the Credo, the litanies of the Holy Name and of the Blessed Virgin, and the acts of faith, hope, and charity. The instructions about the priests and their conduct indicate a reformed tendency. In 1810 when the newly consecrated first suffragan bishops held their first meeting with the new metropolitan, Archbishop Carroll, no real change in these matters was suggested, but there was an added note of severity against attendance at public plays, the theater, and the reading of novels. The faithful at that time were also warned against joining the Freemasons.[2]

By 1829 there were between five and six hundred thousand Catholics among the approximately twelve million people in the new nation. They were for the most part poor people. They had not brought with them any church organization, although most of their priests were immigrants like the laymen themselves. The formation of most congregations was haphazard, which led to undesirable financial relations and the threat of lay domination—the celebrated controversy over lay trusteeism.

Undoubtedly the disturbing factor arising from the immigrant character of American Catholicism was foreign nationalism—Irish nationalism chiefly, although there were at times some manifestations of French and German nationalism. Irish nationalism was dangerous in the eyes of the native and the English and French clergymen of Baltimore because they did not want to have an Irish ethnic church and because so many of the recalcitrant clergymen of the region were Irish. The most serious disturbances tended to combine arrant nationalism and lay trusteeism. The Sulpician archbishops of Baltimore felt sure that a council called to meet these problems would be dominated by Irish ecclesiastics, the most forceful of whom was Bishop John England of Charleston, South Carolina; Bishop England on his part was quite sure that a coun-

2. Ibid., pp. 25–28.

cil was the only real cure for the disorders. Ambrose Maréchal, archbishop from 1817 to 1828, refused to call a council, and Archbishop James Whitfield, his successor, called the Council of 1829 chiefly at the insistence of Roman authorities. The acts of the council decreed what was already taking place: the establishment of regular jurisdictions and the formation of the clergy into diocesan organizations. The bishops ended the threat of lay trusteeism by requiring the deeding of church properties to the bishops and the abolition of any right of patronage in the appointment of pastors. The other decrees merely reaffirmed the custom sanctioned in 1791 and 1810.[3] These early councils contain the clearest evidence of what was noticeably American in Roman Catholicism in this country. Adaptations were scarcely official until sanctioned by a decree of a provincial and, later, of a plenary council.

American Catholicism at the end of the 1850s consisted to a great extent of peasant people with a few English, Irish, and German persons who had achieved a certain local respectability. The unity that most of the bishops sought was to find expression in the First Plenary Council of 1852.[4] Besides the native Americans there were Irish, French, German, and Belgian bishops. Not one of the six archbishops was a native of America. The beliefs and practices of the American church were summed up in the first decree as being those of the Council of Trent as interpreted in the papal constitutions. The other decrees were intended to complete the uniformity of practices in the country by prescribing the use of the Roman ritual as the American ceremonial. Further uniformity was suggested by the establishment of diocesan consultors, instead of the European chapters, and the erection of chancery offices. Among other significant recommendations were the establishment of Christian doctrine schools for youth, the erection of a parish school for each church and the formation of seminaries for the diocese (or at least for the province), the adoption of a uniform set of ceremonies for benediction of the Blessed Sacrament and the

3. Ibid., pp. 31–92.
4. Ibid., supplement (1853), pp. 3–72. Cf. also Peter Keeman Guilday, *A History of the Councils of Baltimore* (New York: Macmillan Co., 1932) for a brief commentary on the conciliar decrees.

special care of Catholics in the army and navy. The regulations against lay trustees were repeated. Absent from these decrees was any statement on the subject of slavery, which was tearing apart several of the Protestant churches, or any statement on the conflicting nationalisms of the Catholic groups, which were provoking some harsh letters from Europe.

The First Plenary Council was more an act of faith than a recognition of a reality. The unity was superficial. Yet in its uniform fidelity to Trent and to Roman ritual American Catholicism could be considered unified in worship and in obedience to one authority, and for that reason it aroused the fears of the Protestant majority. In turn, the activities of anti-Catholics provided the stimulant necessary to bring the various Catholic groups together and make them loyal to their Catholic faith.

In 1853 Archbishop Cajetan Bedini,[5] papal nuncio to Brazil, was sent to the United States to explore the possibility of the establishment of a papal nunciature in Washington. Although received diplomatically by the president, he was harshly treated by the public. He had also been asked by the papal authorities to examine the condition of the Catholic church in the country. In his report on the condition of the church he made some comments on the growth in the number of Catholics:

> The erection of forty Bishoprics scarcely enough for the needs of the Diocese, when just a half century ago there was only one, gives evidence of a most consoling and undeniable increase. But this increase is not due to conversions, which as far as I know have not been *in massa* but of individuals, who for their position and merits are, and have been, very worthwhile. I think much must be attributed to the increasing prosperity of the Catholic people, who by building religious houses and by more intense worship have put themselves more in evidence than before, and this activity has rekindled their zeal.[6]

Yet he admitted that there were great losses among these immigrants, although he had no figures.

5. James F. Connelly, *The Visit of Archbishop Gaetano Bedini to the United States of America (June, 1853–February, 1854)* (Rome, 1960), contains a good account of the visit and gives a translation of Bedini's report.
6. Ibid., p. 206.

The archbishop was keenly aware of the problem of nativism. He noted:

> The Bishops who are not born in the United States must have greater fame in learning, zeal and piety to obtain the sympathies and esteem of the natives. The native American Bishops find things much easier. It is unbelievable to see how the native Bishops can escape the complications created by local authorities. However, the foreign born are always a little suspect and treated with native repugnance. The good Catholics do not consider this difference but the Protestants do. And the priests themselves find it difficult to avoid this nationalistic feeling. They try to include in the number of native Americans those who came to America when very young or who were educated in American institutions. On certain occasions though, even these are not exempt from being tagged as foreigners. I had the chance to witness the fact that the Americans value the advice and demands of the native-born Bishops more than that of foreigners and these American-born Bishops are more courageous and more persevering in the frequent controversies that arise. The American Bishop realizes that he has his nationality on his side.[7]

The bond of American Catholicism between the First and Second Plenary Councils was the common Tridentine faith. Few had the time to engage in theological discussion. Orestes Brownson, a layman, was probably the most active theologian. In the midst of the Know-Nothing reaction to Catholicism, the bishops were anxious to restrain Brownson from asserting the indirect power of the pope in temporal matters. Some of the bishops also disagreed with Brownson when he attacked Newman's theory of development of dogma.[8] The chief organs of discussion were *Brownson's Review,* from which the bishops withdrew official approval when he began to criticize the Irish as well as the nativists, and the *Metropolitan,* a monthly publication published with the approbation of Archbishop Francis Patrick Kenrick in Baltimore. Neither of these, nor any of the several weekly papers published under the bishops' patronage, could be considered an official

7. Ibid., pp. 225–26.
8. There is not yet a satisfactory biography of Orestes A. Brownson. The most authentic is by his son, Henry F. Brownson, *Orestes A. Brownson,* 3 vols. (Detroit, 1898–1900). The discussion about Newman is mostly in vol. 2.

Catholic publication, but they did keep alive some theological discussion during the decades of Catholic expansion preceding the Civil War.

American Catholicism on the eve of the Civil War was a loosely united body whose bond was a set of religious doctrines taught absolutely, combined with a fidelity to authority in the persons of the pope and his bishops. The doctrines were still those of the Council of Trent, but how they reached the ordinary Catholic, outside of the Sunday sermons, depended much upon the circumstances of the individual Catholic. Already Catholic schools were beginning to appear, although the chief teachers of Catholic children were their parents, the priests in the Sunday sermons, and the weekly Catholic press. The faithfulness of so many under such circumstances was remarkable.

Although fidelity to the pope was an outstanding characteristic of the multinational American church, there were times when the leaders of the American body were uneasy in their loyalty. When Pope Pius IX issued his encyclical *Quanta Cura* on December 8, 1864, and accompanied it with his syllabus of errors, the English press was quick to attack the syllabus as a condemnation of democracy and progress. American papers followed the English papers and implied that the syllabus was opposed to American democracy. The syllabus was not easy to defend to a hostile audience because the eighty condemned propositions were statements of opposing opinions taken from various documents written by the pope himself. They were negative in form, and their condemnation did not mean that the opposite was true. The American bishops generally faced a difficult task in trying to explain the meaning of the syllabus. Probably the clearest discussion of the syllabus was Archbishop Martin John Spalding's pastoral letter dated February 8, 1865.

Spalding pointed out that the papal document was an answer to the teachers of "Naturalism" who rejected the supernatural and revelation; it had been written against "the self-styled Liberals." The most important passage of Spalding's pastoral rejected the opinion that there was a conflict between the papal teaching and the ideals of the American government.

> The founders of our government were, thank God, neither Latitudinarians nor infidels; they were earnest, honest men; and however much some of them may have been personally lukewarm in the matter of Religion, or may have differed in religious opinions, they still professed to believe in Christ and His Revelation, and exhibited a commendable respect for his observances. Therefore, their action could not have been condemned, or even contemplated, by the Pontiff, in his recent solemn censure, pronounced on an altogether different set of men with a totally different set of principles—on men and on principles so very clearly and emphatically portrayed in the document itself, which every sound canon of interpretation requires to be construed.
>
> All other matters contained in the Encyclical, as well as the long catalogue of eighty propositions condemned in its appendix, or *Syllabus,* are to be judged on by the same standard.[9]

Archbishop Spalding had been a Southern sympathizer, although in public he maintained a careful neutrality. One of his first proposals as archbishop was to hold a national council in order to show that the Catholic body was united and to provide a statement of Catholic doctrine suitable for the American scene.

The decree of the council began with a summary of the chief doctrines of Roman Catholicism, with special attention to the nature of faith, about which Catholics differed from their Protestant neighbors, to the role of Sacred Scripture, and to the place of the Blessed Virgin in Catholic life. As a kind of appendix, the next decrees discussed what could be considered the chief heresies on the American scene, beginning with the Protestant acceptance of sects whom the Roman church now invited to unity. The other evils given special attention were indifferentism (a result of the division into sects), unitarianism and universalism, transcendentalism and pantheism, the liberal Protestant sects, the practice of superstitious animal magnetism, and spiritism.

9. Martin John Spalding, *Pastoral Letter of the Most Rev. Martin John Spalding, D.D., . . . Promulgating the Jubilee Together with the Late Encyclical of the Holy Father and the Syllabus of Errors Condemned* (Baltimore, 1865), pp. 10–11.

In the section of the decrees that dealt with zeal for souls there was a special chapter on attention to the Negroes. There was disagreement as to what could be done. In the council a proposal had been made that there be a special director whose authority would be above that of the diocesan organizations. While this did seem to be the only solution, because the Catholic Negroes were so widely scattered, bishops pressed by the burden of newly arrived immigrants in their own dioceses were unwilling to accept a supradiocesan organization.[10]

Since these decrees were not published in translation, the document that most affected the faithful was the pastoral letter. Its chief stress was on the necessity of religious authority and the powers of the hierarchy, and it advised the faithful on certain topics then before the public. Of particular interest was the statement on the relations between church and state.

The enemies of the church represented "her claims as incompatible with the independence of the Civil Power, and her action as impeding the exertions of the State to promote the well-being of society." The church, said the pastoral, does hold that the civil power is limited, but in general obedience to the civil power is held by the church to be "a religious duty founded on obedience to God, by whose authority the Civil Magistrate exercises his power. This power, however, as subordinate and delegated, must be exercised agreeable to God's law."[11]

On June 29, 1868, the pope convoked a council at the Vatican to meet on December 8, 1869, the first ecumenical council since that of Trent. Of the fifty-five bishops active in the United States, forty-eight accepted the invitation and went to Rome. It soon became evident that the most important act of the council would be a declaration of papal infallibility.[12]

10. Edwardo J. Misch, *The American Bishops and the Negro from the Civil War to the Third Plenary Council of Baltimore (1865–1884)*, Excerpta ex Dissertatione . . . (Rome, 1968).
11. Martin John Spalding, Pastoral letter, in *The National Pastorals of the American Hierarchy (1792–1919)*, ed. Peter Keeman Guilday (Washington: National Catholic Welfare Council, 1923), pp. 205–7.
12. The latest study of American participation in Vatican I is James J. Hennesey, *The First Council of the Vatican: The American Experience* (New York: Herder & Herder, 1963).

Despite the traditional devotion of American Catholics to the pope, Orestes A. Brownson insisted that several of the early American prelates were Gallican; that is to say, they acknowledged the spiritual supremacy of the pope but denied any political power. As leaders of a minority, the American prelates were generally loyal to the pope and accepted the doctrine of papal infallibility. One important example was Archbishop Martin John Spalding, the holder of the primatial see. There was no doubt in his mind that the pope was infallible when he spoke as pope, but he did not want the council to use the positive word *infallible* in its definition. On the other hand, Archbishop Peter Richard Kenrick of Saint Louis did not seem to believe that the doctrine was sufficiently contained in Scripture and tradition to warrant declaring it a dogma of the church. Many of the American bishops felt that the defining of the pope as infallible was inopportune under existing conditions, particularly since it might create hostility toward the church in countries where it was a minority, as in the United States. Nevertheless, that definition of the dogma was made, and only one American bishop, Edward Fitzgerald of Little Rock, voted against it. The twenty-five American bishops who were present voted for the dogma. Several American bishops who had opposed the definition in earlier voting were absent from the final vote. Subsequently, however, all the American bishops sent in to Rome their acceptance of the definition. American Catholics generally manifested publicly their support of the pope, who had become the "prisoner of the Vatican." Spalding did not long survive the council, dying on February 7, 1872.

The relations between bishops and their priests and the building of the parish schools were only two of many American problems that were reported to Rome in the 1880s. There was a feeling in Rome and among some Western bishops that the holding of a plenary council in the United States would be profitable. Rome listened to the suggestions of the Western bishops and on May 22, 1883, called a meeting of the archbishops or other bishops to prepare the agenda for a plenary council to be held in 1884. When the American prelates met in Rome with the officers of the Sacred

Congregation of Propaganda on November 12, they were presented with a summary (under thirteen heads) of matters to be considered in the coming council.

These proposals amounted to an imposition on the American church of a more traditional and Roman set of doctrines and rules. Archbishop James Gibbons[13] took the lead in presenting American objections to the proposed decrees. Gibbons was acting in a primatial way, even though he had not been granted such powers. When the Americans objected to an Italian presidency over the council, Rome decided that Gibbons would preside.

After receiving a letter from Pope Leo XIII (dated January 4, 1884), Gibbons called the hierarchy into session (on November 9). Gibbons also sent out the materials prepared in Rome, a chapter to each archbishop and his suffragans, to be prepared for the November meeting. The council held thirty-one private and five public sessions. The opening decrees accepted the decrees of the Vatican Council.

The other chief accomplishments were the regulations that one out of ten parishes was to be an irremovable rectorship and that a parish school was to be erected within two years for each parish church. They were the answers to the chief problems that had been taken to Rome before the council. Another important decision called for the erection of a Catholic university.

There was no disagreement among the bishops on what Rome had demanded. But the Roman superiors had no deep understanding of the more intimate problems facing the American bishops in their efforts to create a united Catholicism out of the masses of people, mostly immigrants, who had been streaming into the United States for more than four decades.

The purpose of the legislation of the Third Plenary Council was to bring American religious life more closely under the supervision of the Roman authorities and to make the rules of the church more Roman, but there were few points in the three hundred articles of the decrees that actually reformed American customs.

13. John Tracy Ellis, *The Life of James Cardinal Gibbons, Archbishop of Baltimore 1834–1921,* 2 vols. (Milwaukee: Bruce Publishing Co. 1952), is the best narrative about the events in the American church during his life.

How American could the church become? There were in general two opinions. The Americans and the Irish—generally speaking, those who spoke English as their native tongue—accepted the American cultural traditions as good, and dedicated themselves to the perpetuation of the liberty of the American way of life. There was a difference within this group because the Irish were not traditionally English, although they accepted the American form of this English tradition in all except its Protestantism. The second Catholic group embraced chiefly the Germans, the Poles, the Italians, and other Slavic and Latin groups. They were happy to be in America but knew that in order to be fully American they had eventually to change their cultural traditions. This change they hesitated to make, for two principal reasons. Some, especially the Germans and the French-Canadians, felt that Americans were un-cultured, particularly in matters of religion. They also felt their own cultural traditions could be retained even when they became Amer-icans. Complicating this cultural problem among these non-English American Catholics was the fact that the dominant group among the clergy was Irish. Generally speaking, the Irish members of the hierarchy and the clergy by this time were of American birth or had been in the country from their youth and considered them-selves fully American. But they were not so considered by either the the Anglo-American Catholics or by the Catholics whose native country was not English-speaking.

Probably the most active of the non-English Catholic groups were the Germans, who were the best situated economically of the immigrant groups. Many of them were prosperous farmers, often living in a German community in the Middle West, or were suc-cessful in business in smaller towns or in the cities that formed the German triangle extending from Cincinnati to Milwaukee to Saint Louis. In their own communities the German church was the parish church, but in the cities where there were enough Germans they had a national parish—which, however, lacked geographical lines and was not considered the equal in law of the regular geographical parish. This distinction between the regular parish and the national succursal parish caused some resentment among the Germans—

and other nationalities—partly because they thought their parishes should have full parish rights and partly because there was a constant leakage of the children of the national parishes to the American parish—sometimes called also the Irish parish.

In the fall of 1886 Father Peter Abbelen of Milwaukee asked Archbishop Gibbons for a letter of recommendation to be used in Rome, where he wanted to discuss the relations between the Irish and German priests. Suspecting nothing, Gibbons gave the recommendation. He learned from Father Denis O'Connell, his representative in Rome, that Abbelen was presenting to the Congregation of Propaganda a letter complaining of discrimination against the national parishes and asking that German parishes be given equality with English-speaking parishes. Abbelen asked for a German vicar general where there were many Germans in a diocese, and for various other changes that would remove any stigma of inferiority from the Germans in the country. Father O'Connell sent word of the petition to Bishops John Ireland and John J. Keane, in London on their way to Rome, and also notified other archbishops and American prelates.

Archbishop Gibbons was disturbed and called a meeting of the Council of Archbishops in Philadelphia on December 16. The letter of the archbishops composed by Corrigan denied any improper or unequal treatment of the Germans in their dioceses. In the meantime, Bishops Ireland and Keane had secured a delay in any answer by the Sacred Congregation to allow the archbishops' answer to be received. The two bishops also prepared and published an answer to the Abbelen petition. The decision of Cardinal Simeoni, the prefect, was sent to Gibbons on June 8, 1887, after Gibbons had had an opportunity to speak to the cardinal, and consisted of nine questions and answers to three. The response granted the right of national parishes to exist in the same area as other parishes and recognized that a national parish could also be one of the irremovable rectorships provided for by the Council of Baltimore. Cardinal Simeoni did not discuss the other complaints of Abbelen.

On May 4, 1886, Archbishop Gibbons was elevated to the Sacred College. The red biretta was conferred in Baltimore on June 30 at the hands of Archbishop Peter Richard Kenrick. Gibbons was, like his predecessors, denied the title of primate, but during most of his life there were no other cardinals in America. Rome did grant the right of the archbishop of Baltimore to preside in gatherings of the hierarchy, and addressed its national letters to him, so he was in function a primate.

One of the problems of great consequence in American life that Gibbons faced when he went to Rome was the attitude of the church toward labor unions. Even though it had passed its peak by 1886, the great labor union of the day was the Knights of Labor, and Terence Powderly, the General Master Workman at this time, was a Catholic. The organization of the Knights extended into Canada, where it met the opposition of the Canadian hierarchy, including Archbishop Elzear Taschereau of Quebec, a newly elected cardinal. The Canadians, on instructions from Rome, treated the Knights of Labor as if they were a secret (and therefore condemned) society, and Taschereau, who went to Rome with Gibbons, intended to ask Rome for a formal condemnation of the Knights. Gibbons arranged for a consultation with the Sacred Congregation while in Rome. Through his close friend Bishop J. Keane of Richmond, Gibbons had secured a statement of the policies held by the Knights before he left the United States. Gibbons had presented this to the Council of Archbishops in Baltimore on October 28. Seven archbishops had been against any condemnation of the Knights. Only two had favored condemnation. According to the rules of the Council of Baltimore, the question had to be referred to Rome. In Rome, with the aid of Bishops John Ireland and John J. Keane and Father Denis O'Connell, Cardinal Gibbons prepared a statement dated February 20, 1887, for the Sacred Congregation in which he pointed out that the Knights were willing to make any adjustments necessary to prevent a condemnation by the church, that the Knights would soon decline, and that any condemnatory action would place the church in a bad light with the laboring people. The Sacred Congregation issued no condemnation of the Knights, and Cardinal Taschereau so notified the Canadian hierarchy. By some means the press, notably the *New York Herald,* obtained a copy of his letter and printed most of it. Cardinal Gibbons was hailed as a friend of labor, and some of the luster that surrounded his action was shed also on the rest of the American hierarchy, particularly on Bishop Ireland, who probably composed the French version of the letter.[14]

The year 1889 marked the centennial of the erection of the American hierarchy, and Cardinal Gibbons planned a celebration in Baltimore. When the word got abroad several laymen, chiefly Henry F. Brownson, the son of the great publicist, and William J. Onahan, proposed that there be held in connection with the celebration a congress of Catholic laymen. To obtain the approval of Cardinal Gibbons and the remainder of the hierarchy, the leaders of the movement obtained the assistance of Archbishop John Ireland, who was emerging as the progressive leader of the American hierarchy. The centennial was celebrated in Baltimore on November 10, and the lay congress met the next two days. Prominent Catholics from all parts of the country participated. Such topics as lay action in the church, the independence of the Holy See, the new social order, societies, and capital and labor were discussed.[15] At the conclusion on November 12 Archbishop Ireland publicly blamed himself for not recognizing sooner the power for good in such congresses and expressed the hope that this would be only the first. Eventually, under much the same leadership, there would be a second lay congress in connection with the Columbian Exposition in Chicago in 1893.

In 1883 Peter Paul Cahensly, a German businessman engaged in exporting, made a special trip to the United States to see about the welfare of the German Catholic immigrants to the country. As a result of his efforts a hospice for German immigrants was

14. The relations between Gibbons and the Knights of Labor is told in detail in Henry Joseph Browne, *The Catholic Church and the Knights of Labor,* Studies in American Church History, 38 (Washington: Catholic University of America Press, 1949), pp. 105–312.
15. *Official Report of the Proceedings of the Catholic Congress Held at Baltimore, Md., November Eleventh and Twelfth, 1889* (Detroit, 1889).

established in New York, and a priest was placed in charge. He continued his interest in this work and in 1891 helped to organize a convention of European immigration societies at Lucerne, Switzerland. The meeting prepared a memorial, dated February 1891, to Pope Leo XIII complaining of the treatment of the German Catholics in the United States and asking, among other proposals, that a certain number of American bishops be appointed from the nations involved. When asked for more information, Cahensly and Count J. B. Volpe-Landi of Italy presented a supplementary memorial in June. Informed of the memorials, Cardinal Gibbon immediately protested, and Archbishop John Ireland not only protested periodically but arranged that a protest be voiced in the Senate at Washington by a Minnesota senator. The pope sent word through Cardinal Rampolla on June 28, 1891, that the petition had been rejected. That ended the movement for a separate episcopate of Germans in the United States, if it ever had existed; but the incident did nothing to quiet the opposition of the Germans to Archbishop Ireland.

In the meantime the open warfare between the two groups of the hierarchy had become known in Rome. The pope was very anxious to heal the breach. An occasion for this occurred when the managers of the Columbian Exposition or world's fair in Chicago sought certain maps from the Vatican library for exhibition in the fair. Pope Leo, through his secretary of state, Cardinal Rampolla, not only loaned the desired documents, but appointed a papal legate to accompany them and to represent the pope at the opening of the fair. Archbishop Francesco Satolli came to the United States under the direction and advice of Msgr. Denis O'Connell, who directed him to Baltimore and to the care of Ireland. Satolli attended the dedication of the fair administration building on October 28, 1892. Archbishop Corrigan gave scant attention to the legate, who remained with Ireland until he came to New York to attend the annual meeting of the archbishops on November 16.

To the surprise of the archbishops, Satolli made two proposals at the meeting. His proposal on Catholic schools, while urging the erection of Catholic schools, would have allowed other solutions to the school problem, such as the public operation attempted by Archbishop Ireland in Faribault and Stillwater. The archbishops rejected this and agreed to send their individual protests to Rome. The second proposal was that there be established an apostolic delegation in the country, probably at Washington. The archbishops rejected that too, and asked Archbishop Gibbons to prepare a soft reply. Retiring to Washington, Satolli began to settle certain clerical problems by authority granted him by Rome. Then on January 14, 1893, he announced the establishment of the apostolic delegation in Washington with himself as the first delegate. Gibbons had already composed his letter rejecting the delegation but was able to recall it after the delegate made his announcement.

On October 18, 1893, Cardinal Gibbons celebrated his silver jubilee as a priest. Gibbons sought to bring the warring hierarchy together by having Archbishop Corrigan give the sermon at the Mass and Archbishop Ireland at the evening celebration. The words of Ireland attracted the ears and the minds of his listeners and the public in general. He played on his favorite theme, "the church and the age."[16] Taking as his theme that Gibbons represented both the church and the age, he pleaded with the American church to reconcile the ideals of the church and those of the age. The ideals of the age he characterized as ambition for knowledge, love of democracy, and the search for social justice. He found the reconciliation of the church and the age in Leo XIII and in Cardinal Gibbons. The speech was quoted widely, especially by the French journals that were backing Pope Leo's appeal for reconciliation between the French Republic and the church. The next year Abbé Felix Klein edited and translated into French a volume of Ireland's sermons under the title *The Church and the Age*.

Archbishop Ireland's ally in this enthusiasm for progress and Americanism, Bishop John Keane, had become involved in a parliament or congress of religions planned in connection with the exposition in Chicago. According to the plan each religion

16. John Ireland, *The Church and Modern Society: Lectures and Addresses*, 2d ed. (Chicago, 1897), pp. 85–113.

was to have its own congress at the fair and then join in a World Congress of Religions. The Catholic Columbian Congress in 1893 was a galaxy of Catholic laymen and laywomen similar to the congress in Baltimore in 1889, at which most of the problems of the Catholic layman had been aired. The hierarchy had also commissioned Bishop Keane to take care of the Catholic participation in the Congress of Religions. Keane, Archbishop Ireland, Cardinal Gibbons, and many others gave papers in the Congress of Religions, trying with little success to imply that Catholics were nevertheless not putting themselves on the level of the other religions represented in the congress. Keane found himself immediately on the defensive, and American Catholics generally did not approve of the participation of Catholics in the congress. In 1894 at the International Catholic Congress of Science at Brussels, Keane defended Catholic participation as overcoming the European divisions of nationalities and races and presenting the Catholic faith to those who otherwise would not have heard of it.

In January 1895 there appeared the first papal letter to the church in the United States, *Longinqua Oceani*. In general it was a testimonial of the admiration and affection of the Holy Father for the faithful in this country, but there was one passage that was not well received by Archbishop Ireland and his friends. Americans were warned not to say that the conditions under which they had made so much progress were ideal.

> For the church amongst you, unopposed by the Constitution and Government of your nation, fettered by no hostile legislation, protected against violence by the common laws and the impartiality of the tribunals is free to live and act without hindrance. Yet, though all this is true, it would be erroneous to draw the conclusion that in America is to be sought the type of the most desirable state of the church, or that it would be universally lawful or expedient for State and Church to be as in America dissevered and divorced.[17]

Later in that year the apostolic delegate asked Pope Leo to send a letter condemning parliaments of religion such as that held in Chicago and the one planned for Paris. The letter was issued

17. See my treatment of the Americanist controversy in *The Great Crisis in American Catholic History, 1895–1900* (Chicago: Henry Regnery Co., 1957).

in September. While it was intended primarily for those in France who were planning the congress of 1900, it had the effect of disapproving the actions of the progressives in participating in the congress of 1893.

Following his reconciliation with the conservative Archbishop Corrigan, Satolli became acquainted with the other side of the argument. The most striking change was manifested in a sermon he gave at the dedication of a German Catholic church in Pottsville, Pennsylvania, on April 25, 1895. This was followed some months later by a speech under German Catholic auspices in Saint Louis. In his speech at Pottsville, the delegate went out of his way to praise the Germans and their loyalty to Catholic ideals.

In a letter to Cardinal Gibbons dated September 15, 1896, Pope Leo XIII stated that it was customary for rectorships of pontifical universities to have a terminal date, and he enclosed a letter to Bishop Keane which announced his removal from the office of rector of the Catholic University and said he could remain in this country or go to Rome and become a member of a sacred congregation. Gibbons summoned Keane and on September 28 gave him the enclosed message. Keane readily accepted the message and prepared to leave the university. It was generally received as a blow to the progressives and their hopes for the university. The only action taken in return by the friends of Keane was to force the resignation of Msgr. Joseph Schroeder, the leader of the Germans at the university, on some minor charge. Keane later decided to accept the proposal, contained in the letter, that he go to Rome. In the meantime there had occurred in France some events that were to have important consequences for the church in the United States.

When the Paulists had Father Walter Elliott prepare a life of their founder, Father Isaac Thomas Hecker, and published it in the *Catholic World* in the beginning of 1890 they asked Archbishop Ireland to write a preface. Later in 1891 the biography was published in book form. Elliott pictured Hecker as a progressive religious leader, but the book attracted only ordinary attention. Elliott then arranged to have the book translated into French through his friend, Viscount de Meaux. De Meaux in turn sought the aid of Count Guillaume de Chabrol.

Guillaume de Chabrol was a member of the small group of French Catholics who had answered the plea of Pope Leo XIII for a reconciliation between the church and the Republic in France, and he saw in the biography a message that promoted the cause of the *ralliement.* He had a cousin, Countess de Ravilliax, prepare a translation of the Hecker biography. She insisted that the translation not bear the name of the translator. Chabrol felt that the translation was too long and lacked force, and he appealed to a French writer, Abbé Felix Klein, asking him to smooth out and shorten the translation and to write a preface for it. After some objection, Klein agreed. In his preface he held up Hecker as the example of the priest of the future. Klein quoted Americans in tribute to Hecker and implied that he was a model worthy of imitation in France. Klein took some care to explain how Hecker's ideals were suited to the modern world and his community was qualified to meet modern conditions. The book appeared in the spring of 1897. To attract attention to the biography, Chabrol, de Meaux, and their friends literally stormed the contemporary Catholic press with reviews and press releases. The book was an instantaneous success and went into several editions.

Msgr. Denis O'Connell, who had been corresponding with Archbishop Ireland about the need of spreading the American idea of Catholicism in western Europe, saw in the Hecker biography an already successful tool for his purpose. He began to plan an Italian translation, and at the fourth Catholic International Scientific Congress at Fribourg in August 1897 he gave a paper entitled "A New Idea in the Life of Father Hecker." The paper claimed that Hecker held the ideas which he called Americanism. He distinguished between political Americanism (roughly, the philosophy of the Declaration of Independence, which was acceptable to Catholic thought) and ecclesiastical Americanism (by which the church enjoyed freedom to teach and to develop). He denied that this Americanism was the condemned liberalism of the syllabus of errors. Bishop Charles Turinaz of Nancy offered objections to O'Connell's thesis, but after Klein rebutted his claims the bishop's remarks were erased from the record. O'Connell's paper was printed in *Quinzaine* and reprinted in English and French in pamphlet form. It attracted wide attention.

Late that fall, on the celebration of the feast of Saint Charles Borromeo in the church of Saint Sulpice, Père Coubé, S.J., deplored the four evils that were threatening the church. One of the four was Americanism as presented in the biography of Father Hecker. The next Sunday there was a similar attack on these evils by another Jesuit, Père Gaudeau, and a third was given the following Sunday at Sacré Coeur. It was rumored that the intervention of Cardinal Richard stopped the attacks. The reviews of the Hecker biography continued in the French religious press, and most were favorable. In the meantime the conservative opposition to this appeal to the success of the church in America claimed that Americanists were teaching a kind of neo-Pelagianism, the condemned liberalism, and separatism. O'Connell and Keane, the latter now in Rome, wrote to their friends against this attack. Suddenly, beginning March 3, 1898, there appeared in *La Verité* a series of articles under the name of "Martel," the first of which was entitled "L'Américanisme Mystique." The articles claimed that the church was threatened with a new heresy, *Américanisme,* which was being propagated through the biography of Hecker and the writings of O'Connell, Ireland, Keane, and Klein. The articles with a few additions were published in book form under the title *Le Père Hecker est-il un saint?* It failed to get an imprimatur from Cardinal Richard. The name of a Roman publisher was placed on the book, and the imprimatur was obtained from Père Lepidi, O.P., the master of the Sacred Palace.

Hearing of the attack on Hecker, Cardinal Gibbons wrote a new preface for the sixth edition of the biography which was also released to the press. Klein wrote a letter of protest, and "Martel," acknowledged to be Father Charles Maignen, wrote a letter in his own defense. The continued sale of the biography and the publication of articles for and against "Américanisme" attracted attention in Belgium, Germany, and Italy. An effort to have the biography placed on the Index was stopped only when the pope decided to intervene. The English version of Maignen's book contained letters of O'Connell's in which he seemed to disown "Américanisme" as it was exposed by Maignen. The pope appointed a commission of cardinals to study the question. When news reached the United States that the pope was to intervene, Cardinal Gibbons sent a letter of protest and Archbishop Ireland set out for Rome. When he reached Rome, he was told that the papal letter had already been mailed to Gibbons.

The papal letter, called after its initial words *Testem Benevolentiae,* while testifying to the pope's affection for the Catholics in the United States, was intended to point out certain matters to be corrected. The pope said that Gibbons would be aware that certain ideas had been spread in connection with the translation of the life of Father Hecker. According to these ideas Catholic doctrines should be modified to make easier the conversion of those outside the church in modern times. This idea the pope rejected, since it is the church, not individuals, that decides what may be changed to suit changed times. He then listed the chief errors that had been drawn from this false premise: that external guidance was no longer necessary in the greater outflowing of grace in modern times; that natural virtues were to be extolled over supernatural virtues and that active virtues were to be preferred over passive virtues (the pope denied that there was such a distinction); that vows of religious life were no longer necessary; and that new ways of attracting souls to religion should be created. The pope stated specifically that he was not referring to the characteristics of the American people and further that he was sure that if the ideas he had condemned were held in the United States, the American bishops would reject them. It was rumored that by changing the beginning and end of the report of the commission of cardinals that investigated the subject, the pope was able to avoid accusing anyone of holding the condemned doctrines and in exempting the ordinary Americanism from criticism.

Archbishop Ireland, who was in Italy, immediately submitted but said he had never held the condemned doctrines. So did Archbishop Keane. Klein withdrew from sale the translation of the biography. Before he left Europe, Ireland gave an interview to the press in which he maintained that no one in America held the condemned doctrines but that the heresy of Americanism, as condemned in the papal letter, was the product of Abbé George Périès, a canonist fired from the Catholic University in Washington.

In the United States, Gibbons released the papal letter quickly, and little attention was given to it. The German bishops of Wisconsin and the hierarchy of the province of New York under Archbishop Corrigan wrote letters thanking the pope for warning the faithful about these dangerous opinions. Some archbishops merely acknowledged the receipt of the papal letter. Cardinal Gibbons in a letter that was not given to the public denied that any educated Catholic in the United States held the condemned doctrines. The effect that the pope had sought was attained; controversy was stilled both in the United States and in France.

In the United States there persisted a further controversy that did not get much into the press: whether the leading Americanists, Ireland, Keane, and O'Connell, actually held the doctrines that were condemned. In a parting shot the German bishops of Wisconsin accused the Americanists of using a Jansenist mental reservation in their denial that they held the condemned doctrines, thus imitating similar charges made in the Jesuit Roman publication *Civiltà cattòlica*. An article signed J. St. Clair Etheridge in the *North American Review* [18] presented Ireland's view of the controversy and was presumed to have been written by him. The two groups remained armed camps, but the public controversy was over.

While the controversy was very much in the American press, and both Archbishop Ireland and Archbishop Corrigan, the two

18. J. St. Clair Etheridge, article in the *North American Review* 170 (1899): 679–93.

protagonists, were front-page characters, there is some doubt that the controversy really affected the ordinary Catholic. Catholics, who were for the most part Democrats, were much more concerned about Archbishop Ireland's statement against Populists and "Free Silver" than they were about his attack on religious orders. And the Germans were much more concerned about his flaming drive for Americanization than about his supposed opposition to parochial schools. Those observers were probably correct who said that the pope should be thanked for distinguishing the real Americanism from the false.

The Catholicism of the overwhelming majority of American Catholics was still the basic Tridentine and Vatican faith which for most of them was contained in the Apostles' Creed, the Ten Commandments, and the acts of faith, hope, charity, and contrition. The condemnation of Americanism did affect those clergy who were trying for a quick conversion of the United States to Catholicism, but it did not check the general movements among the Catholic populace.

One reason why the condemnation of Americanism had little effect on American Catholicism at the time was that no institution was suppressed by the letter and no doctrine held by American Catholics was condemned. There were no special American doctrines of Catholicism.

How the Catholicism of these ten millions was maintained remains a source of wonderment, especially as it did not manifest the literary or artistic qualities of European Catholic areas. American Catholicism had some external supports. There were 980,670 children listed as attending Catholic schools, but there are no estimates of the Catholic children who attended public and non-Catholic schools.[19] Critical observers of Catholic education were deploring the failure of Catholic children to go on into high schools and into higher educational institutions.[20] There were ten institutions carrying the title of university, but only the

19. "General Summary," *The Catholic Directory, Almanac, and Clergy List: Quarterly for 1900* (Milwaukee, 1900).
20. James A. Burns, C.S.C., "Catholic Secondary Schools," *American Catholic Quarterly Review* 26 (1902): 485–99.

Catholic University was prepared to give graduate work, properly speaking, and that university had suffered serious losses in its faculty in the controversies during the first decade of its operation.

Unquestionably the formation of American Catholicism during the first decade of the twentieth century was in the hands of the directors of American seminaries. Not every seminary was able to obtain superior scholars, and much of the work done in them was the insistence on the fundamental Tridentine and Vatican I faith as contained in some dogmatic and moral theology textbook. But there were on the staffs of some of these seminaries men who could be said to have formulated what there was of American theological thinking. Besides the Catholic University, with its *University Bulletin,* there were five notable seminaries: Saint Mary's in Baltimore; Saint Bernard's in Rochester, New York; Saint Joseph's Seminary in Dunwoodie, New York; Saint Charles Seminary in Philadelphia; and Saint John's Seminary in Brighton, Massachusetts. They had a limited clientele and did not form any special school of theological thought, but they gave the Catholic multitude the beginnings of religious leadership. They had few outlets for their studies. The *American Ecclesiastical Review* founded by Father Herman Heuser at Saint Charles Seminary in Philadelphia was technically a magazine for priests and devoted most of its pages to pastoral problems, yet it did attempt to keep abreast of the technical journals of western Europe. The *Catholic Encyclopedia* was formally begun in January 1905, and while it was not an American product, in its more delicate theological writings it did testify to the intellectual ferment that was growing in the church in America. Also in 1905, the faculty of Saint Joseph's Seminary in New York began to publish the *New York Review,* subtitled *A Journal of the Ancient Faith and Modern Thought.* It attracted not only ambitious Catholic writers from the United States, but such European writers as Vincent McNabb, Pierre Batifol, Henri Brémond, and Wilfrid Ward. Among the American contributors were Francis E. Gigot, John A. Ryan, Francis P. Duffy, and Edward J. Hanna.

Following the Spanish-American War there were definite Catholic interests at stake in the settlement of the claims of the religious orders to lands that had been taken over by the new government in the Philippines. Since the Catholic viewpoint seemed underrepresented in the press, it seemed desirable to muster Catholic opinion in an organized effort. Under the leadership of Bishop James McFaul of Trenton and of Bishop Sebastian Messmer of Green Bay an effort was made to line up all Catholic societies into a federation. This was partly an imitation of the *Verein* of German societies that had been quite successful; by creating a federation the plan would avoid the strongly centralizing efforts of the Americanists. The Knights of Saint John, a German social and insurance society, made the first move. The Irish Catholic Benevolent Union cooperated. Preliminary meetings were held at Trenton, Cincinnati, Philadelphia, and Chicago, and the American Federation of Catholic Societies was launched in Cincinnati on December 19, 1901.

The federation had to meet two serious objections. Some thought the leaders were trying to organize a Catholic political party somewhat like the Center party in Germany. A more serious objection grew out of the nature of the organization. It was just a federation of societies, and the general organization never had much authority over the individual members. Also, it failed to attract into its federation the Knights of Columbus. The annual meeting of the federation was a pompous affair, usually attended by Cardinal Gibbons, the apostolic delegate, and a few bishops, and consisted in fervent speeches. There were no abiding accomplishments. It was faced with a need for serious reorganization when it was replaced in 1917 by the National Catholic War Council.

The condemnation of Americanism had only slight influence on the teaching and writing of American theologians. Although Archbishop John Ireland had been critical of religious orders, he had not attacked them theologically. In most of his fervent appeals for progress and for cooperation with the spirit of the age, no new theology was implied. The same could be said of Archbishop John

J. Keane, although in his defense of his participation in the Congress of Religions he had praised the fact that in the United States the people were abolishing national and confessional lines. Yet his warnings to Klein when under fire show that Keane had no idea of creating a new Catholicism. If there was to be a new development theologically in the United States it would have to come from those who were engaged in theological study. These were the faculty of the Catholic University theological schools and the faculties of the other seminaries of the country. The unsigned articles on Scripture and the new theology in the *American Ecclesiastical Review* and some of the editorial comments in the *Catholic World* had manifested an interest in the "new" theology. Only the *New York Review* might seem involved in the new criticisms of Scripture and theology. When the *Lamentabile* and the *Pascendi* appeared, the *New York Review* soon ceased, and all manifestations of interest in the "new" theology disappeared from the Catholic literary journals. Prompted by further decrees from Rome, there began the dismantling of whatever American theological efforts had been created.

The effect of the Modernism decrees on the seminaries was simply to quiet any voices or pens that might have expressed themselves during the next five years. Whether every diocese set up a council of vigilance or not, the purpose of the decree had been attained. At the Catholic University, partly because of the ability of Fathers William J. Kirby and John A. Ryan, a safe field for research—and a profitable one for American Catholicism—was founded in applying the principles of Pope Leo XIII's *Rerum Novarum* to the field of industrial relations. Modernistic tendencies were severely checked, and outside of the writings on industrial ethics writings in theology were few until the promulgation of the 1918 Code of Canon Law opened that new field for theological effort.

When the United States entered World War I, the Council of Archbishops meeting in Washington sent to President Wilson a formal promise of cooperation in the war effort. While there was no doctrinal change in American Catholicism during the war, the acceptance of American nationalism was more clearly felt. On the surface it seemed that the Catholic hierarchy was a united force which could mold the Catholic minority into a strong force for Catholic purposes. But these were only appearances. There were many bishops who opposed any centralizing power, some bishops gave only nominal cooperation, some of them regarded an institution such as the National Council Welfare Council, successor to the Catholic War Council, as an interference in the proper diocesan power of the individual bishop. Some bishops complained to Rome of this interference in diocesan affairs, and in March 1922 the national council was suppressed. Other American bishops, especially Bishop Joseph Schrembs, went to Rome to explain more fully the nature and the work of the council. As a result the council was restored in June 1922, but its name was changed to National Catholic Welfare Conference, and membership in it of bishops and their dioceses was made voluntary.

The shutting off of immigration, the formation of the National Catholic Welfare Conference, and the general prosperity of the country were factors in the development of a mild Catholic self-consciousness in the United States. The pastoral of the bishops of 1919 together with the Baltimore Council Catechism expressed the faith of the American church about as completely as it has ever been stated. There was little of Americanism in either.

There was one other development of the twentieth century that changed the quality of American Catholicism. Catholics in the United States had always generally fulfilled the obligation of attendance at Mass on Sundays and certain other feast days, but frequent attendance at the Communion table was not common until after the decree on frequent and daily Communion in 1905. Coupled with the decree on frequent Communion was the allowing of children to receive the sacrament. Over the period of a decade this changed the character of active Catholicism in the United States. No longer could a man pretend to be an active Catholic unless he attended the sacraments. At the same time there was an increase in popular devotions such as novenas and in public demonstrations of devotion. Probably the peak in this manifestation was the international Eucharistic Congress held in Chicago on June 20–24, 1926, at which twelve cardinals, hundreds of bishops, and thousands of priests and lay people joined in what was a grand manifestation of faith without any political or commercial purpose.

Another important factor in the growth and organization of the Catholic body was the enforcement of the new Code of Canon Law. Prior to the promulgation of the code, canon law had been for most American clergymen a labyrinth through which only an expert could find his way. The code gave order not only to the law but also to the means of enforcement. Legislation about the building of and the attendance at Catholic schools, the church's rules about marriage, the proper relation of people to their pastor and the pastor to the bishop and the religious to his superior, were clarified. Bishops and superiors of religious communities soon sent select younger priests to Rome and to the Catholic University to become adept in the new legislation. The orderliness of American Catholicism amidst the growth of external devotions in the next two decades can best be explained by the effective enforcement of the Code of Canon Law. The code was above nationality and class; while it was cold, it was impartial. Thus there emerged in the period before the Second World War a Catholic organization in the United States without many national traits yet with a uniformity that was a great surprise to European Catholics and a source of wonderment to non-Catholic Americans.

As the nation approached participation in World War II, American Catholicism could be said to form a real unity for the first time. The foreign language enclaves were gradually disappearing as the children of the second and third generation of the foreign-language parishes failed to master the old languages and, even if they remained in the parish, ceased to use the languages of their parents. The enforcement of the canonical requirements about schools had created a real network of Catholic elementary educational schools in all parts of the country, with diocesan superintendents supervising the fulfillment of state requirements as well as diocesan regulations. In the Middle West and in some large cities elsewhere there had grown up also a system of Catholic high schools. The Catholic colleges were generally not under episcopal supervision, since they were founded and run by religious communities. There was a greater percentage of Catholic high school graduates going to college, but probably more than half of the Catholics who went to college attended public or non-Catholic colleges. Thus the new canon law had contrived to control Catholics as children during primary or secondary education, but there was really no Catholic agency that reached out to the adult layman. The constant plea for Catholic lay leadership received no adequate reply.

Clerical education also was well organized by the code and was still under the influence of the Counter-Reformation following the rise of Modernism. The complete seminary program consisted of four years of high school, four years of college (which included at least two years of philosophy), and four years of theology. The high school and first two years of college were devoted to the study of classical writers, without the science proposed by the *Pascendi*. Philosophy was usually taught from a textbook derived from Saint Thomas Aquinas. The theology was based on some compendiums of dogmatic and moral theology, also quite Thomistic and written in Latin. The introductions to Scripture and to church history were rudimentary. The discipline of the seminary was basically what Rome had demanded as an aftermath of the Modernism crisis.

There were in the country a few new evidences of an American Catholic culture. *America,* published by the Jesuits, and *Commonweal,* published by laymen, were the chief literary and critical weeklies. The *Catholic World* and the *Ave Maria* were the main literary periodicals, and there were several other periodicals devoted to missionary endeavors. The *Catholic Historical Review,* the *New Scholasticism, Thought,* the *Biblical Review,* the *Thomist,* and, just before the war, the *Review of Politics* gave some promise of a new cultural flowering among American Catholics. The pastoral character of the *American Ecclesiastical Review* and the *Pastoral and Homiletic Review* indicated that clerical intellectual pursuits were not strong.

American opposition to Catholicism generally was still nativistic and reached a new peak when Alfred E. Smith was the Democratic nominee for president in 1928. There was an overtone of popular religious bigotry in the anti-Catholic actions, but there was no real discussion of theological differences between Catholic and non-Catholic groups. The depression had one good effect on religious bickerings. Since there was no money to spend on this kind of warfare and since the economic problems ignored religious lines, religious differences were more or less forgotten in the efforts to recover from the depression. The legislation and public action of the recovery period did not destroy Catholic unity but shored it up. At the same time, they emphasized the nationalism that was to become a characteristic of American Catholicism. By the time the nation entered World War II, American Catholicism had acquired a certain devotion to the American character, and Catholics appeared as popular leaders in most ordinary patriotic endeavors. This created the notion that American Catholics were isolationists in world affairs. Some of this came from ancestral Irish and German opposition to England, America's chief ally, and the ordinary immigrants' children's lack of interest in foreign affairs.

As the nation drew near to participation in World War II there was an intensification of Catholic patriotism. An organization to direct Catholic services to the nation already existed in the National Catholic Welfare Conference. A second factor was the reorganization of the Military Ordinariate under Archbishop Francis Spellman of New York and his auxiliary, Bishop John F. O'Hara, C.S.C. Thousands of priests were drawn into the services and by their ministrations kept the great body of Catholic men in the armed services loyal to the church. Catholics of all ancestries were quite patriotic during the war, furnishing according to some estimates more than their share of men, holding off only on the question of cooperating with the Soviets. The huge task of shifting Catholic men and the priests who had ministered to them back to civilian life was done almost without incident. Thousands of young Catholics took advantage of the GI bill and attended colleges, Catholic or non-Catholic. The young newly married Catholic couples moved with the others of their class and age to the suburbs, where young priests were sent to establish parishes.

Something seemed to happen to American Catholicism in the reconstruction period after the war. It was not theological, although the growth of interest in scriptural and theological studies seemed to be part of this new movement. So far as the laymen were concerned, there was a continued interest in the liturgical services, a kind of desire to participate more than earlier American generations had participated in the life of the church. They were encouraged by some younger clergymen, especially in the Middle West—in Chicago, at Notre Dame, and at Saint John's of Collegeville, Minnesota. Then came Pope John XXIII and his decision to hold a council. The dust has not settled from these eruptions in American Catholic life, although the council is already in the past.

American Catholicism in this age of instantaneous world communication has much in common with world Catholicism. It accepts the documents of the council and follows the leadership of the pope and the bishops. But the democratic milieu in which the present generation of American Catholics has been formed has caused some change. While there are no new dogmas, there is a new critical attitude toward the old dogmas. The liturgical movement has taken hold of the changes of Vatican Council II and tried to make them fit the postwar American scene. There is not yet an American theology, and there may never be, in the sense that new dogmas will be evolved. Even the civic loyalism so prominent in American Catholicism through World War II has become self-critical. The refusal over so many decades to look outside the walls of Catholicism has been upset by the lowering of the walls. The fact that the old catechism is not being used in studying Catholicism is more than symbolic, and the demand for a new canon law fits in with the many rebellions against the old rules. The majority of American Catholics have not changed, but the active ones have.

4

The New Quest
of American Catholicism

DOROTHY DOHEN

Commentators who have rejoiced at the Americanization of the Catholic church and those who have taken a more reserved attitude toward this phenomenon in the past have agreed that today Catholicism has become fully at home in American life. While in 1960 it was still a subject for prolonged comment that a Catholic should run for president of the United States, it is interesting to note that eight years later, when Senators Robert Kennedy and Eugene McCarthy were slugging it out in presidential primary contests, no notice was taken of their mutual religion, and when another Catholic, Senator Muskie, was nominated for vice president his religion remained a matter of personal biography rather than public issue.

It is true that as late as 1961 Gerhard Lenski could publish the results of his sociological inquiry [1] which purported to indicate that Catholics had significantly different value orientations from Americans of other religious persuasions, but shortly thereafter other sociologists produced evidence to show that Catholics are no different from other Americans in regards to values of achievement and worldly success.[2] Catholics as "fish-eaters" seemed to preserve the

1. Gerhard Lenski, *The Religious Factor* (Garden City: Doubleday & Co., 1961).
2. Marvin Bressler and Charles F. Westoff, "Catholic Education, Economic Values, and Achievement," *American Journal of Sociology* 69 (1963): 225–33; Andrew M. Greeley, "Influence of the 'Religious Factor' on Career Plans and Occupational Values of College Graduates," *American Journal of Sociology* 68 (1963): 658–71. See also Andrew M. Greeley and Peter H. Rossi, *The Education of Catholic Americans* (Garden City: Doubleday & Co., 1968).

76

mark of a different subculture for a longer time; however, while the airlines continue to serve kosher food to Orthodox Jewish travelers, Catholicism had bowed to the exigencies of the skyway long before the abrogation of universal Friday abstinence.

On another, formerly important, matter differences are diminishing; the fertility of American Catholics is falling into line with that of other Americans. There is evidence that even the fertility patterns of Roman Catholic women of college background, which during the post–World War II period were markedly different from their peers of other religions, are conforming to the American norm. When the *Reader's Digest* polls of the 1950s indicated that American Catholics were becoming as tolerant of the use of contraceptives as other Americans, both clergy and laity may have been shocked, but so much is it taken for granted today that Catholics in America have accepted artificial contraception that polls on this topic are no longer newsworthy. Teaching in a Catholic university, I felt no surprise that a survey showed that the students in a nearby Catholic men's college shared the same doubts as to the existence of God and the same approval of premarital sex as other American males.

Over a period of nine years it has become more patent to me that Catholic students in introductory sociology courses are less and less able to differentiate between the values and behavioral patterns of American Catholicism as a subculture and those of American culture as a whole. While the authors of sociology texts may have good reason for continuing to label American Catholicism as a subculture, this reason is less and less apparent to Catholic students, who after much thought can only think of the issue of abortion as marking Catholics out as different from their fellow Americans. (If the instructor cannot resist prodding them, and asks if they agree with the author of the text that "money" and "achievement" are the most important values in American culture and, if so, whether these values are congruent with Catholicism, it becomes evident that this is something they have never thought about. They themselves do not experience any cultural conflict, nor do they perceive any conflict in the lives of their fellow

Catholics. One student, noting that charity—"love"—is supposed to be the highest value of the Catholic and that in practice Catholics are no different from anybody else, commented: "Maybe the hippies are right after all. If they are, and love is the highest value, then there should be conflict.")

In the face of this convergence of American Catholicism with the American way of life, it is evident nevertheless that American Catholicism as an institution to a certain extent goes its own way, has its own interests, maintains its own flourishing resources, and faces its own problems. In New York State the Catholic bishops' lobbying against the Blaine Amendment and abortion reform testifies to the fact that not all interests have converged. The crowded urban and suburban Catholic churches on summer Sundays show that American Catholics have not yet, at any rate, taken the same relaxed attitude toward hot-weather worship as many other American Christians. The endless debates on priestly celibacy in the Catholic press, the confrontations of clergy and hierarchy in such diverse cities as San Antonio and Washington, the personal agonies of sisters leaving their convents, as well as the doubts, perplexities, and experiences of the ordinary Catholic in the post-Vatican II period, evidently testify that there are problems which are peculiar to American Catholics.

Yet if these problems are viewed in greater depth are they really that peculiarly Catholic? The celibacy issue may distract priests from realizing that they are facing the same vocational crisis in which their Protestant colleagues are involved. At least one Protestant clergyman, commenting on the celibacy issue, raised rather ruefully the question as to what priests are going to do when they get married and find that—like married ministers—they have still to solve the pastoral problem of the churches. Vatican II may have precipitated changes in the Mass, but liturgical renewal is a Protestant as well as a Catholic concern. The American Catholic who has attended a Eucharist where the priest does not wear vestments, and where the congregation sings "A Mighty Fortress Is Our God," compares notes with her Lutheran cousin whose innovating minister had introduced vestments and Gregorian chant!

In American Catholicism cleavages between the "traditionalists" and the "progressives" may have different manifestations than in Protestantism but they are a reality in Protestantism as well. The old pastor may have trouble with his new curate, but then the "generation gap" affects us all. The crisis of authority may be especially acute in a hierarchically structured church, but are the discontents of Roman Catholic seminarians basically different from those of their counterparts at Union Theological Seminary? Or, for that matter, any different from those of the students at Berkeley, Columbia, or Harvard? The union leader whose members shock him by rejecting the contract that he has won from management sees a crisis of authority and says: "You can't be sure of anyone anymore." Indeed, the formerly docile religious who rebel against their superior or the priests against their bishops may more surely be analyzed as a case in common with the union members than as a phenomenon particularly Catholic, and the struggle for "priest power" may be understood as a variation of the generic struggle for power by students and blacks. In a year when the teachers, the firemen, the policemen, and the sanitation department of one city have gone on strike, the suggestion that priests should stop saying Sunday Mass until the bishop accedes to their demands is not too surprising.

Sociologists may use the single word *anomie* to describe this present state of American society, but it is a word with many connotations, pointing as it does to the present "normlessness" in American life: people are not only not sure of the rules, but are also not sure any longer what meaning there is—whether indeed there is a meaning at all—behind the rules. This crisis of meaning —or, in the religious context, "crisis of faith"—is perhaps most obvious in Catholicism, where in the halcyon days immediately following Vatican II, renewal was looked upon simply as a changing of rules (liturgical rubrics, laws of abstinence) in order to get at meaning. The inflexible, antiquated rules had subverted the meaning, it was argued; change them, and the meaning will become clear once more. But soon the crisis was perceived in reality to be on a much deeper level. In the case of the Catholic this is symbolized by the reaction to the vernacular liturgy: "Now that we know what we believe we are not sure that we believe it." It is instructive that in the religious survey at Manhattan College more students doubted the existence of God than the existence of the Trinity. But the former had become a "real" question to them, as had the problem of Christ's presence in the Eucharist, which they also doubted in large numbers.

This crisis of faith, this crisis of meaning, is not peculiarly Catholic; it affects all Americans to some extent, though admittedly various parts of the population more or less spectacularly. Thus, the student protesters and the adolescents who have turned off religion may testify more openly than the adults to the anomie, the lack of meaning, in American society, to the failure of American churches to provide them with a faith which transcends the "faith in the American way of life" which they now reject. But to see the crisis of meaning as limited to the young is to miss its deeper implications. The literature of America, as well as the literature of other cultures, is replete with adolescent crises of faith and their concomitant, adolescent conversions. What seems significant now is not that the high school boy doubts his faith, but that the religious brother who is teaching him also doubts. Put another way, it would not be terribly important that the young rejected the tradition of their middle-aged parents if the middle-aged were themselves confident of the meaning and the worth of this tradition. A society is indeed anomic when the young cannot really test their parents' values by rejecting them because they are not sure what the parents' values are.

The thrust of our argument is that, for better or for worse, American Catholicism today reflects American society, suffers from the problems of American life, and cannot be analyzed fruitfully apart from this American context. Moreover, even the solutions to which it turns have an affinity for those adopted by other religious and secular institutions in American society. Thus, the sisters who have done away with superiors and whose convents are run by consensus, the priests who are urging their bishops to allow them a voice in the government of their diocese as well as in the selection

of their own assignments, the lay people who want the parish council to become a vehicle for popular sharing of parochial responsibilities—all speak in the terms of "participatory democracy." The
desire for community, the need to find one's identity among those
who care, which seems to play a large part in the motivation of
students in rebellion against large, impersonal universities, moti-
vates also those Catholics who refuse to go any longer to Mass at
the huge urban parish where anonymity prevails, and turn instead
to informal groups for the celebration of the liturgy. The vocabu-
lary of relevancy has been adopted by the Catholic as well as by
his secular counterpart.

In fact, so similar is the ferment in American Catholicism to the
ferment going on in American society as a whole, that it seems
deceptively easy to analyze it exclusively as an *American* phenomenon. It is possible to interpret the trends in American Catholicism as a full flowering of the Catholic church in American
soil. The present emphasis on the self-fulfillment of the individual
nun or priest wishing to use his gifts at the job he desires can be
viewed as the Catholic assimilation of the American value of individualism; the stress on the participation of every member in the
government of the parish, diocese, the religious community, as
congruent with American democratic and egalitarian values. If
"blind obedience" is out and "doing your own thing" is in among
American Catholics, according to this interpretation, it is not
because they are Catholics, but because they are Americans. Indeed, according to some commentators, practically all that is
necessary to complete the renewal of the Catholic church in this
country is the full Americanization of the structure of the church.[3]
In that way, the church can once again become relevant to modern
man.

Leaving aside for the moment possible reservations about
"Americanization" as a solid basis for religious renewal, one can
legitimately question whether the trends among American Catholics intent on renewal can be properly called "Americanization" at

3. Joseph Scheuer and Edward Wakin, *The De-Romanization of the Catholic Church* (New York: Macmillan Co., 1966); Andrew M. Greeley, *The
Catholic Experience* (Garden City: Doubleday & Co., 1967).

all. True enough, it was under the leadership of the American Jesuit theologian John Courtney Murray that the Vatican Council's document on religious liberty came into being. However, respect for the conscience of the individual, demand for participation of the individual in church affairs, and, in general, a democratization of ecclesiastical structures and cooperation with Christians of other religious traditions seem more marked in Europe than in America. It is in Holland that democratically elected representatives of the laity, priests, and religious argue publicly with Cardinal Alfrink about church policy and government. It was in Germany that thousands of Catholic laymen at the annual *Katholikentag* following the issuance of *Humanae Vitae* voted to express their disagreement with the encyclical. The collective hierarchies of Germany, Austria, Belgium, and France were forthright in affirming the rights of conscience in the birth control crisis, while the statement of the American hierarchy about the encyclical emphasized the authority of the pope. If one is going to label the trend toward democracy in the church as an "Americanizing" trend, then one has to face the paradox (or irony?) that it is more marked in Europe than in the United States.

Rather, it would seem that the emphases on collegiality, on decentralization, and on personalism in the church are "internationalizing" trends, if you view them positively; de-Romanizing trends, if you view them negatively.

In Catholicism worldwide solutions are being offered to what is perceived to be a worldwide religious crisis. It is not possible—nor, indeed, necessary—in this paper to analyze that crisis. Social scientists, theologians, and other scholars have devoted vast effort to analyzing the worldwide industrialization, urbanization, and secularization processes [4] which have severely shaken traditional religion and have caused what Peter Berger calls its "plausibility structure" to crumble. If Berger, incidentally, has summed up the plight of the churches most pithily in noting that they are competing for a shrinking market, he is not the only analyst to note that

4. See Bryan R. Wilson, *Religion in Secular Society* (Baltimore: Penguin Books, 1969); and David Martin, *The Religious and the Secular* (New York: Schocken Books, 1969).

increasingly modern man is dispensing with their services, not because he views them with hostility, but because he sees them as being beside the point.[5] The efforts that Catholics throughout the world are making to rediscover the relevance of religion are generated by the same perception of crisis they share with other Christians, but in the case of Catholics there is an attempt to relate religion to modern culture in a way that was tried by the Protestant reformers some four centuries ago. Whether the Catholic church on a worldwide scale will be able to succeed where the Protestants apparently failed, and preserve the transcendental aspects of the Christian faith while making them immanent in modern society and culture, is a moot question.[6]

But it is the American Catholic aspect of this general world crisis which is our concern here. We have tried to show that what American Catholics are experiencing today is not unique to them as *Catholic* Americans nor as *American* Catholics. Put another way, it is not that the crisis American Catholics face is unique to them nor that the means that they take to overcome it, or the values they stress in renewal, are really different from those of their European counterparts. However, it is our contention that because of the special experience of Catholics in America, the American Catholic reaction to this crisis is different. It is against this historical background of Catholics in America that one must view what otherwise would seem to be the rather strange anomalies, reactions, and possible overreactions that occur among American Catholics today.

Item One: In December 1965 Cardinal Spellman, upon returning from his annual Christmas visit to the troops in Vietnam, is quoted by reporters as saying: "Right or wrong, my country." In the summer of 1969 a Catholic pastor gives a sermon on the divine mission of America, castigating as communists all who would refuse to partake in this mission or who would demonstrate

5. Peter L. Berger, *The Sacred Canopy: Elements of a Sociological Theory of Religion* (Garden City: Doubleday & Co., 1967 [paperback]).
6. For an insightful analysis of the possibilities in Catholicism for dealing successfully with this crisis, see Thomas F. O'Dea, *The Catholic Crisis* (Boston: Beacon Press, 1968).

against the war. Yet the incidents of burning of Selective Service files have thus far all been led by Catholics.

Item Two: A sophisticated Catholic sociologist hails John F. Kennedy as having become on the day of his inauguration "the leader of the American Church."[7] Can one imagine his French counterpart hailing de Gaulle as head of the French church, or a German Catholic sociologist proclaiming Adenauer leader of the German church?

Item Three: While bishops throughout the world acknowledge publicly that they disagree with the pope on the birth control issue, only one American bishop takes a similar stand. He resigns from his diocese, and later marries a woman who has been married three times before.

Item Four: An old Irish-American lady, crippled with arthritis, says she has to go to confession because there was a snowstorm last Sunday and she could not get to Mass. A Catholic studying for a master's degree in religious education says he deliberately stays away from Mass on Sunday to prove to himself that he does not consider it a mortal sin.

Item Five: Overheard in an interfaith discussion of prayer, the rabbi of a liberal synagogue: "Prayer all depends on if God exists." Responds a middle-aged nun: "That's a big *if*. What's important is that you know the people you're worshiping with. I refuse to go to Mass where I don't personally know the priest who's celebrating."

Item Six: A bulletin put out by traditionalist American Catholics urges its readers to subscribe to *L'Osservatore Romano* as the only newspaper which speaks the truth. It also remarks that even if all the bishops in the world are in schism the church will continue under the pope. A liberal Catholic newspaper pokes fun at the pope in cartoons and written comment.

Item Seven: Well-dressed, miniskirted American sisters, elegantly coiffured, take a stand for salaries that meet the (secular) going rate, while the New York Archdiocese issues a report on parochial schools which suggests that in order to survive they must

7. Greeley, *The Catholic Experience*, p. 286.

attract lay volunteers who would offer their services for a stated period in the manner of the Peace Corps.

These items, selected for their exaggerated character, are suggestive of some of the characteristics of American Catholicism which must be placed in historical perspective. It is a Catholicism marked by self-consciousness. Throughout their history, American Catholics have experienced an identity crisis (Are they Catholics? Are they Americans? How do they relate the two?) which continues into modern times, at least among Catholics over thirty, and which reveals itself in their being unable to take either the nation or the church "for granted." Immigrants to a country where they very much wanted to be at home, they were aware that in comparison with the Protestant majority they were newcomers, and they felt the need to prove themselves.[8] A kind of hyperloyalty to the country (American Catholics are wont to point out that they have been represented in the armed forces in a number far in excess of their percentage of the total population) [9] was matched by an equally intense loyalty to the pope—Catholics nowhere outshine Americans in their fidelity to the papacy. Given this condition the possibilities of mature dissent are severely limited. In this respect, American Catholicism is still adolescent. It is evident that many American Catholics have not moved—to use the conceptualization of Jean Piaget—from a relationship of constraint to a relationship of consensus. They find it very hard to disagree with the parent (nation, pope) without kicking him in the teeth.

American Catholicism has always been a churchgoing Catholicism. In a country whose religiosity was remarked upon by Tocqueville and other European visitors from at least the early nineteenth century, Catholics outdid themselves as churchgoers. American Catholicism has been preeminently Irish-American Catholicism. Irish-Americans, whose ancestors had persisted in attending Mass in Ireland in spite of the steady persecution of those who were once religious and national enemies, could revel in the opportunity to practice their religion in a climate of freedom and were able to set

8. See Dorothy Dohen, *Nationalism and American Catholicism* (New York: Sheed & Ward, 1967).
9. See ibid., chap. 6, "First in War."

the pattern of Sunday Mass attendance for the more easygoing Catholics from southern and eastern Europe who were to follow them in migration to America. (The factor of social control is so strong in this regard that Joseph P. Fitzpartick, S.J., professor of sociology at Fordham University, has remarked that it takes as much courage for a man in an Irish village to stay away from Mass on Sunday as it does for a man in a Puerto Rican town to go to Mass.)

The Irish-American Catholic parish was, for a few generations, a genuine social community for its members as well as a place to worship God. But, in modern times, in the larger city parishes this is no longer the case. The habit of Sunday Mass has persisted, but increasingly for a growing number of dissatisfied Catholics the church has become a "sacramental filling-station" (to use Michonneau's pungent phrase) where they feel little or no sense of community, little or no human involvement with the other ten thousand or so parishioners. A Protestant, James Bissett Pratt, could suggest that Catholics offered "objective worship" (that they went to church for God's sake) in contrast with Protestants, whom he saw as being involved in "subjective worship" (they went to church for the personal satisfaction they got out of it), and he could remark that paradoxically the Catholics ended up with greater subjective satisfaction as well.[10] But Pratt made this analysis in the 1920s, and today many Catholics would disagree with it. A new generation of Catholics is rebelling against compulsory Mass attendance. They reject the club of "mortal sin" and increasingly look directly for subjective satisfaction in liturgical participation. A reaction against the impersonality, the "overobjectivity," of Catholic worship has set in, while at the same time educated Catholics, attuned to psychological nuances, reject the church's right to assign guilt. Yet they cannot completely free themselves from feeling the guilt which they deny exists.

10. James Bissett Pratt, *The Religious Consciousness* (New York: Macmillan Co., 1920), pp. 290–309, 334–36. These sections have been reprinted under the title of "Objective and Subjective Worship," in *Religion, Culture and Society,* ed. Louis Schneider (New York: John Wiley & Sons, 1964), pp. 143–56.

The socialization of Catholics in families, parishes, and parochial schools took place in a context which assured the internalization not only of Catholic values but also of the sanctions which protected them. If elsewhere in the world bishops and pastors took a more relaxed attitude, in America in the nineteenth century (and until this day) the captains of the bark of Peter ran a tight ship. Ministering to largely uneducated immigrants, they sought to protect them from the religious ravages of what must inevitably have seemed to them a Protestant country, even though it ostensibly held out the promise of religious freedom to all. That the hierarchy and clergy, many of Irish origin, should view Protestants with suspicion and distrust needs no prolonged explanation. The "persecution" of Catholics by Protestants during the nineteenth century in America was not merely something which existed solely in Irish memories. Ray Allen Billington[11] and John Higham[12] have documented the reality of nativism in the United States and the difficulties, discrimination, and long travail faced by Catholic immigrants. The nativist riots of the 1840s and the burning of Catholic churches may have done as much to send the Catholic church in a sectarian direction as any pastoral fears that the faith of Catholic immigrants would be lost in an alien environment. Whether the Catholic hierarchy proceeded to adopt the policy of setting up a set of institutions for Catholics parallel to their Protestant and secular counterparts because they were not welcomed into the latter, or because they did not choose to participate, need not be decided here. The point is that, for whatever reason, the Catholic church in America tended for a long while to exhibit a strong sectarian tendency, strange indeed for an institution which Troeltsch viewed as the example, par excellence, of a "church."

Unable to fill the traditional function of a church which "both stabilizes and determines the social order,"[13] the Catholic church

---

11. Ray Allen Billington, *The Protestant Crusade* (New York: Macmillan Co., 1938).
12. John Higham, *Strangers in the Land: Patterns of American Nativism, 1860–1925* (New Brunswick: Rutgers University Press, 1955).
13. Ernst Troeltsch, *The Social Teachings of the Christian Churches* (New York: Harper & Row, 1960 [paperback]), 1:331.

in America sought to protect its members from being swallowed up in their environment by establishing schools, hospitals, orphanages, and a vast array of organizations which assured that only in occupational life would immersion in the larger society be complete. But if this sectarian tendency was the policy of the church as a whole in America, it was a policy that was constantly being fought by the liberals in the church.[14] Prelates like Cardinal Gibbons and Archbishop Ireland pointed to the opportunities that American society offered the Catholic church; at the same time they somewhat self-consciously reassured American society that it had nothing to fear from the church. If, in resisting the sectarian temptation, these prelates in reality settled for denominational status for the church—allowing it to become, according to Herberg's interpretation, "one of the three denominations of the common religion of the American Way of Life"—they did so unwittingly. Certainly their loyalty to Rome was unquestionable. Indeed, to the present writer it seems especially unfortunate that the end result of the so-called Americanist heresy crisis was to make the American hierarchy even more outspokenly docile to the pope rather than more detached and objective in their views of American society and culture. But given the historical context in which this crisis occurred, such a result is not surprising in view of the ambiguity of the Catholic position in America and the ambivalence of Catholic bishops and clergy toward a society which had grown up apart from Catholic influence. Loyalty to the pope and loyalty to the nation were assiduously cultivated in separate Catholic institutions, where too often distrust of the world in relationship to narrowly conceived Catholic interests prevailed over evaluation of the world in the light of Christian values.

The reaction to this "ghetto Catholicism" is understandable enough. While separate and parallel institutions are still with us, increasingly they are viewed as inevitable, necessary, and good only by conservative Catholics who apparently are fighting a rearguard action. At their worst, these Catholics seem to confuse Christian values with the specific Catholic interests they are fighting to de-

14. Robert D. Cross, *The Emergence of Liberal Catholicism in America* (Cambridge, Mass.: Harvard University Press, 1958).

fend. At their best, they are struggling to realize the results of a faith which, in the present universal crisis, they have trouble articulating. But it can be questioned whether the liberals fare any better than these conservatives. Evidently triumphant in the effort to quash, once and for all, the sectarian tendency in American Catholicism, the liberals seem to face—apparently without fear— the possibilities, the challenges, the difficulties, and the rewards of the secular society in which they claim a part. In 1965, with Harvey Cox, they unabashedly "celebrated the secular"—to an extent which made Martin Marty remark three years later that Catholics alone continued to embrace secular theology after Amerian Protestants had come to realize it was a dead end.

But such overreaction is understandable. Ghetto Catholicism had warned that the world was a danger to faith, but it had not prepared Catholics to evaluate the world. Once the progressives had come to realize that the modern world was not anti-Catholic (it couldn't care less!), it is understandable that they became uncritically accepting of the world—the concrete American world. It may be no more than a curiosity of history that at a time when American hippies are affecting sandals, long robes, and beards, American Catholic religious are getting into contemporary American dress; but the hippies themselves view dress as symbolic of values, and are manifesting their rejection of core American values: achievement, affluence, appearance. The problem today may be that liberal Catholics are too busy in the intramural fight with their more conservative brethren, attempting to change those characteristics of religion which render it irrelevant to the world at the present time, to have the time, energy, or insight to evaluate that world critically. While one would on first thought expect progressives to be prophetic, there is no real reason that this should be so. Furthermore, there may be some practical difficulty in protesting against two establishments at once. Undoubtedly, of course, there are some Catholic liberals whose stand over against the secular establishment matches the prophetic indignation which they feel toward the ecclesiastical status quo. However, the more usual reaction seems to be the one evidenced at the Conference on the Underground Churches which took place in Boston in the spring of 1968. While the organizers had been careful to include papers dealing with extramural concerns of war and poverty, it was evident to this writer that such papers did not provoke the interest from the participants which was generated by such intramural topics as hierarchical authoritarianism.[15] That this was so seemed to be especially ironic in view of the audience's indignant reaction to Rocco Caporale's report of his research on underground churches, in which he concluded that they were largely middle class and introverted, not oriented to social concerns.

But perhaps American Catholics are still working out their problems of identity and marginality. If in the past the Catholic who made a success of his participation in the "world" tended to be marginal to the church, at present the Catholic who is witnessing against what he considers to be the evils of the ecclesiastical structure may still be too marginal to the American world to be critical of it. However, this observation does not seem to apply to Catholics under thirty. As Theodore M. Steeman, one of the organizers of the Boston conference, noted, considering that the conference was held on a college campus it was remarkable that there was a total absence of young people in the audience. Apparently they do not find ecclesiastical reform a pressing concern. Perhaps this augurs well for the future in the sense that it may indicate that young Catholics, having no identity problem and not feeling marginal to the world, will be free to assume a prophetic attitude toward the world precisely because they "can take it or leave it," in the same way as today—much to their elders' concern—they can "take or leave" the church.

Perhaps, too, once American Catholic identity is no longer an issue there will be a greater toleration of diversity in the church. It will no longer be at issue whether American Catholics should withdraw from or should participate in American culture. If in the past the sectarian tendency to withdraw seemed to prevail, today the churchly tendency to "form and be formed by the culture of the

15. For an interpretation of this conference see Theodore M. Steeman, "The Underground Church: The Forms and Dynamics of Change in Contemporary Catholicism," in *The Religious Situation, 1969,* ed. Donald R. Cutler (Boston: Beacon Press, 1969), pp. 713–47.

world" apparently predominates. But if Demerath is right, for religion to accomplish its mission both tendencies are necessary.[16] The sectlike tendency keeps the churchlike from a total merger with secular society, while those with a churchlike orientation prevent their more sectarian-oriented brothers from total escape from the exigencies of earthly, cultural reality.

Demerath, like sociologists before him, notably Talcott Parsons, finds the genius of the Catholic church in its traditional ability to make room for both churchlike and sectlike elements. The consensus of sociologists of religion seems to be that in the Catholicism of the past it has been the religious orders which fulfilled the function of the sect, of withdrawal, of protest against the values of the world. The religious orders kept the cutting edge of religious transcendence sharpened, while through the lives of the laity the church remained immanent in the world. But certain currents in American Catholicism at present pose an interesting question: If the thrust toward renewal in religious orders continues along present lines with female as well as male religious concerned mainly about penetrating the world, will they no longer be within the church the functional equivalent of sects? And will other groups, at present unknown and probably unborn, arise to take their place in providing transcendental witness?

At the end of a recently published work, Thomas F. O'Dea expressed the hope that institutionalized religion will contribute to the goal of "authentic transcendence and genuine community" which Christians need if they are to rediscover the relevance of their heritage to the modern world.[17] The claims of transcendence and community make for a tension similar to that posed by the contrasting churchlike and sectlike tendencies. As has already been noted, the present emphasis on community among dissatisfied American Catholics succeeded the period in American Catholic history when the focus was on transcendence, and community was taken for granted. However, there may be some grounds for

16. N. J. Demerath III, *Social Class in American Protestantism,* (Chicago: Rand McNally & Co., 1965), pp. 183–89.
17. Thomas O'Dea, *Alienation, Atheism, and the Religious Crisis* (New York: Sheed & Ward, 1969), p. 188.

wariness that transcendence can be taken for granted while community is being emphasized. But possibly among young Catholics today there is some evidence that the tension between the two will return. Certainly they are not lured to participate in liturgical experiments out of hopes of experiencing community, at least not in the same proportion as their middle-aged fellow Catholics. There is no evidence that the liturgical group will become for them a compensation for the lost *Gemeinschaft* or the family which has proved itself to be an unsatisfactory primary group. They still can drink beer with the boys or go on LSD trips with the girls, and who knows if with one of the latter they cannot begin a happy family? Consequently, they do not look to religion for community.

They are not the generation Herberg wrote about, the generation which he thought found in the Catholic church their identity as Americans, as well as viable community, during the religious revival of the fifties. That era is gone. Now the search for community is much more conscious, for those over as well as for those under thirty. But for the latter, the locus of their search for community is no longer the religious group.

And for these young American Catholics, as well as for their church, this is probably a good thing. The present writer shares the opinion of Schneider and Dornbusch that when the latent functions of religion become conscious purposes they are less likely to be attained.[18] Translated into our present context, this means that participation in religion in order to achieve community is less likely to give community, and meanwhile it negates the purpose of religion. But if young Catholics are not hung up on community like some of the middle-aged folk, can we claim that it is because they see religion as a transcendental reality? Evidence for a negative response to this question is abundant. Young Catholics who see no need to attend Mass, who apparently are deserting the church in droves, who in an increasing number of Catholic colleges are freeing themselves from any requirement that they take courses in Catholic theology, do not seem to be interested in any dimension

18. Louis Schneider and Sanford Maurice Dornbusch, "Inspirational Religious Literature: From Latent to Manifest Functions of Religion," *American Journal of Sociology* 62 (1957): 476–81.

of religion—transcendental or otherwise. But there are at the same time indications of a countertrend. Catholic college students may reject traditional theology courses, but they crowd into courses in Oriental religions. They read *I Ching* avidly, and they are searching beneath the superficialities of what looks at first sight like passing fads for something around which to orient their lives. The search for something "Other" does not, of course, mean that they will return to active participation in Catholicism, but it does hint that they are groping toward the Object of all religions.

A university chaplain wrote recently: "We are beginning to see that Bonhoeffer was wrong, that *homo religiosus* is one of the abiding definitions of man. We expected that an ever-deepening and self-sustaining secularism was the inevitable course of the future, but now we are discovering (as Becker predicted in 1957) that when our ruling values become ordinary, desacralized, and relativized, man will again undertake the quest for the sacred."[19]

For those young people of Catholic origin whose families are still "making it," the secular values which they gain with their accession to middle-class status may, for a time at least, obviate the necessity for a religious quest. But for more thoughtful young Catholics who share the malaise of their generation in the face of the successful secularism of America, the search for the sacred may take on new urgency. Where it will lead them we do not know.

The future of American Catholicism? Possibly more of the agony which committed Catholics experience at present as they face the crisis of meaning, the crisis of faith. But possibly it is not a vain hope that the future will bring ecstacy as well as more agony. If American Catholics no longer have an identity problem, if American Catholicism no longer functions as a means of social control for the church as well as for American society, if Catholics are really free—socially and psychologically—to belong or not to belong to the church, there will probably be many fewer worshipers. But, given the remnant, will there be a rediscovery of religion, and then will "transcendence in community" become a reality?

19. Myron B. Bloy, Jr., "Alienated Youth and the Chaplain," in *The Religious Situation, 1969*, p. 661.

5

Jerusalem in America

JACOB AGUS

Whether or not there is a specifically American pattern of thinking and feeling remains for us an open question. At various times, perceptive observers have identified diverse and even contradictory qualities as components of the American spirit. In nearly every case, the observer has been compelled to qualify his adjectives to the point of extreme ambiguity. So, Gunnar Myrdal described the American temper as being marked by "practical idealism," "bright fatalism," "moral optimism," etc. He is certain "that most Americans have most valuations in common"—a thesis that is surely not self-evident.[1]

Henry Pratt Fairchild maintained that "Americanism" was a definite "spiritual reality" that needed to be protected against debasement by uncontrolled immigration. He argued that the following traits of Americans were generally acknowledged: "such things as business honesty, respect for womanhood, inventiveness, political independence, physical cleanliness, good sportsmanship, and others less creditable, such as worship of success, material-mindedness, boastfulness."[2] Except for the less pleasant qualities, Europeans would hardly agree.

Ralph Barton Perry regarded the central American quality as being "collective individualism," a readiness to break fresh ground together with others. "The appropriate term is not 'organism' but 'organization'; *ad hoc* organization, extemporized to meet emer-

---

1. Gunnar Myrdal, *An American Dilemma: The Negro Problem and Modern Democracy,* 2 vols., Negro in American Life Series (New York: Harper & Bros., 1944), 1:xliv.
2. Henry Pratt Fairchild, *The Melting-Pot Mistake* (Boston: Little, Brown, & Co., 1926), pp. 201–2.

gencies, and multiple organizations in which the same individuals join many and surrender themselves to none. Americans do not take naturally to mechanized discipline. They remain an aggregate of spontaneities."[3] Perry's analysis is an extension of William James's emphasis on the metaphysical roots of the freedom of the individual, an emphasis that was consciously opposed to Rousseau's concept of the "general will" and the Germanic reverence for the absolute. To James, the fullness of empirical existence is pluralistic in character: "The truth is too great for any one actual mind, even though that mind be dubbed 'The Absolute,' to know the whole of it. The facts and worths of life need many cognizers to take them in . . . . The practical consequence of such a philosophy is the well-known democratic respect for the sacredness of individuality."[4]

Perhaps what impressed the immigrant most was the atmosphere of dynamism and hopefulness that he encountered when he first stepped on these shores. The air was electric with fresh possibilities. Hopes rather than habits guided men's actions. Among religious groups millenarian movements proliferated, and these were often secularized into some vision of the good society. Occasionally, these hopes lent force to American visions of national destiny. Abraham Cahan, the famous founder and editor of the *Jewish Daily Forward,* wrote of his first day in this country: "I had moved from the ordinary world into a special world—America."[5]

But while the spirit of emergent America was an exhilarating force, ethnic loyalties were not suppressed. On the contrary, the parochial loyalties of the new immigrants were free to develop in America, precisely because their cutting edge was directed toward distant lands—toward a free Ireland, a renascent Czechoslovakia, an independent Poland, and a reborn Israel in the land of Zion. So the immigrants tended to cluster together in their diverse enclaves

3. Ralph Barton Perry, *Characteristically American,* University of Michigan William W. Cook Foundation Lectures (New York: Alfred A. Knopf, 1949), p. 13.
4. Raph Barton Perry, *The Thought and Character of William James,* 2 vols. (Boston: Little, Brown, & Co., 1935), 2:265–66.
5. Abraham Cahan, *The Education of Abraham Cahan,* trans. L. Stein et al. (Philadelphia: Jewish Publication Society of America, 1969), p. 217.

seeking solace in each other's company. And while they climbed toward higher levels of well-being they continued to nurture warm feelings toward their compatriots of the "old country," at least in a nostalgic and occasional sense. In fact, the so-called Hansen's law maintained that the third generation of immigrants sought to regain that which the second generation had discarded—but, we may add, in a vague, sentimental way that did not imply a physical return to the ethnic enclave and its ways of life.

This paradoxical commingling of assimilation and ethnicism was paralleled by a similar development in the domain of religion. The physical act of removal to a new land entailed for many an immigrant a considerable cooling toward his specific religious tradition.

Yet the prevailing social atmosphere in America was exceedingly favorable to "religion in general." Also, the immigrant was likely to find within his own particular faith the moral help and companionship that he needed in order to feel truly at home in his new land. Consequently, the immigrants reinforced the emergent American faith, as the spiritual bond between themselves and their new neighbors, even while they cultivated their own particular heritage.

The character of the American faith is clear enough. It is "faith in faith"—a generalized reverence for the "common core" of Western religions. The classic sources of the American ideal reflect not this or that denomination but the Judeo-Christian tradition as a whole: its faith in a higher law and a Supreme Being whose will is wrought in the life of nations or of individuals; its faith in people, who need only to know the facts in order to find their way in life. Yet this faith is countered by a deep awareness of human sinfulness and a consequent belief in the majesty of the law. Radical faith in people is balanced by an equally radical faith in the institutions of law. Polarity and tension are characteristic of an "enlightened" faith, in which traditionalism and skepticism are kept in balance. One may speak of an American faith in the sense of pointing to this restless, ever shifting, central part of the spectrum between the poles of rationalism and supernaturalism. It is as far from the iconoclastic passion of atheists as it is from the dogmatic insularity of "true believers." For the liberal forces of America never had to storm the rigid ramparts of an entrenched church, and at least some representatives of faith have always been found in the forefront of the crusade for new horizons of freedom.

Turning now to an examination of the American impact on Judaism and Jewish people, we have to remember the famous adage, "Jews are like other people—only more so." While the various waves of Jewish immigrants were subject to the same sociological forces as other ethnic and religious groups, they usually found themselves in a more complex situation. As Jews, they had a bond of unity that transcended the political boundaries of Europe. And their ethnic consciousness was rooted in a dreamland that was as close to their hearts in America as it was in Europe.

In the transfer of a religious culture from the old country to the New World, the inner tensions of the faith are pulled tightly in opposite directions. The rate of change is accelerated, the inner tug-of-war between traditionalists and modernists is exacerbated, ethnic and sociological factors enter into play, distorting the serene dialectic of theologians. Let us look more closely at these factors.

First, tension between openness to changes and resistance to innovation mark the life of every religious culture, with the calls for change coming from the younger generation, those born in the new land and fully acculturated in it. In an immigrant culture, this appeal is intensified by the consciousness of the need to adapt in many ways to the new environment. The psychic mechanism of adaptation is carried over into religion. The immigrant feels that he is in a dynamic situation, engaged in a process of transmutation. Hence, he reacts positively to the very notion of change, in and by itself. Also, the intellectual leaders who dare to cross the ocean in order to serve on the periphery of civilization are likely to be pioneers and innovators in spirit. The boldness and vision of Rabbi Isaac M. Wise, who described himself as an "American before he came to America," is a case in point. He, David Einhorn, Max Lilienthal, Samuel Hirsch, and many others of their colleagues had endeavored to modernize congregational life in their native lands.

97

When their efforts proved abortive, they transferred their hopes for a free and dignified way of life to this country. On the other hand, the normal resistance of a conservative person to change is also magnified in the case of the immigrant by his nostalgia for the religion of "the good old days." With the passage of time, especially as he begins to resent the ways of his more acculturated children, he is likely to view the ways of the old country through the tinted glasses of fond enchantment. So the polarization between the old and the new is initially accelerated.

Similarly, normal contacts between different faiths are multiplied in the case of the immigrant. In a stable society different groups may live side by side without ever getting to know one another. This was particularly true for Jewish immigrants, who in the lands of Germany and central Europe were surrounded by invisible walls of implacable hatred. In this country, they found themselves in a fluid and restless situation, where new interpersonal and intergroup relations looked promising. Some account had to be taken of those who differed in faith and historical background. So, the normal osmosis of interaction between different faiths was enormously stimulated. At the same time, the traumatic process of transplantation awakened the fear of the progressive loss of identity. Group-survival became problematic. Hence there emerged an impassioned clinging to the symbols of particularism that separated the group and shielded it from the acids of the melting pot.

The high social mobility that is characteristic of America adds its momentum to the wheels of change. The second generation is always eager and usually able to move out of the area of first settlement. For them, the customs characteristic of their new homeland possess the symbolic appeal of their new status. They have arrived, they have acquired new roots, they have become founding fathers of a new tradition. This mood is deepened by the realization that the various branches of their people have brought different customs to their new country. "The American way" must be a new blend of the diverse versions of the faith in the old lands. At the same time, the desire to recapture the past and to counter the gray formlessness of a life without style and bereft of tradition begins to reassert itself, at least among the children of the third generation.

Finally, the effect of the spread of higher education in the highly industrialized cities of America pulls the strings of tension taut. The initial effect of the ongoing educational explosion is to weaken the bonds of loyalty to one's ancestral religion. The free atmosphere of secular learning dazzles the newcomers, who find themselves living in a new society where the old taboos appear strange and even ludicrous.[6] All particularities fade into the limbo of unenlightened antiquity. Only the common core of faith may still be tenable. Hence, an eagerness to strip one's heritage down to its essentials, abandoning the outer shell for the sake of the inner core. But it is also the new vision of secular ideals that reawakens and reinforces the ethnic cultural components of the old religious culture. The emerging secular viewpoint brings into a fresh focus the ethnic loyalties that underlie the historical faith. In the American cultural climate, the subcultures of ethnic groups are rarely scorned and at times are cherished as valued heirlooms belonging to the total treasury of the nation as a whole.

Ethnic loyalty in America tends to be romanticized and glorified precisely because it lacks the sting of social separatism. It is ethnicism at one remove, loyalty to the loyalty of others: to the nationalist ambitions of the Irish in Ireland, the Italians in Italy, the Ukrainians and Lithuanians in Russia, to the Zionist dream of a reborn land of Israel. The political ambitions of the group in other lands are favored, but the possibility of organizing permanent separatist, ethnic enclaves in this country has long been regarded as neither desirable nor possible. Depoliticized ethnicism is a cultural-philanthropic phenomenon which can grow and even luxuriate in America. Precisely because in practice, even if not in theory, ethnicism is intended for one's kinsfolk in other lands, it can be glorified and extolled without any awareness of derogation to the American ideal or nation.

6. Milton M. Gordon, *Assimilation in American Life: The Role of Race, Religion, and National Origins* (New York: Oxford University Press, 1964). Gordon treats the society of intellectuals and academics as a distinct subculture, paralleling those of the Protestants, Catholics, Jews, Negroes, and Mexicans (pp. 224–32).

As the descendants of the immigrants acquire the self-confidence of natives they seek to recapture the charm of the quaint ways of their forebears, and through the curious logic of sentiment they tend to magnify and sanctify the ethnic interests of their faith-community. Thus, the Zionist sympathies of the immigrants usually underwent a period of dormancy before they reappeared in a new guise as the unique policy of pro-Zionism that is characteristic of contemporary American Jewry.

In sum, the impact of American civilization upon Judaism consisted in a heightening of the historical tensions within the hearts of Jewish people, deepening the ideological divisions of the past, even while reinforcing the substratum of ethnic cohesion and its organizational superstructure.

The formation of Brandeis University is a case in point. It was organized not for the purpose of fostering the specific beliefs of the Jewish faith but to mobilize the educational concerns of the Jewish ethnic community. Yet it is not separatist in any sense; neither its faculty nor its student body is exclusively Jewish. And its orientation is toward the deepening of American culture, as well as toward the promotion of the cultural components of a Jewish subculture.

Throughout the three centuries of its existence, the American Jewish community has been in continuous contact with its European roots. The first group of Jews that settled in New Amsterdam in 1654 consisted of merchants who were accustomed to deal with firms across the Atlantic. In the beginning of the nineteenth century, Mordecai Manuel Noah presumed to solve the problem of Jewish homelessness with his plan for the settlement of European Jews on an island in the Niagara River. The beautiful town of Charleston was among the first to form a Society of Friends of Reform. Rabbi David Einhorn, who settled in Baltimore, was among the originators of the Reform movement in Germany. Rabbi Isaac M. Wise, the great organizer of the American Reform movement, was educated and ordained in Germany. Rabbi Max Lilienthal achieved renown as an educational consultant to the Russian government in connection with Jewish affairs before he settled in Cincinnati. At the end of the nineteenth and in the first generation of the twentieth century, the American Reform community was almost entirely composed of German Jews, the subethnicity of Germanism forming the substratum for their liberal theology. Classical German philosophy, with its grand generalizations, imposed its abstract categories upon their ideology of Judaism.

In the course of time, the Reform movement has become thoroughly American. It is far less ideological than German Reform was and far more pragmatic in its approach to all-Jewish problems. If one compares the Columbus Platform, adopted in 1937, with the Pittsburgh Platform, adopted in 1885, one notes an increased awareness of all-Jewish unity, a repudiation of the sectarian mood, a recognition of the ethnic factor in Jewish life and a sympathetic attitude to Zionism. While the Pittsburgh Platform was certainly more inwardly consistent, the Columbus Platform is more attuned to all the complex factors that impinge upon the Jewish faith.

The Pittsburgh Platform conceived of Judaism as a body of doctrines centering around "this God-idea" which is "the central religious truth for the human race." The Columbus Platform defined Judaism in more ethnic and historical terms as "the historical religious experience of the Jewish people," insisting however that "its message is universal."

While the Pittsburgh Platform accepted "as binding only the moral laws" of the sacred tradition, the Columbus Assembly heard calls for a "return to *Halachah,*" though these calls were purely homiletic in character.

The most bitter dissension arose over the resolution to accept the Zionist thesis. The earlier platform spoke of the messianic era in terms of "the kingdom of truth, justice, and peace among all men" and asserted that "we consider ourselves no longer a nation, but a religious community, and therefore expect neither a return to Palestine, nor a sacrificial worship under the sons of Aaron, nor the restoration of any of the laws concerning the Jewish state."

The later platform did not specifically counter these assertions, but it affirmed that the upbuilding of Palestine as a Jewish homeland gives "promise of renewed life for many of our brethren."

While it did not call on American Jews to become part of the emerging state, it asserted the duty of assisting others to do so. "We affirm the obligation of all Jewry to aid in its upbuilding as a Jewish homeland by endeavoring to make it not only a haven of refuge for the oppressed but also a center of Jewish culture and spiritual life."[7]

The Reform movement in Germany was intellectually virile but practically helpless. In the twentieth century, it was reduced to two congregations. Jewish communal organizations in Germany included all the Jews of a city or a province; hence, the inescapable obligation to resort to a strategy of compromise and mutual accommodation. To be sure, the extreme Orthodox faction seceded from the communal organization, but the liberal-minded were not that bitterly sectarian. As a result, most became Conservative and the synod convened in 1870 under the chairmanship of Prof. Moritz Lazarus was in fact dominated by Conservative rabbis.

In the United States the free choice of the individual Jew was axiomatic. Congregations were organized on the basis of likemindedness by laymen and rabbis. The Reform movement was able to build its institutions freely, save that the German provenance of its following limited for some decades the penetration of the movement into the broader strata of the Jewish community, which after the turn of the century was overwhelmingly of eastern European descent.

In the past generation, the movement has come to lay ever greater stress on the nonrational and the ethnic components of the Jewish heritage. Efforts are made in every congregational school to teach Hebrew, both as the spoken tongue of Israel and as the language of Holy Scriptures. In theology, Buber's glorification of

7. All quotations are from Jacob Bernard Agus, *Guideposts in Modern Judaism: An Analysis of Current Trends in Jewish Thought* (New York: Bloch Publishing Co., 1954), pp. 51–84; and the *Yearbooks* of the Central Conference of American Rabbis (New York), 1935 to 1937. See also Julian Morgenstern, *As a Mighty Stream* (Philadelphia: Jewish Publication Society of America, 1949); David Philipson, *The Reform Movement in Judaism,* rev. ed. (New York: Ktav Publishing House, 1967); and Samuel Cohon, *Judaism: A Way of Life: An Introduction to the Basic Ideas of Judaism* (New York: Schocken Books, 1962 [paperback]).

the Hasidic movement has found a sympathetic audience. The extreme rationalism of men like Emil G. Hirsch is not favored by the contemporary teachers of theology. Prof. Jacob Petuchowski of the Cincinnati school insists on the transcendence of the revelation at Sinai. Prof. Eugene Borowitz centers his reflections on the existential reality of the covenant between Israel and God.[8] The American Reform movement has always emphasized the ideal of community-mindedness.

Rabbi Isaac M. Wise, founder of the Union of American Hebrew Congregations, the Central Conference of American Rabbis, and the Hebrew Union College, was eager to put the quest of unity above every doctrinal consideration. His prayer book, *Minhag America,* made only minor changes in the liturgy, in order to give as little offense as possible to the Orthodox. While in his own view only the Ten Commandments were given at Sinai, he was willing to concede many a point of belief and practice if through such compromises the Jewish community could be kept from splintering. In terms of the church-sect continuum, he opted for the avoidance of sectarianism, if at all possible.

In spite of Wise's readiness for compromise, the Conservative and Orthodox congregations did not join the union. In 1881, there were approximately 200 congregations in the United States, and 123 of them joined the Reform movement.[9]

Reform rabbis provided leadership for the formation and growth of the vast philanthropic network of American Jewry. In nearly

---

8. See Jacob Petuchowski's *Ever Since Sinai: A Modern View of Torah* (New York: Scribe Publications, 1961); Eugene Borowitz's *New Jewish Theology in the Making* (Philadelphia: Westminster Press, 1968); and Ben Hamon's "The Reform Rabbis Debate Theology: A Report on the 1963 Meeting of the C.C.A.R. [Central Conference of American Rabbis]," *Judaism,* Fall 1963, p. 479. Prof. Alvin J. Reines has been reasserting the strict rationalism of Reform in recent years. He defines God as the totality of possibilities and the feeling of the holy as an awareness of the future. See his *Elements of Reform Judaism* (mimeographed).

9. See *The Jewish Encyclopedia,* 12:541, for the life and works of Isaac M. Wise. The source of the statistics quoted is Uriah L. Engelman, "Jewish Statistics in the U. S. Census of Religious Bodies," *Jewish Social Studies* 9, no. 2 (April 1947): 130–34. A similar figure is found in Louis Finkelstein, ed., *The Jews: Their History, Culture, and Religion,* 2 vols. (New York: Harper & Bros. 1949), 1:383.

every community across the length and breadth of the country, a Reform rabbi is likely to be remembered as one of the chief builders of its philanthropic institutions. This pragmatic or "secular" emphasis is still characteristic of the movement. In a recent study of the attitudes of Jewish seminarians, those of the Reform colleges gave the highest priority to the need of cultivating "the social and ethical values of American Jews."[10]

The Reform movement led the way in the formation of the ideal image of the rabbi in America. In the premodern world, the rabbi was primarily a scholar in the domain of ritual and religious civil law. He presided over a court that dealt with the problems of ritual, the laws of marriage, and commercial disputes. Only in the most exceptional circumstances, and under external duress did he have to interpret the law to the non-Jewish world. Learned laymen would generally head the various study circles in the community, and itinerant preachers would travel from town to town delivering sermons in the synagogues.

In contrast, the American rabbi is pastor, preacher, and teacher, expounding the ideals of his faith to his congregation and to the general community. His prime concern is no longer the law, be it cultic or civil, but the ideals and sentiments that underlie the law. Under his guidance, the synagogue has become the major locus of the religious life of his people. He is the pastor of his followers, grappling with their personal problems. He is also their spokesman to the larger community, articulating the import of their faith in regard to the issues of their day.

The pragmatic, nonideological character of American life is reflected in the interdenominational character of the Jewish community, which is structured to serve the philanthropic needs of Jews in this country and abroad. In recent years, the various federations have been increasingly supporting the causes of Jewish education on a nondenominational basis, financing religious schools and even establishing chairs in Judaica in several universities. As a general rule, denominational boundaries are transcended in fraternal or-

10. "The Training of American Rabbis," in *The American Jewish Year Book, 1968,* vol. 69 (Philadelphia: Jewish Publication Society of America, 1968), p. 101.

ganizations as well as in Israel-centered projects and in agencies of antidefamation.

The lines of demarcation between the Orthodox, Conservative, and Reform movements are by no means clear and distinct.[11] In many communities, a considerable segment of the community will be members of a Conservative or a Reform temple as well as of an Orthodox congregation. Many members of Orthodox congregations are not observant according to the norms affirmed by the ideology to which they subscribe. On the other hand, some Conservative congregations, including members of the faculty of the Jewish Theological Seminary, are staunchly Orthodox in practice as well as in theory. Denominational boundaries are transcended by the network of philanthropic, antidefamation, and Israel-centered projects, which for the most part are conducted along nondenominational lines.

The ebb and flow of Orthodoxy in this country is a most interesting reflection of the impact of American culture on Judaism. The mass migration of eastern European Jews from the eighties of the last century to the first decades of the twentieth century brought to these shores three major ideological groups: the provincial traditionalists who had been barely touched by the modern world; labor groups that were predominantly socialist and oriented to the

11. Jack Porter's study of the Philadelphia Jewish community showed that synagogue affiliation did not coincide with the actual convictions of laymen. Those affiliated with Conservative congregations accepted 41 percent of Orthodox teachings and 45 percent of Reform teachings. The Orthodox-affiliated accepted 71 percent of Conservative teachings and 37 percent of Reform teachings. The Reform-affiliated accepted 21 percent of Orthodox teachings. (Jack Porter, "Differentiating Features of Orthodox, Conservative, and Reform Jewish Groups in Metropolitan Philadelphia," *Journal of Jewish Social Studies,* July 1963.)

In a similar study of Baltimore Jewry, which is still unpublished, Manheim S. Shapiro posed this question to his respondents: "Regardless of your actual affiliation and membership, would you consider yourself an Orthodox, Conservative or Reform Jew?" Of the Orthodox-affiliated, 28 percent considered themselves Conservative. 3 percent Reform, and 3 percent as "none of these." Of the Conservative-affiliated, 3 percent regarded themselves Orthodox. 9 percent as Reform, 3 percent as "none of these." Of the Reform-affiliated 3 percent regarded themselves as Orthodox, 8 percent as Conservative, and 1 percent as "none of these" (p. 13).

The survey of Kansas City by the same researcher disclosed a similar situation. The percentage of Orthodox-affiliated there was 25 percent, while in Baltimore the percentage was closer to one-half.

nascent Yiddish culture of the Pale of Settlement; and the Hebrew-Zionist middle classes that dreamed of the rebirth of Jewish culture in its ancient homeland.

The Orthodox masses of the first group organized small congregations as well as central communal institutions. Their ideal was to engage a rabbi for the entire community, who would preside over all its cultic and educational institutions. They sought to adapt the communal pattern of organization (*kehillah*) in the European town to the cities of America. Generally, their efforts proved abortive. On two different occasions, the Jews of New York City tried and failed to form a *kehillah,* an overall community organization.[12]

Wherever such efforts succeeded, the communal organizations proved to be short-lived, their leading members drifting into the ranks of the Conservative and the Reform. Until the past decade, the movement away from Orthodoxy was steady and irresistible, with only the largest Orthodox synagogues being able to withstand this trend of relentless acculturation.[13] More and more Orthodox synagogues adopted first the outer symbols of Conservatism and Reform: family pews, worship in the vernacular, formal services led by a cantor and a rabbi, sermons dealing with contemporary issues. Gradually many of them accepted the inner import of these practices, the conviction that religion is an evolving body of ideals and sentiments, which must be repondered, reexperienced, and rearticulated anew in every generation.

The massive attrition to which the Orthodox community has long been subject has resulted in the formation of a firm core of committed "Torah-true" people who are passionately devoted to

12. On engaging a rabbi for the entire community, see Abraham J. Karp, "New York Chooses a Rabbi," *Publications of the American Jewish Historical Society,* March 1955, pp. 129–98. On community organization, see Maurice J. Karpf, *Jewish Community Organization in the United States: An Outline of Types of Organizations, Activities, and Problems* (New York: Bloch Publishing Co., 1938); and Harry Sebee Linfield, *The Communal Organization of the Jews in the United States, 1927* (privately printed; New York: American Jewish Committee, 1930).
13. Charles S. Liebman, "Orthodoxy in American Jewish Life," in *The American Jewish Year Book, 1965,* vol. 66 (Philadelphia: Jewish Publication Society of America, 1965), p. 13.

their way of life and their institutions.[14] This group has been reinforced by postwar refugees from the European holocaust. They are sustained by the aristocratic feeling of belonging to "the saving remnant." With the growing appreciation in the sixties of the exotic and the nonconformist, they and others no longer view their basic posture as being somehow "un-American." The Habad-Hasidim organize college weekends and retreats in the endeavor to expand their influence and win more followers for their uncompromising faith. In Williamsburg the saying is they recognize only two kinds of Jews—"devout, totally observant Liubavich Hasidim and potentially devout, potentially observant Liubavich Hasidim."

The "committed Orthodox" today constitute an estimated 4 percent of the American Jewish population.[15] They form the nucleus of a vague grouping roughly ten times as large which may be described as "nonobservant Orthodox." The majority of the Orthodox are oriented toward American life in general. Apart from the self-segregating "sects" of Hasidim, they are mildly ideological, willing to cooperate with other Jewish and non-Jewish groups in the areas of social concern.[16] Their greatest institution is the Yeshiva University of New York, a unique American enterprise where educators, scientists, and physicians are trained under Orthodox auspices.

While the vast majority of the descendants of the originally Orthodox immigrants are now either Conservative, Reform, or generally nonobservant, the children of the Yiddish-socialist and the Hebrew-Zionist immigrants have joined the religious congregations. The ideological sharpness of European socialism did not strike deep roots in the soil of America. In 1910 the leading Yiddish daily, *Forward,* which enjoyed a circulation of nearly a quarter-

14. See Liebman, "Orthodoxy in American Jewish Life," p. 18; and Solomon Poll, *Hasidic Community of Williamsburg: A Study in the Sociology of Religion* (New York: Schocken Books, 1962).
15. Liebman, "Orthodoxy in American Jewish Life," p. 18. The figure is an educated guess.
16. The policy of cooperating with the non-Orthodox rabbis has been debated anew at nearly every convention of the Union of Orthodox Congregations in the past two decades.

million, was dogmatically Marxist, printing weekly essays which ridiculed Jewish faith and practice. Gradually, the fervor of socialism was drained into the channels of welfare and labor legislation. The Yiddish press, theater, and other cultural institutions enjoyed a brief and glorious period of efflorescence. However, with the growth of acculturation, the values and ideals of the erstwhile socialist dreamers were channeled into the institutions of religion, philanthropy, and the Jewish centers, which sponsor an amazing variety of social, athletic, and cultural programs acceptable to all or nearly all Jews. Some Jewish centers have opened their membership rolls to non-Jews as well.[17]

The Hebrew-Zionist immigrants were in all probability the smallest group numerically, but their influence was out of all proportion to their numbers. The percentage of intellectuals in their ranks was large, and their concern with the upbuilding of the "homeland" was in accord with the relentless pressures of modern history which squeezed so many European Jews out of their native lands. Their Hebraic nationalism was subtly transmuted by their new environment into that peculiar brand of ethnic-cultural and philanthropic concerns that is so characteristic of America. When the state of Israel was founded, very few of the Zionists of America proceeded to settle in the land of their dreams. In spite of insistent pleas from Israel, appealing to their declared "ideology," as formulated in the literature of the movement, they insisted on their own version of American Zionism, which consisted of a sympathetic interest in and an arduous support of the upbuilding of the Holy Land. While classical Zionism negated the worth as well as the viability of Jewish life in the Diaspora, American Zion-

17. See Louis Kraft and Charles Seligman Bernheimer, eds., *Aspects of the Jewish Community Center,* National Association of Jewish Center Workers Publication (New York: National Jewish Welfare Board, 1954); and Oscar Isaiah Janowsky, *The Jewish Welfare Board Survey, with the Report of the JWB Survey Committee* (New York: Dial Press, 1948). The latter book was based on a survey in depth of the goals and programs of the Jewish community centers. It recommended an intensified emphasis on the cultural and ethical values of the Jewish tradition, within a secular framework.

ists rejected the logic of the movement, although they supported its program "for others." [18]

The philosophy of American Zionism was best formulated by Louis D. Brandeis in 1915.

> We must protect America and ourselves from demoralization, which has to some extent already set in among American Jews. The cause of this demoralization is clear. It results in large part from the fact that in our land of liberty all the restraints by which the Jews were protected in their ghettoes were removed, and a new generation left without necessary moral and spiritual support. And is it not equally clear what the only possible remedy is? It is the laborious task of inculcating self-respect . . . to develop in each generation of Jews in America the sense of *noblesse oblige* . . . . That spirit can best be developed by actively participating in some way in furthering the ideals of the Jewish renaissance; and this can be done effectively only through furthering the Zionist movement.[19]

Most of the Hebrew-Zionist adherents flocked into the synagogues of the Conservative movement.

So in the space of two generations the pattern of polarization between the Orthodox and the secularists has given way to the American pattern in which only small groups remain at the two extremes, while the vast majority are drawing together toward a central position in the spectrum of Jewish ideology.

The Baltimore study, referred to above, shows that native-born Jews regard as "essential" to being a good Jew the following items in their order of frequency and importance: leading an ethical and moral life, belief in God, identification as a Jew, knowledge of fundamentals of Judaism, winning the respect of Christian neighbors, belonging to a synagogue or temple, supporting all humanitarian causes, attending services on the High Holidays, marrying

18. Robert Gordis, *Judaism in a Christian World* (New York: McGraw-Hill Book Co., 1966). Gordis states: "When it is authentic, secular Zionism has only one plank in its program for Diaspora Jewry, as David Ben-Gurion has always insisted: all Jews have the obligation to migrate as quickly as possible to the state of Israel where alone Jewish life can be truly lived" (p. 29). Religious Zionists and American Jews generally regard Jewish life in America as being both viable and challenging; how to live in spiritual authenticity in an environment of "freedom within freedom" (p. 20).
19. Louis D. Brandeis, "The Jewish Problem and How to Solve It," in *The Zionist Idea*, ed. Arthur Hertzberg, Temple Books (New York: Atheneum Publishers, 1969 [paperback]), p. 521.

within the Jewish faith, promoting general civic improvement, working for equality of all minority groups, contributing to Jewish philanthropies, supporting Israel, attending weekly services, observing the dietary laws.[20]

The Conservative sector is more a segment of a spectrum than it is a movement. Its central institution, the Jewish Theological Seminary, is nonideological in character, and its rabbinic, as well as its congregational, constituency covers a wide range in its practices and programs.

The Conservative sector is a typically American outgrowth. Its hallmark is not a specific creed but the practice of men and women worshiping together, without a partition *(mehiza)* between them. Strangely, the issue of constructing a partition separating the women's section from the main sanctuary has become the most visible distinction between Orthodox and Conservative congregations. This issue appeared in the days of Philo, when the Theraputae erected such partitions in their synagogues. "This common sanctuary in which they meet every seventh day is a double enclosure, one portion set apart for the use of the men, the other for the women." [21] The impact of American pragmatism may be seen in the circumstance that an issue of this type looms larger in practice than the distinction between literal revelation and general inspiration.

Conservative congregations observe the dietary laws, but with some relaxations that are intended to promote commensality with the nonobservant and with non-Jews.[22] Certain emphases are

20. We must not read too much in this schematization of values, since the events of the day may determine the mood of the people. Thus, the ideal of "supporting Israel" may move to the forefront when the existence of the state and the lives of its people are threatened.

21. Philo, *Philosophical Works,* vol. 3, *De vita contemplativa,* Loeb Classical Library (Cambridge, Mass.: Harvard University Press, 1960), p. 32.

22. The prohibition of non-Israelite wine was originally due to the pagan practice of offering oblations to the gods. However, at a later time, wine as well as oil, milk and its products, and all things baked and cooked by Gentiles were interdicted for the purpose of diminishing social intercourse between Jews and non-Jews and lessening the danger of intermarriage. (Aboda Zara 35*b.,* 38*a.* Maimonides' Commentary on the Mishnah, Aboda Zara, II, 6. Aboda Zara 36*b.*) From the very beginning, the liberal school of rabbinic thought opposed these injunctions. (Aboda Zara 36*a.* and Tossafot ad hoc. Shabbat 17*a*).

characteristic of this sector, such as the promotion of a historical approach to every doctrine and practice, the recognition of the nonrational components of religion, the appreciation of the role of diversity within a balanced faith, and the positive estimate of law *(Halachah)*—but as a living process of legislation and interpretation that allows room for growth and adaptation even while providing firm guidelines for its constituency. As in the overall American faith, the goal of the Conservative branch of Judaism is to balance the enlightened freedom of the individual with the discipline of communal law that is itself conceived as a living process.

The Reconstructionist movement grew out of the liberal wing of the Conservative sector, although its influence within the Reform movement is quite considerable. It is pragmatic in philosophy, liberal in religion, ethnicistic as well as humanistic in its conception of the American dream. It conceives of Jewish civilization as being like a cluster of inverted pyramids, all based on the one fulcrum of ethnic-spiritual unity and diverging into all areas of culture, concern, and faith. The general purpose of Reconstructionism is to bring together within a unifying structure all that is vital and creative in Jewish life on the assumption that a free and democratic community will produce the diverse institutions and patterns that are most expressive of its vitality. Naturally, this view rejects the very ideal of a monolithic Judaism. It aims to persuade all branches of Judaism to acknowledge their inner unity and to accept some unifying disciplines. The difficulties in the way of this unification are many. In addition to differences in observance and doctrine, there are diverse views as to the desirable mode of communal organization between those who favor an "organismic" structure and those who prefer the maximum of individual freedom in thought and expression. However, it is the hope of Reconstructionism to provide an organizational counterpart to the concept of the Jewish people as a worldwide fellowship.

In its evaluation of central religious themes, the Reconstructionist movement aims to discover their operative meaning in contemporary life as well as in the past. This emphasis leads to an interpretation of the rituals and doctrines of the past that focuses on the psychological equivalents of ancient sancta. The world Jewish community is conceived as an evolving religious civilization, with responsiveness to changing circumstances as the heartbeat of the living faith. The term *religious civilization* is intended to call attention to the secular, ethnic dimension of Jewish life. In the land of Israel, the religious culture of Judaism may be expected to grow and unfold in new ways, developing new symbols, institutions, and rites. In the Diaspora, Jews will learn to live in two civilizations, balancing the sancta of their religious culture as Jews against the sancta of the American society. While American civilization is largely secular, it also possesses a religious dimension which consists of the Judeo-Christian tradition and the secular humanist ideal. Indeed, there is no religion without a secular base, and no society without an incipient religious quest. Both Jewish and American loyalties are open-ended; that is, Jewish loyalty is open to critical evaluation in the light of religious and humanist values, and American loyalty is similarly open to the same critique, as well as to diverse supplementary loyalties. The "chosenness" of the Jewish people can only be regarded as exemplary, not as exceptional in character. All nations should regard themselves as "covenanted" unto the Lord, fulfilling their specific vocations within the society of mankind.[23]

Taken as a whole, American Judaism is open, flexible, and optimistic. It is open to new influences and new loyalties. The

23. The Reconstructionist philosophy is presented in many books, particularly in Mordecai Menaham Kaplan, *Judaism as a Civilization: Toward a Reconstruction of American-Jewish Life* ([orig. 1935] New York: Schocken Books, 1967). In *The Future of the American Jew* (New York: Macmillan Co., 1948), Kaplan respects the Diaspora-negating type of Zionism, asserting that the Jewish way of distilling religion out of historic experience will ultimately be followed by America. "This means that there must henceforth be two standards of normality for Jewish life; one standard for Eretz Israel, where Jewish life can be lived out fully as a complete civilization that provides those who live by it with all the elements of life necessary for their self-fulfillment and happiness; and a second standard for countries like the United States, where they must look for economic and social security to American citizenship, which in turn expects them to find their moral and spiritual security elsewhere. That security they can for the present find mainly within their own Jewish people and its tradition. In time, however, with American democracy having achieved more self-awareness and consistency, it too will become for Jews, as well as for the rest of the population, a source of inner peace."

feeling of living in exile, wandering in alien fields, has given way to a feeling of at-homeness and fulfillment. And the concept of covenantal loyalty as a moral-religious collective vocation may well be extended to America as a whole. The predominant feeling of American Jews is that Americanism at its noblest is one with the creative élan of Judaism, that America is not another nation but the vital nucleus of humanity, by virtue of its multiethnic composition, its humanist tradition, and its relative power. Here at last we have the opportunity to realize the age-old prophetic vision of mankind united in freedom, in faith, and in fraternity. Tactically and temporarily, Americans may shift from isolationism to internationalism and back again. Right now, our young people are struggling to emerge from the despondency of the Vietnam entanglement. But essentially we feel as Americans that we are "chosen" for singular tasks in behalf of mankind. Ours is the major part of the burden of steering mankind into a glorious future, in accord with the Judeo-Christian faith, to build "Jerusalem in every land." And this goal is to Jewish people altogether compatible with the task of building the city of Jerusalem in Israel, as the spiritual capital of the world, the Holy City of three great faiths.[24]

24. It must be admitted that at this moment the radiance of Israel reborn casts into the shade all other aspects of the messianic dream. The Six-Day War shocked many of our theological writers into a new acceptance of the biblical hope of restoration in its literal sense. Prof. Abraham Joshua Heschel gave expression to this renascent myth in his prose-poem, *Israel: An Echo of Eternity* (New York: Farrar, Straus, & Giroux, 1969). "July, 1967 . . . I have discovered a new land. Israel is not the same as before. There is great astonishment in the souls. It is as if the prophets had risen from their graves. Their words ring in a new way. Jerusalem is everywhere, she hovers over the whole country. There is a new radiance, a new awe" (p. 5). "The God who hides Himself, went forth from His place of hiding. Must God apologize for His audacity in performing wonders in 1967?" (p. 209).

Heschel is ready to center the entire messianic ideal around Israel reborn, since it was first announced in the streets of Jerusalem. But his mood is poetic, theological only insofar as religion celebrates and sanctifies the metaphors of poetry. In the fashion of the psalmists, he projects the understandable exultation of the moment into the metaphysical scheme of things. Heschel's impassioned concern for social justice in America is an expression of the universal phase of his messianism.

In a serious vein, a modern theologian cannot but regard all lifesaving and life-enhancing events as manifestations of the hidden God. The long, hard fight against Hitler was certainly such a manifestation. Without the

The oneness of Jewish and American consciousness is still an emergent—but very real—phenomenon. Most analysts have overlooked it, especially in view of the upsurge of interest in Israel after the June war. The anguish of dual loyalties, so characteristic of Jews in other lands and times, is remarkably absent in the minds of American Jews. Whatever the theoretical justification for this conviction may be, the fact itself is clear enough. The repression of Judaism in the Soviet world and the emergence of Israel as a sanctuary of freedom have helped to mold this widespread belief in the past two decades.

More and more American Jews are beginning to conceive of their religious heritage as an integral part of their country's spiritual élan. And they view their intense concern for the state of Israel as an ideal that is American as well as Jewish. In their messianic vision, the goal of history is the emergence of a universal society in which ethnic groups as well as individuals will be able to attain fulfillment. Israel is the hope of fulfillment for Jews as a historic, worldwide community, one in which the prophetic genius of Judaism will be articulated in the arts of state-building. America constitutes the nucleus of the universal society, insofar as individual freedom and opportunity are concerned. Different as these two aspects of the universal society are, they are not mutu-

brave resistance of the British to Hitler's threats and blandishments, and without the resurgence of liberal forces in America, Hitler would have won. At the same time, the theologian must acknowledge and excoriate the intertwining of the demonic with things divine.

No events in history are purely theophanic. If there is glory in wearing the crown of thorns, there is tragedy in the hearts of those who force it on their victims. If the radiance of triumph crowns the Israeli victors, the dark burden of humiliation weighs heavy on the heads of the victims. And the cries of injustice from the hapless refugees mingle with the shouts of exultation in the troubled land. While poetry has its place, life has a way of restoring the normal cadences of prose.

But we must not forget that for the Orthodox the messianic vision in all its literalness is dogma, not poetry. And the complex panoply of Orthodox symbols and dogmas exerts a powerful momentum, which is shared in increasing degrees by those whose posture has shifted under the impact of recent events from rationalism to existentialism, to ethnic mysticism, and thence to the vagaries of sanctified myths.

As to the Orthodox, the recently published work of Kasher's fits the events of Israel's emergence into the ancient categories of the *eschaton*, with due allowance for physical resurgence under the "Messiah son of Joseph" and the final advent of "Messiah son of David" in 1990 or so (Menachem M. Kasher, *Hatekufah Hagedolah* [Jerusalem, 1969]).

ally contradictory. Somehow, the ideals of ethical nationalism and of universal humanism will have to be blended in our vision of the good society, if mankind is not to lose the enhancing impetus of nationalism and the harmonizing principle of cosmopolitanism. Nor is their blend in our contemporary vision fortuitous and ephemeral. For more than a century, the Jews of the Western democracies considered the expansion of humanism as the modern secular form of the biblical messianic vision, while the Zionists localized their dream of redemption in the Holy Land. Both secularist versions of the messianic ideal were fragmentary and one-sided. In America, as a result of the shattering events of the holocaust, the emergence of Israel, and the manifest imperative of establishing a universal society in the race against nuclear suicide, the two conceptions are now being blended in one many-splendored vision.

6

Protestant Clergy, the First Amendment
and Beginnings of a Constitutional Debate, 1781–91

JAMES H. SMYLIE

The ratification of the new Constitution of the United States was the occasion of the Grand Federal Procession in Philadelphia on July 4, 1788. One observer was impressed favorably with the way in which the clergymen took part.

> The Clergy formed a very agreeable part of the procession. . . . They manifested, by their attendance, their sense of the connexion between religion and good government. They amounted to seventeen in number. Four or five of them marched arm in arm with each other, to exemplify the Union. Pains were taken to connect Ministers of the most dissimilar religious principles together, thereby to shew the influence of a free government in promoting Christian charity. The Rabbi of the Jews, locked in the arms of two ministers of the gospel, was a most delightful sight. There could not have been a more happy emblem contrived, of that section of the new Constitution, which opens all its power and offices alike, not only to every sect of Christians, but to worthy men of every religion.[1]

Free government was already proving itself very effective. It was even beneficial in producing "Christian charity" through the specific stipulation in Article 6 of the Constitution which reads that "no religious Test shall ever be required as a Qualification to any Office or public Trust under the United States." [2]

1. [Francis Hopkinson], *Account of the Grand Federal Procession* (Philadelphia: Carey, 1788), p. 21.
2. *Documents Illustrative of the Formation of the Union of the American States* (Washington: Government Printing Office, 1927), p. 1001.

This raises the question of the relation between religious societies and the civil magistrate under the Constitution of the United States. The provision regarding a religious test is the only one the writers of the Constitution thought to include in order to deal with this problem. Even this was resisted by one member of the convention as unnecessary because of the "prevailing liberality" of the times which was a "sufficient security agst such tests." [3] But the liberal age showed vestigial remains of an illiberal past which caused dissenters to suffer civil disabilities for religious opinions. In only two out of thirteen original states were full rights of conscience conceded without legal qualifications. In Rhode Island such freedom had become a habit; in Virginia, it had recently been won. In contrast with this, five states, viz., New Hampshire, Massachusetts, Connecticut, Maryland, and South Carolina, maintained a religious establishment through a legalized and supposedly equal policy of assessment. Beyond this there were provisions in state constitutions supporting religious tests for holding office. Six states—New Hampshire, Connecticut, New Jersey, the two Carolinas, and Georgia—insisted on an acceptance of Protestantism. Delaware and Maryland widened this to Christianity as a whole. In Pennsylvania and South Carolina officials had to believe in one God, and in a heaven and hell, while Delaware demanded assent to the doctrine of the Trinity. Three states —New York, Maryland, and South Carolina—excluded clergymen from holding civil office.[4] Although in most areas vigorous forces opposed many of these provisions, the "prevailing liberality" did not prevent the continuation of tests in state constitutions. It is clear that many of the supporters of the Constitution considered the provision concerning religious tests an adequate safeguard for the rights of conscience in the national government. Moreover, at this time the writers followed a precedent established by the Articles of Confederation which left religious affairs a matter of local option.[5]

3. "Debates in the Federal Convention of 1787 as Reported by James Madison." in *Documents*, p. 647.
4. See Sanford H. Cobb, *The Rise of Religious Liberty in America* (New York: Macmillan Co., 1902), p. 507.
5. Ibid., p. 27.

How did the First Amendment come into existence? Not until 1791 did the words "Congress shall make no law respecting an establishment of religion, or prohibiting the free exercise thereof" become a part of the law of the land.[6] The story of the ratification of the amendment has been related many times.[7] It has been interpreted in as many different ways. What did it mean? Did Americans stumble into religious freedom? [8] Was the First Amendment a "carefully defined equilibrium of church and state" and an "article of peace"? [9] Was its intention to establish a "tradition of free co-operation between government and religious bodies—co-operation involving no special privilege to any group and no restriction on the religious liberty of any citizen"—or a "co-operative separatism" involving "institutional separation" and "functional interaction"? [10] Did it mean a high and impregnable "wall of separation" or a "line of separation" between the civil magistrate and religion? [11] Did it mean a separation which guarantees freedom, and a freedom which requires a separation? [12]

6. *Documents,* p. 1604.
7. See Cobb, *The Rise of Religious Liberty;* Philip Schaff. *Church and State in the United States* (New York: G. P. Putnam's Sons, 1883), p. 161; Evarts B. Greene, *Religion and the State* (New York: New York University Press, 1941), p. 172; Max J. Kohler, "The Fathers of the Republic and Constitutional Establishment of Religious Liberty," in *God in Freedom,* ed. Luigi Luzzatti (New York: Macmillan Co., 1930), pp. 670–705; Leo Pfeffer, *Church, State, and Freedom* (Boston: Beacon Press, 1953), p. 675; Anson Phelps Stokes, *Church and State in the United States,* 3 vols. (New York: Harper & Bros., 1950), 1:538–52; George Slater Coleman, "The Religious Background of the Federal Constitution" (Ph.D. diss., Harvard University, 1933).
8. Perry Miller, "The Location of American Religious Freedom," *Religion and Freedom of Thought* (Garden City: Doubleday & Co., 1954), p. 15.
9. Winthrop S. Hudson, *The Great Tradition of the American Churches* (New York: Harper & Bros., 1953), p. 9; John Courtney Murray, *We Hold These Truths* (New York: Sheed & Ward, 1960), p. 56.
10. Roman Catholic Bishops of the United States, "The Christian in Action" (1948), reprinted in *The National Catholic Almanac* (Paterson: St. Anthony's Guild, 1949), p. 91; Paul G. Kauper, *Civil Liberties and the Constitution,* (Ann Arbor: University of Michigan Press, 1962), pp. 3–51; *Church and State: A Lutheran Perspective* (New York: Board of Social Ministry, Lutheran Church in America, 1963).
11. Thomas Jefferson to the Danbury (Connecticut) Baptist Association, January 1, 1802, Jefferson Papers, Library of Congress, Washington; Sidney E. Mead, "Neither Church nor State: Reflections on James Madison's 'Line of Separation,' " *Journal of Church and State,* vol. 10, no. 3 (1968), pp. 349–63.
12. Pfeffer, *Church, State, and Freedom,* p. 604.

It is the purpose of this paper to illuminate the problem of the meaning and significance of the First Amendment through a study of Protestant clerical opinion during the period surrounding its formulation and ratification. Did Protestant clergymen have anything to do with writing the clause? Did they have anything to do with creating the climate of opinion in which it was framed? What did the clause mean to them? And how might the First Amendment be interpreted in light of the struggles which were going on during the latter part of the eighteenth century in America over the problem of the rights of conscience?

THE MAKING OF THE AMENDMENT

When the Constitution of the United States was being debated for adoption not all state delegations were enthusiastic. Some representatives wanted changes. So hot was the opposition in some states that Federalists took the initiative to overcome hostility by proposing or at least favoring certain immediate alterations in the document. Led by the Massachusetts convention, Maryland, South Carolina, New Hampshire, and New York proposed amendments, while Virginia and North Carolina recommended amendments with a Bill of Rights which included an article guaranteeing the rights of conscience.[13] While these suggestions were not mandatory alterations to be enacted before ratification, the states placed pressure on the new government to act upon the modifications. Clergy were not amendment-mongers.[14]

For the most part, the clergymen who attended state conventions for ratification and who favored a stronger central government were willing to accept the Constitution as it stood.[15] They seemed to take for granted, along with Federalists generally, that religious liberty was secured by civil liberty embodied in a Constitution establishing a limited government. The Baptists were exceptions to a general clerical silence. They had been persistently

13. *Documents*, pp. 1030–31, 1047.
14. John Bach McMaster, *A History of the People of the United States*, 5 vols. (New York: Appleton, 1888); 1:532.
15. See Jonathan Elliot, ed., *The Debates in the Several State Conventions*, 4 vols. (Philadelphia: J. B. Lippincott Co., 1836), 2:155, 174.

engaged in a struggle for religious liberty in Virginia and Massachusetts. When the Constitution appeared they expressed dissatisfaction that the rights of conscience were not adequately protected.[16] John Leland, articulate Virginia Baptist, amplified opposition when he wrote:

> What is clearest of all—Religious Liberty, is not sufficiently secured. No Religious test is Required as a qualification to fill any office under the United States, but if a Majority of Congress with the President favour one System more than another, they may oblige all others to pay to support their System as much as they please, and if Oppression does not ensue, it will be owing to the Mildness of Administration and not to any Constitutional defence, and if the Manners of the People are so far Corrupted, that they cannot live by Republican principles, it is Very dangerous leaving Religious Liberty at their Mercy.[17]

Among Baptists this concern did not abate after the adoption of the Constitution. Apparently in Virginia reports circulated among them that James Madison, one of the chief authors of the Constitution and one who gained the support of Virginia Baptists for its ratification, had ceased to be a "friend of the rights of conscience." Hearing that George Eve, a Baptist preacher, was disposed to discourage this rumor, Madison communicated with him in order to encourage his constituency. He admitted that he had never seen the dangers in the Constitution. The rights of conscience were sufficiently protected by the limitation of the powers of the national government. He opposed alteration during the debates because any other strategy would have given enemies of the instrument the opportunity to promote dissension among the states. He assured Eve, however, that the Constitution provided for the possibility of change and ought to be amended now that it had been secured. The first Congress ought to make satisfactory provisions for essential rights, including "the rights of conscience, in the fullest latitude, the freedom of the press, trials by jury, security

16. See Robert B. Semple, *A History of the Rise and Progress of the Baptists in Virginia* (Richmond: John O'Lynch, 1810), p. 77; H. J. Eckenrode, *Separation of Church and State in Virginia* (Richmond, 1910), p. 164.
17. [John Leland], Enclosure (1788), Madison Papers, Library of Congress, Washington.

against general warrants, etc." [18] Madison had given ample evidence of his sympathy and his sincerity in his continual defense of the rights of dissenters and his drive in previous years against the establishment even of a system of equal assessment in Virginia.[19] But when Baptist Isaac Backus, staunch opponent of assessment in Massachusetts, visited Virginia in August 1789 he had to reassure Baptists that their rights were safe even after Madison had initiated the amending process.[20]

Acting under such pressure, the first Congress hammered out the First Amendment. Except for Frederick Augustus Muhlenberg, a Lutheran who had exchanged his clerical gown for the parliamentarian's gavel as presiding officer in the House of Representatives, clergymen had no part in formulating it. On June 8, 1789, Madison introduced in the House a series of constitutional amendments to be incorporated into the body of the Constitution itself. Among them were the following provisions:

> The civil rights of none shall be abridged on account of religious belief or worship, nor shall any national religion be established, nor shall the full and equal rights of conscience be in any manner, or on any pretext, infringed.
> No State shall violate the equal rights of conscience, or the freedom of the press, or the trial by jury in criminal cases.[21]

The "full and equal" rights of conscience were not to be infringed by the institution of civil disabilities for belief or worship, nor by the establishment of a "national" religion. Madison wanted to encourage those people who were anxious about the broad lawmaking power of the new government. "Congress should not establish a religion," he explained, "nor compel men to worship God in any manner contrary to their conscience." [22] The second provision extended equal rights of conscience to citizens in all

18. James Madison to George Eve, January 2, 1789, Madison Papers, Library of Congress, Washington.
19. Irving Brant, "Madison: On the Separation of Church and State," *William and Mary Quarterly*, 3d ser., 8 (1948):7–11.
20. James Manning to James Madison, August 1789, Madison Papers, Library of Congress, Washington.
21. *The Debates and Proceedings in the Congress of the United States*, 42 vols. (Washington: Gale & Seaton, 1834–56), 1:451–52.
22. Ibid., pp. 757–59.

states, presumably those in which some policy of establishment did exist.[23] The House finally altered the amendment excluding any reference to the practices in the various states: "Congress shall make no law establishing religion, or to prevent the free exercise thereof, or to infringe the rights of conscience." [24]

In this shape the House submitted the proposal to the Senate for concurrence, along with the other amendments to the Constitution. Fortunately, a record of the recommended alternatives indicates something of the debate which must have taken place in the Senate over this particular amendment. Three suggestions were made. Each was rejected in turn. At first one senator wished to strike out "religion, or prohibiting the free exercise thereof," and to insert "one religious sect or society in preference to others." [25] This change was rejected. Others proposed this phraseology: "Congress shall not make any law infringing the rights of conscience, or establishing any religious sect or society." [26] This recommendation was also voted in the negative. Another motion was made to amend the article to read: "Congress shall make no law establishing any particular denomination of religion in preference to another, or prohibiting the free exercise thereof, nor shall the rights of conscience be infringed." [27] After rejecting this proposal, the Senate produced a form of the amendment which read: "Congress shall make no law establishing articles of faith or a mode of worship, or prohibiting the free exercise of religion." [28]

Both branches of Congress hit upon the final formula: "Congress shall make no law respecting an establishment of religion, or prohibiting the free exercise thereof." This was locked with guarantees of the freedom of speech, of the press, of assembly, and of petition for a redress of grievances. Civil liberty was connected

23. Ibid., pp. 783–84.
24. Ibid., p. 796.
25. *Journal of the First Session of the Senate* (Washington: Gale & Seaton, 1820), p. 70.
26. Ibid.
27. Ibid.
28. Ibid., p. 77.

inseparably with the exercise of the rights of conscience in religious matters.[29]

It is impossible to ascertain much more fully what the lawmakers had in mind by this final statement because of the lack of extant comment. Two things seem evident. On the one hand, the framers of these words desired to protect the rights of conscience. Both aspects of the amendment concerning religion seem to be instrumental to this end. No establishment was necessary for free exercise; free exercise required no establishment. The terms *establishment of religion* and *free exercise thereof* are nowhere defined. On at least two occasions Congress declined to simplify the question of the interpretation of the amendment in terms of the nonpreferential establishment of religious societies. Legislation would have to be tested continually to determine what laws respected an establishment of religion, or prohibited its free exercise. On the other hand, in this final formulation, the framers turned down Madison's earlier proposal that national protection of the rights of conscience be extended to the individual states. The new government followed the Articles of Confederation in curbing congressional intervention in state affairs, and in allowing the continuation of state laws. The proposed amendment had no effect except as check and example. The amendment, along with eleven others, was submitted to the state legislatures late in 1789. Of the thirteen original states, Massachusetts, Connecticut (both of which had policies of assessment), and Georgia failed to make returns. Nine states agreed to ten amendments, including the one discussed here, and they became part of the law of the land.[30]

Few clergymen left records of their opinion of this process. James Madison, bishop of the Protestant Episcopal Church, wrote the other James Madison that he approved of changes in the Constitution if they made for greater stability and prosperity, and

29. William Linn, *Discourses on the Signs of the Times* (New York: Thomas Greenleaf, 1794), p. 12.
30. Muhlenberg thought these amendments covered those which the opponents of the Constitution had in mind. He hoped for an early restoration of harmony. (Frederick Augustus Muhlenberg to Benjamin Rush, August 18, 1789, Miscellaneous papers, Historical Society of Pennsylvania, Philadelphia.

if they rendered the theory of government as perfect as possible.[31] Jeremy Belknap of Massachusetts was insulted. Philadelphian Nicholas Collin displayed some indifference.

Congregationalist Belknap considered agitation for new amendments to the Constitution an exhibition of lack of confidence in the new government. After rehearsing the outline of the amendments to ensure the rights of conscience, the right of the press, the right to keep arms, and protection from seizure of persons and property, Belknap complained:

> Should a Man tell me that he devoutly wished I might not break into his house & rob his desk . . . I think I should have a right to suspect that he viewed me in no better light than a Burglar. . . . So if a Man publicly expresses a *devout* wish that the new government may not rob him of his personal & domestic rights . . . I think it not uncharitable to conclude that he has a jealousy of its intentions.[32]

Of course this was exactly the point with many citizens. With Shays's Rebellion fresh in mind, Belknap muttered: "The *dear* insurgents must be treated with tenderness because they mean well tho' under some mistakes—but the staunch, tried defenders of America's Liberty must be guarded against with a 'devout wish' that they may not violate personal & domestic rights!"[33]

Nicholas Collin, a Lutheran clergyman, did not think the time propitious for a debate over amendments to the Constitution. Furthermore, he shared the views of Federalists that the Constitution itself included guarantees enough for civil and religious rights. In commenting he discussed the First Amendment particularly. It would be very "unjust and pernicious to establish any religious system in the united states." This possibility was slight at the national level because Congress did not have by construction or inclination any such power. Moreover, denominations would perform themselves the office of a *censor morum* over each other

31. [Bishop] James Madison to James Madison, August 15, 1789, Madison Papers, Library of Congress, Washington.
32. Jeremy Belknap to Paine Wingate, July 6, 1789, Boston Public Library.
33. Ibid.

and on the encroachments of Congress upon the rights of conscience.[34] It was advisable that Congress guarantee liberty of conscience in each state, since it was "much more probable that superstition, mingled with political faction, might corrupt a single state, than that bigotry should infect a majority of states in congress." [35] This Congress refused to do.

Collin was strongly of the opinion in his interpretation of the amendment that certain conduct based on religious belief should be stopped by the civil magistrate. Religion may be a transaction between a man and his maker; but when any person claims "from religious principle, the right of injuring his fellow-citizens, or the community at large, he must be restrained, and, in atrocious cases, punished. If he is a fool, or a madman, he must not be a tyrant. It is impossible that God could order him to be unjust, because he commands us all to be just and good." [36] No bold and artful prophet pretending a commission from heaven ought, "from his tender conscience, cut our throats and plunder our property." Although he lived in a "civilized era," Collin was ready to admit that "the human heart, is very wandering, and the fancy of mortals very whimsical." [37]

That so few clergymen seem to have recorded their thoughts about amendments and the amending process is disappointing. But the relation between religious societies and the civil magistrate was both a previous question and a continuing problem. Clergymen during the decades before the adoption of the First Amendment showed much concern over the rights of conscience. They helped to create the climate in which the amendment was drafted and finally ratified. They were of different minds, often, as to what the rights of conscience happened to be, clergymen of the same denomination not being in agreement. It is possible to discern at

34. Nicholas Collin in *American Museum*, September 1789, pp. 235–36. Cf. Thomas Jefferson, *Notes on the State of Virginia* (Paris, 1784–85), p. 293.
35. Collin, in *American Museum*, pp. 235–36.
36. Ibid.
37. Ibid.

least three basic approaches to the problem, each of which may illuminate the problems which were confronted by the congressmen who framed the amendment to the Constitution under which Americans live.

NONPREFERENTIAL COOPERATION ALLOWING FREE EXERCISE

In interpreting the problem of the rights of conscience, some clergymen were concerned for the promotion of virtue which religion alone could condition. They insisted that religion and virtue were necessary for civil government and maintained the right of the people to invest the civil magistrate with the power to require religious belief and worship, and thereby the teaching of virtue throughout the community. Adapting themselves to the circumstances of the time, clergymen who supported this position pressed for the maintenance of religion through a nonpreferential cooperation whereby the civil magistrate could assess citizens for the support of a religious society of the individual's choice. They firmly believed that this encouraged free exercise of religion without curbing the rights of conscience. This position was best represented by those whose societies had enjoyed special status before the law in colonial America. Congregationalists and Episcopalians were supported by some Presbyterians sympathetic to the presuppositions of the case.

Congregationalists, for example, were in a strong position in the postwar world because of their support of the Revolutionary cause. Ever since they had swarmed to New England in the seventeenth century they had been jealous for the religious monopoly they claimed, and zealous that no heresy pervert the purity of the New England way. God had revealed truth to them out of his Word, which was characterized peculiarly by a Congregational polity. Because of their view of the rights of conscience in face of the truth, they felt perfectly justified in impressing it upon the whole community. Freedom of conscience in earliest days meant that all dissenters had "liberty to keep away." [38] Belknap put

38. Nathaniel Ward, "The Simple Cobbler of Aggawam," in *The Puritans,* ed. Perry Miller and Thomas H. Johnson (New York: American Book Co., 1938), p. 227.

this view succinctly when he retold the "bloudy" debate between John Cotton and Roger Williams in a novel entitled *The Foresters.*

"Come, come," John Cotton (alias John Codline) complains to Roger Williams (alias Roger Carrier), "none of your idle distinctions: I *say* you are in the wrong, I have *proved* it, and *you know* it: you have sinned against *your own conscience,* and therefore you deserve to be cut off as an incorrigible heretic."

"How dost thou know," replies Roger, "that I have sinned against my own conscience? Canst thou search the heart?"

Thereupon Williams experiences the "logic of the foot" when enraged Cotton gives him "a smart kick on the posteriors, and bade him be gone." [39]

Congregationalists thought it quite logical for the civil magistrate to compel conformity to the truth. In 1790 Samuel Seabury, first bishop of the Protestant Episcopal Church in the United States, called attention to what appeared to be an inconsistency in their case and some unfinished business on their agenda. "Nor have I a word to say against liberty of conscience," he wrote.

> I pray God to preserve it to us all; nor do I think it improbable that they [early Congregationalists] came to America to enjoy greater liberty of conscience than they could obtain in England. They had certainly set their hearts on it; at least the principal men and the ministers had done so; for they no sooner obtained in America that liberty of conscience which they sought, than they endeavoured to monopolize it all to themselves; and with their good will, would not suffer a neighbour to have an atom of it. [40]

Time and circumstance modified the situation. Dissenters who came to stay slowly pressed the states controlled by Congregationalists and Episcopalians to modify their legal status. By the time of the Revolution Congregationalists in New England had been forced by an ever increasing population of those who did not have the Congregationally informed conscience to allow the existence of different societies. Somewhat grudgingly, Massachu-

39. [Jeremy Belknap], *The Foresters: An American Tale* (1792) (Exeter: S. Hardy, 1831), pp. 27–28.
40. [Samuel Seabury], *An Address to the Ministers and Congregations of the Presbyterian and Independent Persuasions in the United States of America* (New Haven: T. & S. Green, 1790), p. 53.

setts (1780), New Hampshire (1784), and Connecticut (1784) relaxed laws—although not granting everything which dissenters desired.[41] Those who sympathized with Congregationalists at this point insisted that public support of religion could be so enacted and administered as not to violate the rights of conscience.

These clergymen seemed to be concerned more with the preservation of civil society than with the maintenance of religious societies. Certainly, they voiced a desire to protect the "natural and unalienable right to worship GOD" according to the dictates of conscience. But in their argumentation for a policy of assessment they continually asserted that the civil magistrate could not long understand or fulfill his function without the cooperation of the religious society as the promoter of the virtuous life.[42] Religion was necessary to the very *"existence"* and *"well-being"* of civil society because it was calculated to operate in a salutary fashion on the character of citizens. This was crucial for a republican society.[43] Congregationalist Joseph Lathrop explained it this way:

> The foundation of all social virtue is a belief of the existence and government of a Deity. A regard to the Deity cannot be maintained without some publick exercises of religion. Social worship is therefore necessary to the happiness of society, and to the easy administration of government, and in this view worthy of attention of every legislature, while in a higher view it deserves the regard of the individual.[44]

Why ought government to have anything to do with religion? Lathrop explained that "religion has much to do with govern-

---

41. Cf. Jacob Conrad Meyer, *Church and State in Massachusetts from 1740 to 1833: A Chapter in the Development of Individual Freedom* (Cleveland: Western Reserve University Press, 1930), p. 276; M. Louise Greene, *The Development of Religious Liberty in Connecticut* (Boston: Houghton 1905), p. 552; Charles B. Kinney Jr., *Church and State: The Struggle for Separation in New Hampshire, 1630–1900* (New York: Teachers College, Columbia University, 1955), p. 198.
42. Kinney, *Church and State*, p. 123. Kinney quotes the 1784 constitution of the state of New Hampshire.
43. Thomas Reese, *An Essay on the Influence of Religion in Civil Society* (Charleston: Markland & M'Iver, 1788), p. 73. Reese was a Presbyterian whose essay received wide circulation throughout the United States.
44. Joseph Lathrop, *A Miscellaneous Collection of Original Pieces* (Springfield: John Russell, 1786), p. 45.

ment." [45] In the same manner David Tappan saw the necessity of government-supported religion. He compared the relationship between Moses and Aaron to that which ought to exist between the civil magistrate and the religious society. He recalled that the "union of friendship, of counsel and exertion in the public cause," which characterized the Hebrew lawgiver and high priest, also distinguished the fathers of New England. Energetic government was the "guardian of freedom," and religion, especially the Christian religion, was the "pillar of both." [46] To deny the right of civil government to shield religion—and even to suppress irreligion, as Tappan saw the matter—would be to deny it the "most essential means of self-preservation." [47]

The magistrate, as a "nursing father" to religion, had the authority to foster virtue through religion.[48] In providing for the "safety of the body politic," [49] the magistrate could justly oblige every member of civil society "to pay something for the support of religion," that is, the religious society of a citizen's own choice.[50]

Implicit in this policy of a pluralistic establishment through equal assessment is the assumption that the rights of conscience could be maintained and protected. This aspect of the case was expressed somewhat negatively by Presbyterian Patrick Allison of Maryland, who fought against the favoritism of the magistrate in that state to the Episcopal church, but did not challenge the legality of taxing on a nonpreferential basis. "Herein lies the sole ground of complaint and cause of fear," he wrote, "the aggrandizement of any one sect above the others, by its holding an illicit commerce with civil power—the obtaining, or striving to obtain, from government, by any one sect, privileges, advantages, preferences, or distinctions, superior to the rest—whether its officers be called pastors or priests, prelates or popes, it matters not a straw. An

45. Ibid., pp. 149–50.
46. David Tappan, *A Sermon* (Boston: State Press, 1792), p. 25.
47. Ibid. See also Nathan Strong, *A Sermon* (Hartford: Hudson & Goodwin, 1790), p. 18; Reese, *Essay on the Influence of Religion*, p. 74.
48. David Parsons, *A Sermon* (Boston: Adams & Nourse, 1788), pp. 12–13.
49. Reese, *Essay on the Influence of Religion*, p. 74.
50. Ibid., p. 79.

attempt of this sort will ever raise a powerful alarm, unless the people are enslaved or asleep."[51]

It was absurd, Joseph Willard protested, while preaching at Harvard in 1785, for anyone to assume "the authority of dictating to another's conscience." [52] Then he went on to applaud the way in which New Englanders, particularly in Massachusetts, had solved the problem:

> Any denomination of Christians, who would endeavor to bring the Civil Authority of the State to grant any peculiar privileges to their church, and to give it a pre-eminence over others, ought to be watched over and guarded against. . . . Happy is it that our excellent Frame of Government in this State provides "That every denomination of Christians, demeaning themselves peaceably, and as good subjects of the Commonwealth, shall be equally under the protection of the law: And no subordination of any one sect or denomination shall be established by law." While this frame of Government continues, no one church or denomination of Christians can oppress another with constitutional law on their side.[53]

Should this be revised, Willard considered it the duty of every citizen to fight such a change until all religious societies were settled equally in the sight of the law.

Episcopalians were pushed by the force of circumstances to adopt a similar attitude about the relation of religious societies and the civil magistrate. The Protestant Episcopal Church in its national organization fully accepted "ecclesiastical independence" as a part of the postwar world.[54] But until the war Episcopalians in the Southern states, like Congregationalists in New England, had enjoyed a privileged position. After the war they were placed on the defensive by powerful groups of patriotic dissenters, and developed more sharply the rationale that religion produced virtue

---

51. Vindex [Patrick Allison], *Candid Animadversions* (Baltimore: William Goodard & James Angell, 1793), p. v. Allison first published his protest in 1783 in answer to a petition presented to the General Assembly of Maryland by Episcopalians William Smith and Thomas Gates.
52. Joseph Willard, "Persecution Opposite to the Genius of the Gospel," sermon preached on September 7, 1785, Widener Library Archives, Harvard University, Cambridge, Mass.
53. Ibid.
54. The Protestant Episcopal Church, *The Book of Common Prayer* (printed in Philadelphia; reprinted in London for J. Debrett, 1789), Preface.

for the good of civil society. John Bissett, for example, an Episcopalian clergyman of Maryland, saw religion as the "foundation" and the "main pillar" of civil government because it controlled the secret springs of action over which government had no control.

> Religion and Government, then, like two allied powers engaged in war against a common enemy, ought to countenance and assist each other. Religion ought to place peaceful submission to the Magistrate among its duties, and to support his lawful authority, as its ablest coadjutor in the great work of rendering mankind virtuous and happy; and Government ought to lend its aid for promoting. that knowledge and sense of Religion upon which the success of its own operations, nay its very existence, depends.[55]

The civil magistrate could justly require this support upon "equal and general principles," and thus, overruling scrupulous but doubtful pleas concerning the rights of conscience, should rescue religion from a precarious voluntarism which would be detrimental to the community at large.[56] Episcopal clergymen attempted to gain governmental assistance for ecclesiastical causes, justifying the use of subordinate or secondary causes, as Devereux Jarratt argued, in the accomplishment of the obvious intentions of God.[57]

Third, a nonpreferential cooperation between the civil magistrate and religious societies did not violate the rights of conscience. Conscience, to claim its rights, should be conscience rightly informed. This was an echo of former times when Christians—for example, Congregationalists, Episcopalians, and Presbyterians—claimed that God's truth was identified easily with their own teachings. At the same time, they asserted with eighteenth century rationalists that God had established laws of nature which could be ascertained by the human mind and which should form part of man's religious consciousness. Therefore, all men ought to know in good conscience that civil government was based upon virtue and that virtue was dependent upon religion. This was God's will, not the will of crafty politicians and priests. No man's conscience

55. John Bissett, *A Sermon* (Philadelphia: T. Dobson, 1791), Appendix, p. 4.
56. Ibid., pp. 11, 14–16.
57. Devereux Jarratt, *Life of the Reverend Devereux Jarratt* (Baltimore: Warner & Hanna, 1806), pp. 154–55.

thus properly informed would be violated if the civil magistrate enacted and administered just laws for the support of religion for this common cause. Insisting that the ruler must make such provisions, Gershom Lyman asked in the affirmative, "Now how are the rights of conscience invaded, if the ruler makes laws to prevent their robbing God in this withholding what he claims for support of his worship, when at the same time the public good requires it, more than when he enforces, by law, the command not to rob men?" [58] David Tappan argued in the same manner, as he urged the support of religious institutions on account of their "transcendent importance to civil government and society." Maintenance through an "equal and liberal plan" did not mean the political establishment of any particular religious belief or worship, nor the invasion of sacred rights.[59] These clergymen took thought to make room for diversity of religious opinion. They assumed, however, that the conscience of all men would agree to the necessity of the civil support of religion. Because of this concern for the common welfare shared by every man, a policy providing for equal treatment before the law would in no way violate the rights of conscience.

Here is one way by which a group of clergymen could interpret the rights of conscience. It implied a nonpreferential cooperation which encouraged the free exercise of the rights of conscience. It would be easy, of course, to sense some duplicity in this position. Many of the clergymen had been dependent upon the magistrate's power to coerce membership for societies, monetary support, and attendance at religious gatherings. Having no habit of independence, Congregationalists and Episcopalians, particularly, faced an uncertain future. Moreover, those who approved a policy of nonpreferential assessment were often too uncritically certain that some just arrangement could be made so that each man could follow freely the dictates of his conscience in religious matters. They were not completely frank about impatience with requests

58. Gershom Lyman, *A Sermon* (Windsor: Hough & Spooner, 1784), p. 15; see also Nathanael Emmons, *The Dignity of Man* (Providence: Bennett Wheeler, 1787), p. 20.
59. Tappan, *A Sermon*, p. 23.

from various religious societies seeking aid and the ever present tendency of those who have the truth to protect the "ignorant," as Belknap wished to do, from the "fits and frights" of their religious convictions.[60] Supporters of this position resisted, in good conscience, interpretations of the rights of conscience in any other way. Clergymen sincerely believed that the civil magistrate needed the support of religion. In the past, the religious society and the civil magistrate had been partners in bringing the community into conformity to truth. Now, in a pluralistic society, they were to continue as partners in permeating the society with the virtue so necessary to government.

Pastor-poet Elijah Fitch summarized the perspective in some poor verse, *The Beauties of Religion.*

> Therefore the patriot in the Christian shines
> Most bright, as diamonds set in polish'd gold;
> Nor can a real patriot exist,
> Unless Religion actuate his soul.
> As soul and body join'd make up the man,
> So virtue and Religion in the man,
> Make up the steady, shining patriot.
> As body without soul cannot survive,
> No more can virtue, when Religion's gone.
> Religion without virtue's but a cheat,
> And virtue at the best is but a shade,
> When separate from Religion shews her face.
> As shades sometimes afford a cool retreat
> From scorching sun-beams, so virtue's shadow
> Oft protects a State from faction's furious rage:
> Her very shadow benefits the world.[61]

FREE EXERCISE EXCLUDING NONPREFERENTIAL COOPERATION

Other clergymen interpreting the rights of conscience were concerned more for the purity of the religious experience, as they saw it, which could be assured only through the autonomy of religious societies. While not denying that religion and virtue were

60. Jeremy Belknap, *An Election Sermon* (Portsmouth: Melcher & Osborne, 1785), p. 20.
61. Elijah Fitch, *The Beauties of Religion: A Poem* (Providence: John Carter, 1789), p. 60.

necessary for civil government, they held religion to be an inner experience, the integrity of which was violated if coerced except directly by God himself. Man's conscience must be free from any legislation which would obstruct full exercise, because this experience is not determinable nor ultimately definable by man. Rights were not protected under any system providing for a non-preferential cooperation between the civil magistrate and religious societies. Dissenters who had suffered civil disabilities under Congregationalist and Anglican establishments during the colonial period articulated the case. It was most fully and forcibly pushed by Baptists in alliance with Presbyterians and Methodists.

As had the Congregationalists, the Baptists bled for the American cause. They emerged from the conflict flexing their muscles and eager to impose rights legislation which conformed to their consciences on the various states in which they found themselves. Unlike the Congregationalists, the Baptists had never enjoyed a privileged status in colonial life. They were opposed to legal assistance on principle, and had made their way in the American environment in spite of harassment by establishments. They stood in the tradition of Roger Williams—although many years removed from his direct influence—as they reminded the civil magistrate that in religious matters *"civill weapons* are improper" and are "never able to effect aught in the *soule,"* except hypocrisy.[62] The civil magistrate cannot "search the heart," to recall Roger Carrier's words to John Codline in *The Foresters.* Baptists were often lampooned because of their constant accent on rights. "The want of a *bill of rights* is the great evil," explained onetime army chaplain H. H. Brackenridge, in analyzing opposition to the Constitution. There was "no occasion for a bill of *wrongs;* for there will be wrongs enough. But oh! a *bill of rights."* [63] Baptists thought they were driving toward the fulfillment of the desires of the earliest

---

62. Cf. Roger Williams. "The Bloudy Tenet of Persecution," in *The Puritans,* p. 223; Isaac Backus, *A History of New England,* 2 vols. (Newton: Backus Historical Society, 1871), vol. 1; Thomas B. Maston, *The Ethical and Social Attitudes of Isaac Backus* (Ph.D. diss., Yale University, 1939), pp. 191–94.
63. H. H. Brackenridge, *Gazette Publications* (Carlisle: Alexander & Phillips, 1806), p. 78.

American settlers. With more nostalgia for the past than regard for history, Baptist Samuel Stillman of Boston eulogized pioneer heroes on the Fourth of July:

> Our ancestors, driven by the violence of persecution from their native country, brought with them to these shores those principles of religion and of government, which have finally ripened by time and by manifold oppressions, into the joyous event which we now celebrate. . . . With them it was a self-evident principle, that all men are and ought to be at liberty to think and act for themselves in matters of religion; and that so long as they lead peaceable and quiet lives, no men whether *court* or *clergy,* have any right to interfere with their creed or manner of worshipping God; except by addresses to their understandings.[64]

These principles were somewhat less "self-evident" to the ancestors than to Stillman in the eighteenth century. As they gained power through the years, however, Baptists were able to make themselves heard and heeded. With evangelical zeal they pressed for legislation which would guarantee their rights. Thus, shortly after the revolution, Baptists, with Presbyterians and some Methodists, helped to disestablish the Anglicans in Virginia and prevent laws of assessment from being enacted.[65] Under the leadership of Isaac Backus and John Leland, who had been trained in lobbying techniques in Virginia, dissenters pressed their case against the annoying assessment laws in New England.[66] In both sections of the country they denied that essential free exercise was possible under a system of nonpreferential cooperation.

Clergymen who desired complete autonomy of religious societies sometimes spoke of the restoration of the situation which had existed in primitive Christian times. Christ alone was head of his church previous to Constantine, in times of prosperity or of persecution. The church lost its purity and its power to the extent that

64. Samuel Stillman, *An Oration* (Boston: B. Edes, 1789), p. 6; cf. Oliver Hart, *America's Remembrancer* (Philadelphia: T. Dobson, 1791), pp. 6–7.
65. Cf. Eckenrode, *Separation of Church and State;* Alvah Hovey, *A Memoir of the Life and Times of the Rev. Isaac Backus* (Boston: Gould & Lincoln, 1859), p. 369; L. H. Butterfield, "Elder John Leland, Jeffersonian Itinerant," in *Proceedings of the American Antiquarian Society, October 15, 1952* (Worcester: American Antiquarian Society, 1952), pp. 155–242.
66. Hovey, *Memoir of . . . Isaac Backus,* p. 243.

it failed to recognize this lordship. Constantine was the culprit. He was accused of undercutting this primary relationship by establishing Christianity as the religion of the realm. Moreover, Morgan Edwards labeled those who had participated in Constantine's councils "usurpers and traytors" because they were "the first set of wretches that arrogated to themselves the prerogatives of their sovereign Jesus." They made "laws for his subjects" and enforced them "with excommunication, deposition, degradations, banishments." [67] Before Constantine Christianity thrived, claimed Baptist Elhanan Winchester as (after the Revolution) he instructed a British audience on the history of the church. Before that time, he confidently preached, "Christianity flourished, conquered its foes, triumphed over all opposition, miracles, and gifts of the spirit were common; but all this beauty faded like a moth, when once the church was established by law. It was soon filled with unworthy members, idle ministers, and vicious proud, domineering ecclesiastics of all sorts: And thus its glory departed, and has never wholly returned since." [68] Constantine had committed a grievous error [69] when he failed to recognize that religion lives best on free and unfettered exercise. Those who broke lances on Constantine believed that it was possible through restoration to approximate the situation into which Christianity had first come and in which men had been Christians because of conviction, not by compulsion.

Furthermore, free exercise could not be fully achieved through any system of nonpreferential cooperation. Those who accepted this viewpoint threw the weight of their influence against policies of equal assessment, which they did not believe to be right by principle or able to be administered justly. In arguing this point, they were not simply thinking about the early church. Dissenters had suffered in the American environment under establishments

---

67. Morgan Edwards to Samuel Jones, July 26, 1785, John Hay Library, Brown University, Providence.
68. Elhanan Winchester, *Of the Glorious, Holy, Wonder-Working God* (London: J. Johnson, 1788), p. 29.
69. John Leland, *The Rights of Conscience Inalienable* (New London: T. Green, 1791), p. 4.

and under systems of assessment.[70] With empirical evidence they opposed those proposals of Congregationalists and Episcopalians which provided for such arrangements between the civil magistrate and religious societies. Some Presbyterians joined the Baptists against the assessment bill to underwrite religious activity in Virginia. "We are fully persuaded of the happy influences of Christianity upon the morals of men," they petitioned,

> but we have never known it, in the history of its progress, so effectual for this purpose, as when left to its native excellence and evidence to recommend it, under the all-directing providence of God, and free from the intrusive hand of the civil magistrate. Its Divine Author did not think it necessary to render it dependent on earthly governments. And experience has shown that this dependence, where it has been effected, has been an injury rather than an aid. It has introduced corruption among the teachers and professors of it wherever it has been tried for hundreds of years, and has been destructive of genuine morality, in proportion to zeal, of the powers of this world, in arming it with the sanction of legal terrors, or inviting to its profession by honors and rewards.[71]

In the struggle against assessment, Baptists were opposed to any "Bitumen to Cement Church and State together; the foundation for Ecclesiastical Tyranny, and the first step towards an Inquisition." They drove their point home asserting the essential freedom of the church: "New Testament Churches, we humbly conceive, are, or should be, established by the Legislature of Heaven, and not earthly power; by the Law of God and not the Law of the State; by the acts of the Apostles, and not by the Acts of an Assembly." [72] The civil magistrate should leave the gospel alone and allow God to perpetuate it. Only if the gospel were offered freely could Christians "convince the gazing world, that Disciples do not follow Christ for Loaves, and that Preachers do not preach for Benefices." [73] Any attempt of the magistrate to legislate for re-

70. Cf. Eckenrode, *Separation of Church and State;* Hovey, *Memoir of . . . Isaac Backus;* Butterfield, "Elder John Leland."
71. Presbyterian Convention to the Virginia State Legislature, August 13, 1785, Virginia State Library, Richmond.
72. Baptist General Committee to the Virginia State Legislature, August 5, 1785, Virginia State Library, Richmond.
73. Ibid. Cf. Leland, *Rights of Conscience,* p. 15.

ligious societies would be presumptuous, an attempt to tolerate God "in his empire of man's conscience, and government of the moral world." Establishment of any type was an attempt to "raise earthly thrones above the third heaven, to govern universal nature, and controul even the Supreme himself." [74] Accentuating free exercise, these clergymen claimed that even nonpreferential cooperation was an infringement upon the rights of conscience.

Although Methodists seem to have sought some protection under the wing of Anglicanism and to have supported its general position on the relation between the civil magistrate and religious societies,[75] some of them were quick to sense the advantages of the dissenter position. Thomas Coke, fresh from England to help organize Methodism in this country, expressed satisfaction that all things religious did not have to be weighed in the "scales of politics." When addressing Francis Asbury at the Christmas Conference in 1784 he reminded him that in England where Christians did not depend upon God alone for the support of the church, clergymen were "the parasites and bottle-companions of the rich and the great . . . faithful abettors of the ruling powers." Now in the United States "intolerable fetters" were struck off and the "antichristian union" which had united church and state had been broken asunder.[76] Free exercise gave Methodists opportunity for an open hearing of the gospel. Circuit rider Ezekiel Cooper reflected in 1789 that nobody in the nation would be able to curtail Methodist preaching by political restrictions. Truth would have "every advantage to defend its cause and gain the hearts of men."[77]

The free exercise which excluded a nonpreferential cooperation was based upon a view of the responsibility of conscience. Man is ultimately responsible to God alone. Therefore, man must always be responsive to the promptings of God, who has promised

74. Solomon Froeligh, *Republican Government Advocated* (Elizabethtown: Shepard Kollock, 1794), p. 10. Froeligh was a Dutch Reformed pastor with strong Jeffersonian sympathies.
75. See Eckenrode, *Separation of Church and State*, p. 47.
76. Thomas Coke, *The Substance of a Sermon* (London: J. Paramore, 1785), p. 6.
77. Ezekiel Cooper, in *Beams of Light on Early Methodism in America*, comp. George A. Phoebus (New York: Phillips & Hunt, 1887), pp. 89–90.

to lead man into all truth. The free activity of God must not, indeed, cannot, be bound by the coercive acts of men who think that they have fully ascertained truth which may be impressed upon the conscience of all other men at the point of the sword. It was not a matter of the conscience rightly informed being free. It was a matter of free exercise of religion in order that man's conscience might be continually informed. "The thoughts, the intentions, the faith and consciences of men, with their modes of worship" lay beyond the reach of the civil magistrate, and were "ever to be referred to a higher and more penetrating tribunal." Presbyterians of Virginia concluded that these "internal and spiritual matters cannot be measured by human rule, nor be amenable to human laws. It is the duty of every man for himself to take care of his immortal interests in a future state, where we are to account for our conduct as individuals; and it is by no means the business of the Legislature to attend to this, for *there* governments and states, as collective bodies, shall no more be known." [78]

John Leland underscored this sense of man's ultimate responsibility before God: "Every man must give an account of himself to God, and therefore every man ought to be at liberty to serve God in that way that he can best reconcile it to his conscience. If Government can answer for Individuals at the day of judgment, let men be controlled by it, in religious matters; otherwise, let men be free." [79] Those clergymen in favor of a nonpreferential cooperation allowing for the free exercise of religion knew also that man was responsible to God. Indeed, because of this they insisted that this responsibility could be fulfilled best through the civil support of religion for the promotion of virtue. They were opposed by those who considered this solemn responsibility seriously impaired by any interference of the civil magistrate.

Clergymen who believed that proper free exercise excluded nonpreferential cooperation between religious societies and the civil magistrate did not show much consciousness of all of the conditioning and contingent elements in the religious experience. Stress-

78. Presbytery of Hanover to the Virginia State Legislature, October 1784, Virginia State Library, Richmond.
79. Leland, *Rights of Conscience*, p. 7.

ing the individualistic approach to the experience, they seem naïve about the political nature of their own lobbying and petitioning against governmental interference in religious matters. They were not fully aware of the significance for their cause of any article in a civil constitution which supposedly guaranteed the rights of conscience. They seemed to forget that the early Christians themselves had not been protected from severe persecution. But they insisted in good conscience that no man should be forced to pick a "soul-guide" under any type of civil management. Cooperation made religion a "mere engine of the state." [80] After the First Amendment had been formulated it was used as a stick, particularly by dissenters in New England, to beat down systems of nonpreferential assessment.

Baptist clergyman David Thomas matched Fitch's doggerel with his own:

> Tax all things; water, air, and light,
> If need there be; yea, tax the night:
> But let our brave heroick minds
> Move freely as celestial winds.
> Make vice and folly feel your rod,
> But leave our consciences to God:
> Leave each man free to choose his form
> Of piety, nor at him storm.
> And he who minds the civil law,
> And keeps it whole, without a flaw,
> Let him just as he please, pray,
> And seek for heav'n in his own way;
> And if he miss, we all must own,
> No man is wrong'd but he alone.[81]

Nonpreferential Protection for Responsible Free Exercise

The official position of the Presbyterian church in the United States of America must be considered. With the Congregationalists and Baptists, they formed a part of the broader English Puritan

80. Cf. Jonathan Maxcy, *An Oration* (Providence: Carter & Wilkinson, 1795), pp. 16–17; Hovey, *Memoirs of . . . Isaac Backus,* p. 243.
81. Poem by David Thomas, quoted in David Benedict, *A General History of the Baptist Denomination,* 2 vols. (Boston: Manning & Loring, 1813), 2:479. According to Benedict, Thomas wrote this verse about the year 1785.

tradition which had shaped the American scene predominantly. The most ardent supporters of the two positions already suggested were the Congregationalists and the Baptists, who were sectarian in their view of ecclesiastical polity. They were able to think of religion in somewhat individualistic terms, either as the exercise of virtue or as a vital encounter between God and man. Presbyterians, who organized nationally in 1788, had to come to terms as a denomination of Christians with the rights of conscience. They did so, not only in terms of the individual, but also in terms of the freedom of the church, as a national organization which wished to preserve a continuity with the past as well as a continuing life. They produced a statement bearing directly upon this problem, the only one of length and significance made by a denomination, rather than by individuals or local bodies. Methodists, Episcopalians, and Reformed Dutch, along with Presbyterians, started to organize during the period of Confederation. Civil magistrates treated this matter with indifference and did not seek to determine or deter the process in any way.[82]

The Presbyterians composed the most representative religious body in the country during the Revolution and the early national period. There were Presbyterians in New England, in the South, and in the Middle States. While Presbyterian immigrants knew something of protection and privilege for religious bodies, not all of them remembered the situation in the Old World fondly. In the New World Presbyterians never knew special status. Wide representation made for inclusiveness of ideas and for much cross-fertilization. The body embraced sectarian as well as churchly, evangelical as well as more rationalistic, attitudes. The denomination's influence grew to such an extent that in 1783 its highest governing body, the Synod of New York and Philadelphia, issued a pronouncement to allay the apprehensions of non-Presbyterians:

> It having been represented to Synod, that the Presbyterian Church suffers greatly in the opinion of other denominations, from an apprehension that they hold intolerant principles, the Synod do solemn-

82. Cf. Stokes, *Church and State,* 1:477-82, for what this meant to Roman Catholic organization as well as for other denominations.

ly and publickly declare, that they ever have, and still do renounce and abhor the principles of intolerance; and we do believe that every member of civil society ought to be protected in the full and free exercise of their religion.[83]

This statement expressed the desire of the denomination that the rights of conscience should be secured to every citizen of the Confederation.[84] This did not keep some Presbyterians from accusing Americans of using their "liberty as a cloak of covetousness."[85]

Presbyterians found theological unity through their adherence to the Westminster Confession of Faith, written in the seventeenth century. Robert Annan, an Associate Reformed Presbyterian, stated the problem which this presented to the denomination. Like Congregationalists and Episcopalians, he was anxious that political life know the ferment of sound virtue. Consequently, religion should be supported by some means.[86] But he claimed that the Westminster Confession in its political statements had given too much power to the civil magistrate in the affairs of the church. Its provisions at this point had no relevance to the American situation.[87] He expressed some pleasure and some displeasure at the negative policy of the United States government: "They have at least given the fullest liberty to religion; that is, they declare they will not hinder or forbid it in any form. This is at least favoring it in a negative way. But surely it is of so much importance to society, as to merit some positive encouragement." [88] He wanted to discover a "medium," however hard to hit, "between an Erastian supremacy and Sectarian anarchy; tyrannical slavery and lawless licentiousness." [89] Presbyterians struggled to do something about updating the Westminster Confession during the period of organization, 1787–88. They restudied the confession and in effect

83. *Records of the Presbyterian Church in the United States of America* (Philadelphia: Presbyterian Board of Publication and Sabbath-School Work, 1904), p. 499.
84. Cf. John Rodgers, *The Divine Goodness Displayed* (New York: Samuel Loudon, 1784), pp. 29–30.
85. Cf. *An Address from the Presbytery of New-Castle to the Congregations under Their Care* (Wilmington: James Adams, 1785), p. 27.
86. Robert Annan, *Brief Animadversions on the Doctrine of Universal Salvation* (Philadelphia: R. Aitken 1787), p. 51.
87. Ibid., p. 50.
88. Ibid., p. 52.
89. Ibid., p. 53.

commented upon it in expressing principles of ecclesiastical polity in a preface to the government and discipline in the Presbyterian church. In all probability John Rodgers, clergyman of New York City, was most influential in the whole development. John Witherspoon, aging revolutionary, may have written the introductory words to the form of government.[90]

Presbyterians reviewed and revised the Westminster Confession of Faith about which Annan had reservations. Without question chapter 20, "Of Christian Liberty and Liberty of Conscience," is the most important for a definition of the problem of conscience, and for an understanding of the Presbyterian approach. In fact, because Congregationalists and Baptists in the United States were under the influence of the Westminster Confession, except when deviating rather obviously in matters of ecclesiology and the baptism of adults, it provides a clue to an understanding of their different approaches to the problem. Presbyterians claimed that the liberty of the Christian man is wrought for him by Jesus Christ. This consists in a freedom *from* the condemning wrath of God, the guilt of sin, the sting of death, and a freedom *for* sonship. Presbyterians reasserted that "God alone is lord of the conscience." This means that God has left conscience free from the commandments of men, which are "contrary to" or "beside" his Word in matters of faith and worship.

When these words were first written, Presbyterian theologians considered them a condemnation of popery, prelacy, and the perversion of independency. They went on to maintain that conscience could be violated in two ways. On the one hand, to believe that which was contrary to or beside the Word "out of conscience" was, in effect, to "betray true liberty of conscience." A man may believe, and be bound to in conscience, only that which is the truth. Congregationalists in colonial America perpetuated the desire among the Puritans to bind the conscience by coercion to those commandments of men which they believe in harmony with the Word. On the other hand, to require an "implicit faith, and

90. Leonard J. Trinterud, *The Forming of an American Tradition* (Philadelphia: Westminster Press, 1949), pp. 292–93.

an absolute and blind obedience" is to destroy "liberty of conscience and reason, also." A man may not believe and be bound by conscience in such a way as to vitiate his critical faculties. Baptists in colonial America preserved this more radical inclination in the Puritan tradition by their insistence that no man be forced to give unquestioning obedience to any other man. It is possible to interpret the Presbyterian position as an attempt to describe in one statement the responsible and yet continually responsive conscience.[91]

The conscience of the Christian man informed by the knowledge of the gospel is not to be exercised by the destruction of, or resistance to, the civil or ecclesiastical ordinances of God.[92] Presbyterians were very much aware of the importance of institutional structure. They were interested in the development of stable and energetic constitutional instruments which would at the same time preserve liberties. Christian liberty was not to be a pretense to oppose lawful power, lawfully exercised.[93] Finding themselves in a new situation in the United States, they tried to define a relation between the religious society and the civil magistrate which would satisfy the conscience. They produced a confessional statement approving a nonpreferential protection by the civil magistrate of religious societies which would provide for a proper free exercise in matters of religion.

This involved, on the one hand, an expression of high regard for the office of the civil magistrate. According to one chapter in the Westminster Confession, "Of the Civil Magistrate," God ordained the office for his glory and the public good. The power of the magistrate, therefore, is not derived from any ecclesiastical authority.[94] On the other hand, the magistrate has no power over the church in the "administration of the Word and Sacraments," over the use of the "keys of the kingdom," or to "interfere in matters of faith." He has the duty as nursing father

91. Cf. *The Constitution of the Presbyterian Church in the United States of America* (Philadelphia: Thomas Bradford, 1789), chap. 20.
92. Ibid.
93. Ibid.
94. Ibid., chap. 23.

to protect the Church of our common Lord, without giving preference to any denomination of Christians above the rest, in such a manner that all ecclesiastical persons whatever shall enjoy the full, free and unquestioned liberty of discharging every part of their sacred functions, without violence or danger. And as Jesus Christ hath appointed a regular government and discipline in his Church, no law or any commonwealth should interfere with, let, or hinder, the due exercise thereof, among the voluntary members of any denomination of Christians, according to their own profession and belief.[95]

In this statement Presbyterians indicated in assembly that they were concerned with religion not merely as the foundation of personal or public virtue or as an unfettered personal encounter, but as involving an institution. They attempted to define the freedom of the church as an organization established by Christ, composed of clergymen and all other "voluntary" members. However, they went on to base the case not only on the right of the church to freedom, but upon the responsibility of the civil magistrate to every citizen under his protection. It is the duty of the magistrates "to protect the person and good name of all their people, in such an effectual manner as that no person be suffered, either upon pretence of religion or infidelity, to offer any indignity, violence, abuse, or injury to any other person whatsoever: and to take order, that all religious and ecclesiastical assemblies be held without molestation or disturbance." [96] This article was finally adopted in 1788. With it Presbyterians sought to accommodate themselves to circumstances in the United States previous to the final ratification of the First Amendment to the Constitution. Adaptation, however, took the form of a restatement of an article of faith by which members of the denomination were bound by conscience. In striving for some consistency they dropped words from the Larger Catechism, which, in answer to a question concerning graven images, forbade "tolerating a false religion." [97] According to Ashbel

95. Ibid.
96. Ibid.
97. Ibid., pp. 79–80; cf. *The Confession of Faith, and the Larger and Shorter Catechisms* (London, 1652), pp. 111–12.

Green's memory of the occasion, these words were stricken by unanimous consent.[98]

Nonpreferential protection meant the possibility of free exercise of the rights of judgment and the pervasive influence of Christian virtue throughout the community for the common good. The preface to government and discipline in the Presbyterian church supplies some commentary on the alterations in the Westminster Confession of Faith. Since God is the lord of conscience, Presbyterians claimed "the rights of private judgment, in all matters that respect religion, as universal and unalienable: They do not even wish to see any religious constitution aided by the civil power, further than may be necessary for protection and security, and, at the same time, may be equal and common to all others." [99] "Rights of private judgment" belong to all men. They may not be taken away or given up. This assertion in the context of an ecclesiastical constitution and in the preface to a form of government and discipline may not be interpreted, without distortion, as rank individualism disassociated from any communal responsiveness or responsibility. Presbyterians asserted the necessity of preserving free access for every man to all the means of grace provided by God for man's redemption, and the personal responsibility of man in decision. The denomination went beyond the Westminster Confession of Faith to express opposition to the civil support of a religious society "further than may be necessary for protection and security" which could not at the same time be granted and be "equal and common to all others." Support of religious societies had to be seen in view of its tendency to promote free exercise of judgment for all.

There was another string to the Presbyterian bow. Free exercise involved the possibility of propagation and of permeating the community with the leaven of Christian virtue. Jefferson was confident that it did him no injury if his neighbor said there were "twenty gods or no god. . . . It neither picks my pocket nor breaks

98. Joseph H. Jones, *The Life of Ashbel Green* (New York: Robert Carter, 1849), p. 184.
99. *The Constitution of the Presbyterian Church*, p. 292.

my leg." [100] Presbyterians disagreed. Wishing to support the best in the Congregational and Episcopalian case at this point, they explained that Christian liberty could not be construed to sanction looseness or license in public.[101] To illuminate this clause in an age in which some believed religion to be without civil effects, they commented that

> truth is in order to goodness; and that no opinion can be either more pernicious or more absurd, than that which brings truth and falsehood upon a level, and represents it of no consequence what a man's sentiments are: On the contrary, They are of opinion, that soundness in the faith lays a proper foundation for holy practice; for, if it were otherwise, it would be of no importance either to discover truth or to embrace it.[102]

This paragraph went through several changes. In 1789, when the final draft was printed, it had been altered to read in a longer, perhaps less pungent, manner:

> Truth is in order to goodness; and the great touchstone of truth, its tendency to promote holiness; according to our Saviour's rule, "by their fruits you shall know them." And that no opinion can be either more pernicious or more absurd, than that which brings truth and falsehood upon a level, and represents it as of no consequence what a man's opinions are. On the contrary, They are persuaded that there is an inseparable connection between faith and practice, truth and duty. Otherwise, it would be of no consequence either to discover truth or to embrace it. [103]

"The thoughts, the intentions, the faith and conscience of men," as Virginia Presbyterians held, might lie beyond the reach of the civil magistrate. But what a man believed made a difference in the way in which he behaved. Religion could not be reduced to an individualistic relation between God and man to the exclusion of corporate life, for faith was inseparably bound to practice, and truth, to duty. Free exercise for Presbyterians included, therefore,

---

100. Jefferson, *Notes,* p. 292.
101. *The Constitution of the Presbyterian Church,* chap. 20.
102. *A Dràught of the Form of the Government and Discipline of the Presbyterian Church in the United States of America* (New York: S. & J. Loudon, 1787), p. iv.
103. *The Constitution of the Presbyterian Church,* p. cxxxiv.

the propagation of the faith which involved the possibility of persuading the community to that truth which is in order to goodness. They maintained, however, that the mission and message of religious societies should have power only "ministerial and declarative." Resting on no civil compulsion, Christianity should derive its force and bind man's conscience only from its "own justice, the approbation of an impartial public, and the countenance and blessing of the great Head of the Church universal." [104]

During this post-Revolutionary period of the making and remaking of constitutions, some Presbyterian clergymen had been urging hearers of their political sermons to "stand fast in the Liberty" by which Christ had made them free.[105] John Ewing of Philadelphia, in a sermon he preached a number of times, drove home a point consistent with the point of view of these Presbyterian statements. He appreciated a well-regulated zeal for civil liberty. This was a noble and generous passion which he coveted for all. He hoped that the spirit of freedom which prevailed under the recently passed American Constitution would never suffer decay. How "negligent and careless," he continued, "are men in securing spiritual Liberty; or a Freedom from the Tyranny & Bondage of Sin? . . . without which no Man, let his Civil Liberty be what it will, can ever be accounted free." [106] Ewing implied that civil liberty in the United States was a possibility because God the redeemer was also God the creator and preserver of the universe. Christian liberty is a gift granted by God through Jesus Christ. The liberty of the Christian man does not depend, therefore, upon the shape of a civil constitution. The liberty of the Christian man does release man to "serve the Lord without fear, in holiness and righteousness" in society.[107]

Some Presbyterian clergymen, after the First Amendment had been ratified, expressed deep dissatisfaction over the religious situ-

---

104. Ibid., pp. cxxxv–cxxxvi.
105. Cf. Samuel Miller, *A Sermon* (New York: Thomas Greenleaf, [1793]), p. 38; Samuel Stanhope Smith, *The Divine Goodness to the United States of America* (Philadelphia: William Young, 1795), p. 38.
106. John Ewing, sermon no. 1, Presbyterian Historical Society, Philadelphia.
107. Ibid. Cf. *The Constitution of the Presbyterian Church,* chap. 20.

ation in the United States. They condemned the "criminal indifference to the inestimable truths of the gospel" which masqueraded under the "specious name of liberality." [108] Charles Nisbet, Scottish immigrant and president of Dickinson College, roughing it on the Pennsylvania frontier, grumbled with some acidity:

> The truth is that Religion is so little regarded in this Country, that the best Schemes for its Support & Encouragement, could not meet with half so many Friends, as a Proposal for its Extinction or entire Suppression. And indeed nothing could serve this Purpose more effectually than that Equality & Indifference of Religious Opinions that is established by our Political Constitutions. It is this that has divided all our Citizens into two great Parties, the Anythingarians who hold all Religions equally good, & the Nothingarians who abhor all Religions equally. And in such a Division, you may easily believe that the Anythingarians having no fix'd Principles to rest on, must soon be put down by the Nothingarians, who are the great Majority in this Country.[109]

But other Presbyterians looked with more hope on the prospect of religious life in the United States. Samuel Stanhope Smith, of the College of New Jersey, had written to Nisbet, while the latter was still in Scotland, deploring religious conditions. But he accepted the constitutional provisions concerning religion as it had been determined by the citizens of the country. He was satisfied that in America religion had been freed from the degenerating influences of restricting civil and ecclesiastical institutions. He interpreted the amendment by writing:

> Among us truth is left to propagate itself by its native evidence and beauty. Stripped of those meretricious charms that, under the splendor of an establishment, intoxicate the sense, it possesses only those modest and simple beauties that touch the heart. . . . In America, a diligent and faithful clergy resting on the affections, and supported by the zeal of a free people, can secure their favour only in a proportion to their useful services. A fair and generous competition among the different denominations of christians; while it does not

108. Thomas Reese, *Steadfastness in Religion* (Philadelphia: William Young, 1793), p. 10.
109. Charles Nisbet to Charles Wallace, October 31, 1797, New York Public Library.

extinguish their mutual charity, promotes an emulation that will have a beneficial influence on the public morals.[110]

Smith sensed the practical implications of the situation. No political coercion meant a coexistence. Coexistence meant in turn a "fair and generous" competitive existence.

Presbyterian efforts to come to terms with the problem of the rights of conscience are significant because Presbyterians attempted to develop a national denominational position. Some Presbyterians were not satisfied with the results. Be this as it may, it is clear that in the statements in the Westminster Confession of Faith and the preface to government and discipline Presbyterians as a denomination claimed that "truth is in order to goodness." Matters of conscience are not merely private matters. And yet they insisted that man possessed "universal and unalienable" rights of private judgment. Presbyterians had suffered disabilities under establishments in colonial America. Consequently, they were undecided and indecisive about the type of positive encouragement they desired from the civil magistrate for the religious life of the community. They sought from the civil magistrate a nonpreferential protection of religious societies, including clergy and laity in their religious practices. They stated this case negatively by disapproving any civil aid to ecclesiastical institutions which would not be "equal and common" to all. Any positive nonpreferential encouragement would have to fulfill such a condition. Congressional or state law, for that matter, would have to be judged on the basis of its tendency "respecting" an establishment of religion, or its tendency "prohibiting" the free exercise thereof. By leaving this problem open, Presbyterians underscored the complexity of life in a pluralistic society and the impossibility of solving by formula a teasing and tension-producing problem as old as the church itself. Presbyterians, with other Americans, were to determine whether or not (to use the words of the Reformed Dutch) religion would be "more effectually patronized in a civil

110. Smith, *Divine Goodness*, pp. 32–33. Cf. Michael Kraus, "Charles Nisbet and Samuel Stanhope Smith—Two Eighteenth Century Educators," *Princeton University Chronicle*, vol. 6, no. 1 (1944), pp. 17–36.

government where full freedom of conscience and worship is equally protected and insured to all men." [111]

The debate about the meaning of the First Amendment, begun in the latter part of the eighteenth century, still proceeds in the latter part of the twentieth. Several conclusions may be suggested from this particular analysis of the early history of the discussion. In the first place, there was much less stumbling during the period than Perry Miller is willing to admit. To be sure, there may have been too few resources and too many denominational bodies to recognize a pluralistic establishment and to impose a policy of assessment for the support of all religious institutions. [112] But the discussion of establishment and the free exercise of religion was an old one extending back in time throughout the whole colonial period, and conceptualization of the problems appears far clearer than hitherto recognized by some historians. Those who engaged in the debate did not produce lengthy treatises on the subject, but they did express their opinions in sermons, pamphlets, petitions, newspaper articles, and correspondence. Mark De Wolfe Howe recently accused the Supreme Court, not of bad decisions, but of bad history with regard to the meaning of the First Amendment. He accused the court of elevating to judicial doctrine the Jeffersonian tradition involving a high "wall of separation" while neglecting the equally important tradition of Roger Williams. [113] While it is unclear—the evidence is slim—whether eighteenth century clergy knew Williams as well as they did Jefferson, Howe is right about the existence of the Williams interpretation alongside the Jeffersonian. Howe is much too narrow, however, in his own analysis. Among Protestant clergy it is possible to ascertain several approaches to the First Amendment indicating the existence of a vigorous religious pluralism.

In this connection, the eighteenth century debate was rich in theological, ecclesiological, and ethical content. John Courtney

111. *The Constitution of the Reformed Dutch Church, in the United States of America* (New York: William Durell, 1793), pp. vii–viii.
112. P. Miller, "Location of American Religious Freedom," p. 15.
113. Mark De Wolfe Howe, *The Garden and the Wilderness* (Chicago: University of Chicago Press, 1965), p. 5.

Murray argues that the First Amendment to the Constitution was an article of peace rather than an article of faith, the establishment of left-wing conceptions of the nature of religious life and institutions.[114] He thereby exposed his own theological, ecclesiological, and ethical presuppositions. It seems very clear that Protestant clergy accepted and interpreted the First Amendment with certain presuppositions, some of which have been systematized in the now-famous Declaration on Religious Liberty of Vatican Council II.[115] One of the most important was that man receives his identity as a person neither from political structures nor from religious institutions, the ancient regimes, but through his relation to God as a responsible and accountable creature. The debate between those who argued for a nonpreferential assessment which would allow free exercise and those who argued that any assessment policy was an infringement of free exercise only disputed the ways and means of expressing that responsibility and coming to that accountability. In a sense, both sides wished to preserve a voluntarism in this relation. It must be noted that the development was not individualistic and completely naïve about corporate Christian life.

This is illustrated in the discussion which went on as the Presbyterians organized the General Assembly of the Presbyterian Church in the United States of America. While the Synod of New York and Philadelphia accepted the voluntarism, it also attempted to face some of the corporate implications of the situation in which Christians found themselves. Presbyterians spoke for others as well as themselves in insisting upon the freedom of the denomination with regard to the administration of word and sacrament and the inner discipline of religious bodies. But the synod's insistence upon protection and security for the denomination and its right to influence society for the public good indicates some sophistication about the necessary functional interaction of the civil magistrate and religious bodies. Thus the Presbyterians in assembly exposed the ambiguities of the debate and implied that

---

114. Murray, *We Hold These Truths,* p. 56.
115. See *The Documents of Vatican II,* ed. Walter M. Abbott (New York: Guild Press, 1966 [paperback]), pp. 675–96.

interpreting the First Amendment would be a continuous debate. Their conclusion seems to be more favorable to Madison's metaphor of the "line of separation" than to Jefferson's reference to the "wall."

The First Amendment of 1791 must be considered from the earlier and more basic perspective—its constitutional context. Most Protestant clergy accepted the Constitution of the United States as an attempt to deal with the problem of power about which they shared the same presuppositions. They accepted power, the dominion of some men over others, as essential to human society. They also believed that power is of an encroaching and corrupting nature. This is true of ecclesiastical as well as civil power. This is true especially of civil power sanctioned uncritically by ecclesiastical establishments, and of ecclesiastical power supported by civil coercion. Power, civil and ecclesiastical, has to be deflated, diffused, and properly related in order to keep it from becoming absolute, arbitrary, and abused.[116] Therefore, the First Amendment with its no establishment and free exercise clauses may be seen as contributing to the proper equilibrium of power. But this must not be considered a static concept. There was a great amount of experimentation during the early years of the nation's history. Generally, Protestants decided that they did not want to be coerced to support the religious institutions of others, much less their own. Given the shifting nature of power they saw that the constitutional problem would be perpetually calling for the eternal vigilance of those who prized religious liberty and liberty of conscience.

116. Bernard Bailyn, *The Ideological Origins of the American Revolution* (Cambridge, Mass.: Harvard University Press, Belknap Press, 1967) p. 56.

7

The Voluntary Establishment of Religion

ELWYN A. SMITH

It might be supposed that the defeat of the Virginia establishment in 1776 and the adoption of the Federal Bill of Rights in 1792 would have undermined established religion and called into question the social philosophy that undergirded the Puritan church-state system. But New England was another country, and its habits were much too steady. In the enthusiasm for the French Revolution that swept the new states after 1789 it seemed for a time that America's old order of ideas would follow the Tories into limbo, but when news of the Terror came the admirers of Rousseau, Voltaire, d'Alembert, and Condorcet were thrown on the defensive and the Calvinists seized the moment.

The Calvinist resurgence was not simply a case of reaction following revolution. Conservative theologians such as Nathanael Emmons of Franklin, Massachusetts, knew that they now lived in a Republic where the people were sovereign. They took comfort in the emergence of a written constitution, seeing in it a conservator of values and a defense against democratic excesses. Such men scarcely realized, however, that religion also was moving toward a social reorientation. Samuel Hopkins published his massive *System of Doctrines* in 1793; yet the order of that system revealed little sensitivity to the need for an interpretation of religion that could persuade effectively in the new conditions of the nation. The future lay with another breed of leadership: practical men who understood that America would no longer accept a religion of authority perpetuated more or less coercively by a clerical-political class but would accept only a religion oriented to persuasion.[1]

The American self-consciousness authoritatively affirmed to each man his freedom. So fundamental a doctrine called sharply into question any social system that intermingled legal coercion with religion. At the same time, very few questioned the dependence of government upon the moral quality of its citizens or the significance of religion as the nursing mother of morals. As they watched the erosion of the establishments in Connecticut and Massachusetts, the New England clergy could not believe that morals could survive the severing of church from state. Yet when the divorce came there appeared a conception of the relation of religion to society that accepted the American commitment to freedom and the voluntary principle in church-state relations without making sacrifice of the precious conception that religion was the essential ingredient of the public weal.

The system of ideas and action worked out by the new Calvinism for the instruction of the public was so comprehensive and effective as to merit paradoxical description as a "voluntary establishment" of religion. While they shrank from the notion of a "national" religion because of its legal overtones, the new leadership believed in the social establishment of Christianity: the Republic—both its morals and its unity, and therefore its power to survive—rested on a pervasive religious and moral consensus. Lyman Beecher, the most prominent advocate of the revived Calvinist order, never considered legal establishment wrong at the root, so long as it did not coerce; but legal religion had become dysfunctional in the nineteenth century. "It was the fundamental maxim of the fathers of this state," he wrote, "that the preaching of the Gospel is, in a civil point of view, a great blessing to the

1. Three articles are particularly crucial to the interpretation of the event whose theoretical foundation is the subject of this paper: James Fulton Maclear, "The True American Union of Church and State: The Reconstruction of the Theocratic Tradition," *Church History* 28 (1959): 41 ff.: Sidney E. Mead, "From Coercion to Persuasion: Another Look at the Rise of Religious Liberty and the Emergence of Denominationalism," *Church History* 24 (1956): 317 ff. and idem, "The 'Nation with the Soul of a Church,' " *Church History* 36 (1967): 262 ff.

community. . . . This law, while the inhabitants of the state were all of one creed, was entirely efficacious and secured to the people of the state at least four times the amount of religious instruction which has ever been known to be the result of mere voluntary associations for the support of the Gospel." It was the "multiplication of other denominations" that wrecked that system and opened the door to a popular refusal of all religious and moral duty. Legal establishment had failed; there was no other way to establish religion in society except through persuasion.[2] The enormous practical success of the voluntary social establishment reached the farthest corners of the expanding nation; it dominates the Protestant mind in large sections of the nation to the present day. The typical Protestant American—Calvinist, Wesleyan, Episcopalian—still seeks the voluntary establishment of his religiousness rather than the radical separation advocated by the Baptists Isaac Backus and John Leland and the Republicans Thomas Jefferson and James Madison.

Puritanism had conceded so much by 1775 that John Adams doubted that what remained of church-state law in Massachusetts could rightly be called an establishment. Both establishment and toleration had yielded to freedom in Connecticut, in Timothy Dwight's opinion, except that there did remain a limited "establishment of the worship of God." [3] Legal preference of the Congregational church nevertheless survived into the nineteenth century in Massachusetts, New Hampshire, and Connecticut.[4]

2. Lyman Beecher, *The Autobiography of Lyman Beecher,* ed. Barbara M. Cross, 2 vols. (Cambridge, Mass.: Harvard University Press, Belknap Press, 1961), 2:200–201.
3. *President Dwight's Decisions of Questions Discussed by the Senior Class in Yale College in 1813 and 1814* (New York, 1833), p. 47.
4. The emergence of religious liberty in these states is recounted in the following works: Charles B. Kinney, Jr., *Church and State: The Struggle for Separation in New Hampshire, 1630–1900* (New York: Teachers College, Columbia University, 1955); M. Louise Greene, *The Development of Religious Liberty in Connecticut* (Boston: Houghton Mifflin Co., 1905); Jacob Conrad Meyer, *Church and State in Massachusetts from 1740 to 1833: A Chapter in the Development of Individual Freedom* (Cleveland: Western Reserve University Press, 1930); Sanford H. Cobb, *The Rise of Religious Liberty in America* ([1st printing 1902] New York: Burt Franklin, 1968), pp. 133–290.

If it was generally ineffective in maintaining religious unity, establishment perpetuated the social and political domination of the clergy. This in part explains why after the election of Jefferson the Connecticut establishment became the target of a general social and political upheaval that brought the Republicans to power in the general ruin of Federalism.[5] Constitutional revision in Connecticut in 1818 totally abolished the establishment of religion. Massachusetts did not lack contestants on both sides of the issue, but it was Connecticut that bred the new theocratic leadership: Timothy Dwight (1752–1817), president of Yale: Lyman Beecher (1775–1863), his student and the most notable church activist of the era; and Nathaniel W. Taylor (1786–1858), professor at Yale and the best theorist of the new Calvinism.

The term *theocrat* does not merely add a dash of polemic seasoning to this exposition; all three of these principal figures defended the Old Testament system of political and religious government as a model adaptable to popular sovereignty in the American Republic.[6] All believed that government per se was ordained of God and was to be obeyed, as taught by Paul (Romans 13). While they were by no means Jeffersonian Republicans, they were friends of free popular government rather than class-oriented. Taylor, in particular, elaborated the concept of human rights in some detail.[7] They vigorously denied any kinship between the Mosaic theocracy and the theory of the divine right of kings; they equally denied any theory of absolute right of the sovereign people and strictly separated civil government as a human and natural institution from God's moral governance. "Nothing is plainer," wrote Taylor, "than [Peter's and Paul's] distinct recognition of the difference between God's authority as a moral governor over men as moral beings, and the authority of civil government over men

5. For this account, see Richard J. Purcell, *Connecticut in Transition, 1775–1818* ([orig. 1918] Middletown: Wesleyan University Press, 1963), passim.
6. See Nathaniel W. Taylor, *Lectures on the Moral Governments of God*, 2 vols. (New York: Clark, 1859), 2:36 ff.; see also John Rainer Bodo, *The Protestant Clergy and Public Issues, 1812–1848* (Princeton: Princeton University Press, 1954), chap. 2.
7. Taylor, *Lectures on the Moral Government*, 2:265 ff.

as its subjects; for both apostles simply employ one kind of authority, viz., God's authority as a moral governor, to enforce submission to another kind of authority, viz., man's authority as a civil ruler. The authority of civil government is simply human authority." [8]

When God ordained that government exist among men, the new theocrats taught, he did not ordain a particular form of government and grant his authority to kings or presidents. Any form of government is in principle acceptable, provided it meets the rudiments of divine law: defends the rights of God's people, etc. Thus the theocrats, despite some confusion of thought arising from strong anti-French feeling, did not rule out social compact—but they did suspect its advocates of the anti-Christian view that government's whole and sole authority for existence arises in the people, exclusive of any natural or revealed obligation to God or to the teachings of the Scripture.

On these assumptions, the new theocrats deftly separated the issue of the legal establishment of religion from their basic commitment to a public order grounded in reason and revelation, and through vigorous public activity they robbed humanist revolutionary philosophy of a victory. Singing the praises of liberty, the Yale Calvinists argued that religion alone could guarantee the high level of public morals indispensable to so fragile an experiment as democracy and mounted a spirited attack on infidelity, Unitarianism, atheism, Pelagianism, Arminianism, Arianism, Catholicism, and French philosophy in general. Less salutary Calvinists such as Emmons saw in the ascendency of Jefferson nothing but national catastrophe, but this was not the mood of the Connecticut leadership. They accepted the authority of fact, exalted utility and experience, and plunged into public propaganda with zest. In company with a less savory revivalism than their own, they swept most of New England and the West for the cause of piety.

The thinking of the Connecticut theocrats, therefore, perpetuated the traditional world view of established religion—but stripped of its historic legal trappings. That tradition did not remain unaltered; the Yale men elaborated the theme of liberty

8. Ibid., p. 58.

in fresh directions, both personal and social; quietly accepted Lockean philosophical assumptions; and modified Puritanism's theory of society. They gave up the notion of a morally superior upper class, an assumption never wholly abandoned by New England theologians of the older caste.[9] If there was to be respect for law, it must be sustained by the free consent of all the people; the best of laws would be futile if discrepant with the public will.

At the philosophical level, the new theocrats abandoned the old metaphysics and accepted the authority of experience, duly melded with revelation. Dwight steered a careful course around the metaphysical doctrine of Adam's "federal headship," a theory that explained each individual's sin as due to no choice of his own but to Adam's alone; he used the notion of man's solidarity with Adam only to make individuals responsible for their acts. "It is evident," wrote this genuinely cheerful man, "that the fundamental principle of moral and political science, so far as man is concerned, is depravity. . . . This is the first and fundamental fact. Because of it arise . . . all his volitions, and all his conduct. . . . No system of regulations can be practically suited to him, or fitted to control his conduct with success, or efficiency, which is not founded on the same principle." [10] So much for Rousseau; yet Dwight's appeal was to fact, not dogma.

9. In his *Errand of Mercy: The Evangelical United Front, 1790–1837* (Chapel Hill: University of North Carolina Press, 1960), Charles I. Foster points to the collaboration of Presbyterians, Episcopalians, and Baptists in the reform movement in Connecticut as evidence that "class interests rather than religious interest were primarily at stake: a new aristocracy was intent upon establishing social, religious, and political control in the pattern of the old, Tory aristocracy." This conclusion does not follow from the premise. Episcopalians had stood apart from the sectarian struggle for religious liberty in Connecticut until discrimination against them by the legislature forced them into the sectarian camp. Cf. Purcell, *Connecticut in Transition*, chap. 8. Baptists never sought a role in any aristocratic coalition but entered into cooperation with formerly state-supported congregations because they believed that God had destined America for his own righteous people. Such an ideal may not be "religious" in some uses of the term, but to the Connecticut evangelicals it was. That Dwight and Beecher in particular were aristocratic in mien and habit did not impose a class character either on Connecticut's Baptists or on anyone else; it was rather that disestablishment after 1818 made collaboration possible among equals. Foster failed to review the sources and the relevant secondary literature.
10. Timothy Dwight, "Depravity of Man," sermon 33 in *Theology Explained and Defended in a Series of Sermons*, 4 vols., 11th ed. (New Haven: T. Dwight, 1843), 1:498. Dwight's full critique of social compact is found in "The Duty of Rulers," sermon 113 in ibid., 3:324.

Beecher was even more unmistakable. "The question . . . is not a question of possible or impossible," he declared, "but a question of FACT." He respected science and its supporting principles. Against the fundamentalists of the era he cried:

> what would be said if in tracing the implications of the Bible, in respect to the qualifications of mind for accountable agency and government by law, we should find them all contradicted? Christianity could not stand before such contradicitions of revelation by science. It would open upon us the floodgates of an all-pervading, irresistible infidelity. . . . It would undermine all confidence in consciousness or argument and terminate in universal scepticism. . . . Our argument against transubstantiation is, that our senses are a correct revelation of the reality and attributes of external things; . . . no written revelation from heaven can contradict the testimony of this constitutional revelation by the senses concerning attributes of external objects, without supposing the conflict of contrary revelations, which would not only destroy the credibility of the Bible, but vacate all confidence in the testimony of the senses.[11]

The standard of utility was deeply suspect to clergymen who were Federalist in politics and theology alike. Noting that Law, Paley, Hume, and Godwin advocated the view that virtue "wholly consists in utility and all its excellences lie, not in its nature, but in its tendency to promote personal happiness," Nathanael Emmons remarked: "Godwin has founded a scheme of sentiments, which carried into practice, would subvert all morality, religion and government." [12]

In the fall of the *ancien régime,* certain radical utilitarians had argued that the command of love had lost its authority, that oaths need not be honored under all circumstances, and that punishment should be abolished, and had advocated other views equally terrifying to New Englanders. Dwight, Beecher, and Taylor, of course, would touch none of this, but their practice was profoundly utilitarian. They habitually abandoned unsuccessful tech-

11. Lyman Beecher, *Views in Theology* (Cincinnati: Truman & Smith, 1836), pp. 87, 209. Idem, *Autobiography,* 1:150.
12. Nathanael Emmons, *The Danger of Embracing That Notion of Moral Virtue Which Is Subversive of All Moral, Religious, and Political Obligations, Illustrated: A Discourse . . . November 29, 1804* (Providence: Heaton & Williams, 1805), pp. 8–9.

niques—the legal establishment of religion, for example—and adopted others that had proved effective—certain tactics of revivalism, for example. The structure of their new Calvinism was powerfully motivated by considerations of utility. They by no means rejected Calvinist teachings for those of utilitarianism; rather, they insisted on a practical Calvinism and were prepared to make the theoretical modifications necessary to effectiveness. Noah Porter, a pupil of Dwight's, put the matter boldly.

> Never for a moment have I doubted the importance of an undisguised declaration of the whole counsel of God, and particularly of those doctrines which exhibit the dependence of fallen man on the sovereign grace of God; but if experience and observation have taught me anything, it is that there is a way of discussing these subjects . . . which does little good; . . . if hearers are not taught their relations to God as accountable subjects of his government, and capable heirs of salvation, and if the obligations and encouragements which belong to these relations, are not carried home to their hearts, a general recklessness as to the concerns of salvation may be expected to prevail. [13]

Notwithstanding these new emphases, the social philosophy of the new theocrats evolved strictly within the New England mainstream.[14] Their master conception was an expression of the venerable Christian doctrine of divine sovereignty: the "moral government of God." Thus did Nathaniel Taylor entitle his theological lectures at Yale, since for him systematic theology was the unfolding of the moral government of God.

The universal moral government of God accounted for man's created nature and defined his depravity; the divine government would be brought to glorious manifestation in the millennium.[15]

13. Noah Porter to William B. Sprague, March 12, 1832, in *Letters of Revivals of Religion*, ed. William B. Sprague, 2d. ed. (New York, 1833), pp. 296–97.
14. A brief and lucid account of the ties of New England Puritanism with medieval and sixteenth century roots is furnished by Joseph Haroutunian, *Piety vs. Moralism* (New York: Henry Holt & Co., 1932), pp. xii–xxv.
15. Cf. Timothy Dwight, *A Discourse . . . August 20, 1812 on the National Fast* (New York: Seymour, 1812), pp. 19, 29. The power of this conception in nineteenth century Protestant thought was to grow. Also cf. George Marsden, "Kingdom and Nation: New School Presbyterian Millennialism in the Civil War Era," *Journal of the Presbyterian Historical Society* (hereafter cited as *JPHS*), vol. 46, no. 4, pp. 254 ff.; James Fulton Maclear, "The Republic and the Millennium" (see next chapter).

This conception of divine governance had always undergirded the Massachusetts theocracy. Any early Puritan might have said with Beecher: "Men are desperately wicked and must be restrained somehow. Civil rulers are ministers of God . . . and found to exercise their best discretion to provide for public safety. The fear of the Lord is the most salutary influence that can be addressed to the human mind." [16]

To the theocratic mind, the government of God was all-encompassing: religion, society, economy, politics. The Connecticut trio accepted the separation of certain rights from the political process; they wanted no man's religious belief or practice submitted to the electorate. But society could not permit rights to operate to the detriment of the general welfare. Fully regulative of the thought of the theocrats was the statement of Jonathan Edwards, the teacher of them all: "The God that is the Creator of the world, is doubtless also the Governor of it: for he is able to govern it. . . . He that first gave the laws of nature must have all nature in his hands." What immediately struck the Yale theologians was Edwards's concept of the voluntary. "God had some end in what he did," wrote Edwards, "when he made the world . . . otherwise he did not act as a voluntary agent. . . . That being never acts voluntarily, that has no end in what he does." [17]

In God and man alike, the nerve of the moral is the freedom of the agent. Taylor defined the moral as the "intelligent, free, permanent, predominant action of the heart in which the agent elects some given object or end as his supreme end, and which is thus directly fitted to promote this end and prevent its opposite." [18] Calvinists had always to assert God's freedom and always to deny that he acted under any necessity whatsoever. Thus volition and freedom were thrown into the foreground of their view of man who was God's image. The voluntary principle thence passed into their social theory.

16. Lyman Beecher, *A Sermon . . . May 20, 1813* (Hartford: Gleason, 1813), p. 16.
17. Jonathan Edwards, "Miscellaneous Observations on Important Doctrines," in *Works*, Worcester Ed. (New York: Leavitt, Trow, 1844), 1:565.
18. Taylor, *Lectures on the Moral Government*, 1:65.

The crucial struggle of New England thought from Edwards through Taylor turned on the issue of human freedom. In his *Freedom of the Will* [19] Edwards conferred on a century of American religious thought its pivotal term for reconciling God's sovereignty and man's freedom: the distinction between natural and moral ability. It was impossible for anyone who claimed the name of Calvinist to deny human depravity: those who did were Arminians or worse. How, then, could a depraved man be free?

"When I say that mankind are entirely depraved by nature," answered Taylor in his celebrated *Concio ad Clerum,* "I do not mean that their nature is itself sinful, nor that their nature is the physical or efficient cause of their sinning; but I mean that their nature is the occasion, or reason of their sinning: —that such is their nature, that in all the appropriate circumstances of their being, they will sin and only sin." [20] Depravity affects not natural but moral ability: that is, the competence of the will to choose and, having chosen, to act to do the good. Man *is* man because of certain defining abilities or faculties: perception, reason, conscience, common sense—the facultative psychology of the era varied. [21] These faculties are natural; without them, man would be animal or even inanimate. The Fall did not cancel God's work of creation. No "physical necessity," therefore, intrudes on the freedom of man: human faculties are not undone. The source of depravity lies wholly in man's will, specifically its domination by perverse "motives." Moral inability, wrote Beecher, is an actual

19. Jonathan Edwards, *A Careful and Strict Enquiry into the Modern Prevailing Notions of That Freedom of the Will Which Is Supposed to Be Essential to Moral Agency, Virtue and Vice, Reward and Punishment, Praise and Blame* (now available as *Freedom of the Will*, ed. Paul Ramsey [New Haven: Yale University Press, 1957). Cf. Sidney E. Mead, *Nathaniel William Taylor, 1786–1858: A Connecticut Liberal* ([orig. 1942] Hamden, Conn.: Shoe String Press, 1967), pp. 194 ff.; and Perry Miller, *Jonathan Edwards* (New York: Dell Publishing Co., 1967 [paperback]). See also Perry Miller, *The New England Mind*, vol. 2, *From Colony to Province* ([orig. 1953] Boston: Beacon Press, 1961 [paperback]), passim; and Haroutunian, *Piety vs. Moralism*, pp. 15–42. 220–28.
20. Nathaniel W. Taylor, *Concio ad Clerum: A Sermon . . . Sept. 10, 1828* (New Haven: Howe, 1821), p. 14.
21. Cf. Emmons, *Works*, 4:156–57, 348; also, Lyman Beecher, *Views in Theology*, p. 27. On the "faculty psychology" that functioned in New England thought from the entry of Locke's thought to William James, see Haroutunian, *Piety vs. Moralism*, pp. 249 ff.

"aversion of the mind to the performance of its spiritual duties, brought upon the race, by the voluntary transgression of Adam, and eventuating in a habit of corrupt will." [22] Man's inability to obey God, Dwight explained, "is completely indicated by the word Indisposition, or the word Disinclination." Oppositely, the disposition to love fulfills the whole duty of man.[23]

Defining sin as "deliberate, total, and obstinate dissent from the government of God," Beecher was teaching as early as 1808 that "all the glory of God, in his Law and Gospel, depend wholly upon this great fact, that men, though living under the government of God, and controlled according to his pleasure, are still, entirely free and accountable for all the deeds done in the body." [24] "It is a matter of universal consciousness," he wrote in 1836, "that men are free to choose right or wrong." [25]

In these reasonings, certain Calvinist types smelled an aroma of Pelagianism, a subtle assertion of man's ability to meet his own needs, if not entirely without divine aid, at least as an active collaborator with God. They reaffirmed the most categorical doctrine of depravity: Adam's sin had polluted the very nature of man. This metaphysic the new Calvinists repudiated. What is depravity but the naked fact that sin universally prevails, as even minimal observation of human conduct will prove? What does dubious speculation add? On this basis, the Edwardeans gave full consent to the traditional doctrine. Wrote Dwight:

> I have been employed in the education of children and youth more than thirty years and have watched their conduct with no small attention and anxiety. Yet among the thousands of children committed to my care, I cannot say with truth, that I have seen *one* whose native character I had any reason to believe to be virtuous; or whom I could conscientiously pronounce to be free from the evil attributes

22. Beecher, *Views in Theology,* p. 115. Cf. Timothy Dwight, "The Sovereignty of God," sermon 16 in *Theology Explained and Defended,* 1:268.
23. Timothy Dwight, "Man's Inability to Obey the Law of God," sermon 133 in *Theology Explained and Defended,* 4:20 ff. Depravity consists in "the want of love to God," said Beecher, *Views in Theology,* p. 161.
24. Lyman Beecher, *The Government of God Desirable: A Sermon . . . Oct. 1808* (New York: Smith & Foreman, 1809), pp. 9, 16.
25. Beecher, *Views in Theology,* p. 42.

mentioned above . . . rebellious, disobedient, unkind, wrathful, and revengeful . . . proud, ambitious, vain, and universally selfish . . . destitute of piety.[26]

Dwight did not deny that at maturity many human beings reveal more winsome traits than these: "natural affection; . . . compassion; generosity, modesty, natural conscientiousness." [27] But even these qualities are subject to the authority of "that controlling Disposition, or Energy, which constitutes the moral character." Man's "disinclination to obedience is still so obstinate and enduring, that it is never relinquished by man, except under the renewing influence of the Spirit of God." [28]

The Connecticut school's refusal of the radical metaphysic of the pre-Edwardeans was absolutely crucial to their system: if man is not in some sense free, there can be no human accountability; and therefore no genuinely moral government of God. Taylor launched an outright assault in his *Concio ad Clerum.* "The doctrine of a corrupt and sinful nature as such has been retained by some. . . . The entire annals of orthodoxy do not contain the doctrine that God creates a sinful nature in man. . . . [We] as fully believe in the certainty of the universal and entire sinfulness of mankind—[we] as fully believe in the inefficacy of moral suasion and in the necessity of the Holy Spirit's agency in regeneration as any other men." To recognize the desperate sinfulness of man does not require a metaphysic that annihilates the very humanity in him; depravity, in fact, is completely explained by the fact that "as free moral agents, we sin knowingly and voluntarily when we become capable of thus sinning." It was Edwardean thought, selectively developed.[29]

26. Timothy Dwight, "Human Depravity: Derived from Adam," sermon 32 in *Theology Explained and Defended,* 1:432.
27. Dwight, "Depravity of Man," sermon 31 in ibid., 1:462.
28. Dwight, "Man's Inability to Obey the Law of God," sermon 133 in ibid., 4:20–21.
29. Nathaniel W. Taylor, *Concio ad Clerum,* pp. 26 ff. Cf. Earl A. Pope, "The Rise of the New Haven Theology," *JPHS,* vol. 44, no. 1, p. 24, and no. 2, p. 106; and Elwyn A. Smith, "The Doctrine of Imputation and the Presbyterian Schism of 1837–38," *JPHS,* vol. 38, no. 3, pp. 129 ff. See also Beecher, *Views in Theology,* pp. 65–66; Haroutunian, *Piety vs. Moralism,* pp. 15–43, 252–53; and F. H. Foster, *A Genetic History of New England Theology* ([orig. 1907] New York: Russell & Russell, 1963), pp. 47–106 and passim.

The thrust of the Yale theology was to establish at almost any price man's accountability for his behavior. Accountability alone makes men "qualified subjects of moral government." It is no part of the Christian religion, argued Beecher, to suppose "that man, after all, is not able to modify and diversify his choice indefinitely, but chooses sin or holiness by a coercive necessity . . . and cannot turn and prefer the Creator to the creature." [30] A benevolent Creator had reached out to fallen man with a Word and Spirit effective to redeem. It would be senseless to suppose that man has no faculty capable of response and cannot be held responsible to say yes. Each man sins for himself; he is not relieved of responsibility because Adam did his sinning for him— as the opposition put it, each had sinned in Adam before any personal choice was ever posed. The moral government of God included a complete scheme of reward and punishment. Dwight did not contend for human responsibility only to thrust the whole issue of reward and punishment into a future state after death. He firmly expected Christ to intervene in human history; he saw divine punishment in the War of 1812. In every detail of life man faced the issue of reward or punishment.

The theory of the moral government of God might have had little significance for American culture at large, and the relation of religion to government specifically, had the theocrats identified the divine government only with an attitude of the individual or the order of a small religious community. The moral government of God reached both of these, to be sure; but its total extent was nothing less than the universe. Dwight declared: "The extent of Christ's kingdom is repeatedly denoted by the phrase 'all things.' . . . Every knee in this vast dominion we are assured will one day bow to Christ; and every tongue found in it will confess, at a future period, that Christ is Lord. . . . This world, therefore, the planetary system, the stellary systems, the highest heavens above, and hell beneath, are all included . . . in the immense empire of which he is the head." Futhermore, there is no limit to Christ's

---

30. Beecher. *Views in Theology,* p. 85. Cf. Haroutunian's judgment of the significance of Taylor's thought, *Piety vs. Moralism,* pp. 254, 266, 281 ff.

authority: "He upholds all things by the word of his power; and directs them with a universal and irresistible agency to their proper ends." [31]

Moral government required that man possess full knowledge of its laws. This was the function of the Bible, which is "so comprehensive as to reach, perfectly, every possible moral action; to preclude every wrong, and to secure every right. . . . Its control extends with the same efficacy and felicity to all worlds, and to all periods. It governs the Universe; it reaches through Eternity. . . . In the Scriptures alone is this Law contained. Nay, the Scriptures themselves are, chiefly, this Law, expanded into more minute precepts and more multiplied by applications." [32] The Massachusetts Baptist Isaac Backus had declared that all iniquitous unions of church and state had been erected on the notion that the Old Testament was an order of grace and was thus applicable as a model of government in Christian nations. To Backus, a theology of religious freedom must emphasize release from the Old Testament order of law into the new freedom of the "gospel law." On these points Dwight, Beecher, and Taylor—particularly Beecher—stood foursquare with the theory of the New England establishments. The Old Testament was full of grace; the New, full of law. Law was absolutely basic to religion as to civil life. In 1820 Beecher wrote:

> It is the object of the law to maintain the social order and happiness of the intelligent universe, by precepts, and rewards and punishments according to deeds. This is all which direct legislation proposes, or in the nature of things, can do. It is the object of the Gospel to provide an influence which shall reclaim alienated subjects, and sustain the influence of the law in the universe of God, while its penalty is averted from those who repeat and believe in the Lord Jesus Christ.[33]

"The Gospel is not . . . an expedient to set aside a holy, just, and good law. [God] sent his Son to vindicate and to establish his

31. Timothy Dwight, "The Character of Christ as King," sermon 59 in *Theology Explained and Defended*, 2:244–45.
32. Dwight, "The Law of God Perfect," sermon 91 in ibid., 3:61–62.
33. Lyman Beecher, *The Gospel according to Paul: A Sermon . . . Sept. 17, 1828* (Boston: Marvin, 1829), p. 5.

holy law, to redeem mankind from the curse, and to bring them back to the obedience of that same law, from which they had revolted. It is the glory of the gospel that it upholds the moral law and moral government of God." [34]

That the gospel should "pardon upon the simple condition of repentance" was unthinkable; it "would break the power of every human government on earth." Besides, nothing is gained in repentance; there is "continued defect." It is the role of the gospel to inject fresh moral strength in man and so to "maintain its influence over sinful minds. . . . The whole must be sustained by its own peculiar rewards and most fearful penalties."

Theocratic thought negated separatist Baptist theory and identified the biblical law with the public order, the nation of Israel with the United States. The biblical revelation correlated with God's natural revelation to America.

"The religion and morality of the Old Testament," Beecher wrote, "preserve in the hands of the people as much personal liberty as ever was or can be combined with a permanent and efficient national government." Elaborating the parallel between the Mosaic order and the American Republic, he noted that "the civil constitution of the Old Testament [is] a federal republic."[35] Beecher advocated the Mosaic theocracy no more than the British monarchy. His reasoning was this: the divine law is obligatory on all government; in a republic it should pass into the public law by elective processes. The establishment of religion, he flatly affirmed, was no part of divine or natural law.[36]

In this system of the moral government of God we may discern something new in America: the republican theocrat. Not that the theological sons of Timothy Dwight were tempted by Jefferson; scarcely a political Republican existed among the Connecticut

34. Beecher, *The Government of God Desirable . . . Oct. 1808* (New York: Smith, 1809), p. 17.
35. Beecher, *Republican Elements in the Old Testament: Lectures on Political Atheism and Kindred Subjects* (Boston: Jewett, 1852), pp. 177–78.
36. Beecher, *The Memory of Our Fathers: A Sermon . . . Dec. 22, 1827* (Boston: Marvin, 1828), p. 11.

clergy.[37] It was rather that the men who fashioned America's fundamental theory of the religion of the Republic in the third decade of the nineteenth century accepted popular power and the voluntary spirit. "God governs mind by motive and not by fiat," declared Beecher.[38] Since that was true, coercion in religion was wrong. Beecher in later life called disestablishment "the best thing that ever happened in the State of Connecticut." [39]

It is useful in this connection to point to some contrasts between these republican theocrats and other schools of Protestant thought. Their differences with the Baptists we have noted: the new theocrats stood within the tradition of establishment, not against it. On the other hand, they sharply opposed the hard imputationists, whose metaphysic of the federal headship of Adam left little ground for human responsibility and accountability. In such a view the new Calvinism discerned mere fatalism.[40] Yet their affirmation of man's universal, habitual disposition to sin set the theocrats apart from every theory, Christian or not, which put its hope in man's actual capability.

More subtle was the distinction between the "consistent Calvinists" of the Edwardean school, principally Samuel Hopkins, and the republican theocrats. Edwardeans of any shape agreed on the distinction between natural and moral ability, human accountability, the necessity of religion (that is, Protestantism) to social stability and even the Lockean philosophical base. Their differences were more subtle. Nathanael Emmons really feared the American masses. "So long as government effectually guards its subjects from too great equality and from too great inequality," he wrote, "it promotes and secures that perfect liberty to which all have a just and equal claim. . . . That liberty and equality are inseparably connected . . . is one of the most wild and absurd [no-

---

37. See Bodo, *The Protestant Clergy*, passim. See also Purcell, *Connecticut in Transition*, pp. 195 ff.
38. Beecher, *Autobiography*, 1: 47, 213.
39. Ibid., 2:252, 336–37.
40. See Charles E. Cuningham, *Timothy Dwight, 1752–1817: A Biography* (New York: Macmillan Co., 1942), p. 320. Cf. Beecher, *Views in Theology*, pp. 138, 156; idem, *Autobiography*, 1:139, 145. Cf. also Dwight, *Theology Explained and Defended*, 1:478; and Haroutunian, *Piety vs. Moralism*, pp. 16 ff., 163 ff.

tions] that ever entered into the mind of man. . . . Rulers should form the character of the people and not . . . the people . . . the character of the ruler." [41] Political Federalism induced such theologians to give priority to doctrines of authority—God's decrees, revelation. They used Edwards's analysis of human abilities only to show the utter fatality of moral inability.[42]

Beecher turned the coin over. "Man is not so constituted as that no choice, good or evil, can be originated by him, which God, by an immediate efficiency does not produce. Nor is he made accountable for a nature created in him by heaven . . . or for moral qualities which are as involuntary as his appetites or his instincts. . . . The dependence of man upon Christ is in no sense the dependence of his deficient constitution as a free agent, but of his deficient character as a sinner—the obstinate perversion of his free agency." [43] Here was a crucial difference of attitude and direction. For Hopkins and Emmons, human free will primarily validated guilt. "When their [Joseph's brethren's] guilt is to be brought into view and condemned, *they* are said to sell Joseph into Egypt," wrote Emmons, "but when the wisdom and goodness of God are to be displayed, *he,* and not *they,* is said to send him thither." [44] To these grave Edwardeans, as to the stern imputationists, man was simply a burnt-out case.

Dwight and Beecher considered the human predicament no less critical, but they were less concerned with fixing guilt than with establishing accountability and human possibility. The Yale theologians brought Edwards's analysis of human freedom into the foreground, not only to justify God, but also to lay the groundwork for the moral renovation of the American people through revivalism, reform societies, the religious press, and sumptuary legisla-

41. Emmons, *Works,* 2:9 ff., 106, 124.
42. Cf. Nathanael Emmons, "Hopkinsian Calvinism," an article in Hannah Adams's *View of Religions,* 2 pts., 2d ed. (Boston: Folsom 1791). Cf. also Mead, *Nathaniel William Taylor,* pp. 105–6.
43. Lyman Beecher, *Dependence and Free Agency: A Sermon . . . July 16, 1832* (Boston: Perkins & Marvin, 1832), pp. 6–7. Cf. Moses Stuart, *A Sermon . . . May 30, 1827* (Boston: True & Green, 1827), pp. 23–24.
44. Nathanael Emmons, *Sermons on . . . Christian Doctrine and Practice* (Boston: Armstrong, 1812).

tion. In their hands, the moral government of God was an optimistic teaching.

The new theocrats did not approve Jefferson, but they believed they knew how to banish the demon of public depravity that was digging the grave of democracy. They agreed that government was a divine ordinance, but did not consider social compact so much a contradiction of that doctrine as a means by which the people would establish the moral government that God had ordained on earth. As an expression of French "infidelity," social compact repelled Dwight; as a form of the divine ordinance, it was accepted.[45] Republicanism, Dwight reasoned, was a fact, and he knew how to deal with it. All sane Americans, not only the elect, were in full possession of their natural faculties; the power of the Bible was as real as that of government; revivalism worked, and Beecher possessed a major organizing talent.

The grand implication of the republicanized system of divine government was that the clergy and supporting action societies should reconquer the nation for God. "This land was settled by Christians," Dwight told his Yale students. "God brought his little flock hither; and placed it in this wilderness, for the great purpose of establishing permanently the church of Christ in these vast regions of idolatry and sin, and commencing here the glorious work of salvation. This great continent is soon to be filled with the praise, the piety, of the Millenium." [46] The corruptions of Rome must never be allowed to bring this vision to ruin; the dooms pronounced in the New Testament applied as much to the papacy as to any ancient emperor. "Our own republic, in its constitutions and laws," proclaimed Beecher, "is of heavenly origin. Our constitution borrows from the Bible its elements, proportions, and power. It was God that gave these elementary principles to our forefathers." [47] The forefathers in question were, of course, the Puritan founders. Furthermore, God had given many signs of his

45. Dwight, *Theology Explained and Defended*, 3:324–28.
46. Dwight, *The Northern Army: A Thanksgiving Sermon ... Dec. 18, 1777* (Hartford: Watson & Goodwin, 1778), p. 13.
47. Beecher, *Republican Elements in the Old Testament*, p. 189; cf. idem, *The Memory of Our Fathers*, pp. 14, 25.

blessing: God had given victory in the Revolution, asserted Dwight;[48] the American acceptance of Jews in full civil equality had a holy significance; and, of course, such leaders as Washington had been raised up by God.

Dwight and Beecher heartily endorsed Washington's view of religion as a force of national importance. "With slight shades of difference, you have the same religion, manners, habits, and political principles," said the retiring president in 1796.

> Of all the dispositions and habits which lead to political prosperity, Religion and Morality are indispensable supports. In vain would that Man claim the tribute of Patriotism, who would labor to subvert these great pillars of human happiness, these firmest props of the duties of men and Citizens. . . . Where is the security for property, for reputation, for life, if the sense of religious obligation deserts the oaths which are the instruments of investigation in Courts of Justice? And let us with caution indulge the supposition, that morality can be maintained without Religion. Whatever may be conceded of the influence of refined education on minds of peculiar structure; reason and experience both forbid us to expect that national morality can prevail in exclusion of religious principle. . . . 'Tis substantially true, that virtue or morality is a necesary spring of popular government.[49]

Dwight believed that virtue was the fundament of a free people; virtue was grounded in the nature of things, and was not a gift of grace. Since virtue was essential to sound society, measures to ingrain it should be taken by government.[50] Yet virtue remained essentially voluntary; it could best be cultivated by the power of the gospel, which "concentrates upon the heart an intensity of motive which it is utterly impossible for law to disclose or apply," as Beecher phrased it.

If the nation could be made virtuous, "what a change would be wrought in this world," sang Dwight. "With what astonishment would we see every debt paid at the time and in the manner in which it was due! every promise faithfully fulfilled! every loan of

48. Dwight, *Discourse . . . Aug. 20, 1812 . . . on the National Fast*, p. 54–56.
49. George Washington, Farewell Address, quoted in Timothy Dwight, *A Discourse . . . Feb. 22, 1800, on the Character of George Washington, Esq.* (New Haven: Thos. Green, 1800), pp. 48–49.
50. Timothy Dwight, "Utility the Foundation of Virtue," sermon 99 in *Theology Explained and Defended*, 3:156–57.

money, utensils, or other property, returned without injury or delay! every commodity sold according to its real value." Laws would be formed only in the interest of the people and equitably administered; the people at large would willingly render the same justice." [51] The new theocrats saw church and state as allies in the great contest for the moral integrity of society. There is no power to restrain sin comparable to the Scriptures, Dwight remarked.

> Civil Government, in a different manner, is employed in promoting the same end and, at times, operates with a superior efficacy. But its influence is felt only within certain limits, and on particular occasions; whereas the Scriptures extend their influence to every place, time and action, seek out the offender in solitude . . . sound the alarm at midnight, . . . enter into the recesses of the bosom, watch the rising sin, and threaten the guilty purpose, while it is yet a shapeless embryo.[52]

It was all very well to agree with Washington that piety was the school of civil virtue, the "foundation . . . of the order and peace on which all social happiness depends," but precisely how should the advocates of religion and morality interact with the lawmaking process? The theocrats were social solidarists in the medieval and Calvinist tradition. Pondering the moral unity of the human race in Adam, Beecher remarked: "There is . . . something of this constitutional social liability pervading the whole moral universe, and inseparable from the nature of mind and moral government. . . . It is probable, that rational beings, constituted as they are, cannot be brought together, so that the action of one shall not in some degree affect the character of others." [53] This constitution of society, in Edwardean thought, was of divine origin. In the light of that fact, Dwight considered the only effective bond of social union to be "belief in the presence and providence of God; and of an approaching state of Reward and Punishment." [54]

51. Dwight, "The Effect of Benevolence on Public Happiness," sermon 98 in ibid., pp. 140–41.
52. Dwight, *Nature and Danger of Infidel Philosophy . . . Sept. 9, 1797* (New Haven: Bunce, 1798), pp. 65, 78.
53. Beecher, *Views in Theology*, p. 180.
54. Dwight, *The Nature and Danger of Infidel Philosophy*, p. 41.

On such understandings, the theocrats could not see in separation of church and state any general principle that set religion aside from society and politics. Religion was more than a purely personal concern. It stood guard over liberty. The voluntary character of religion assured its purity. In a larger sense, Taylor was to argue, separation reflected a fundamental distinction between the spiritual and the temporal, but this concept did not figure materially in the thought of Dwight or Beecher. It remained for the Catholic tradition to relate American separationism to its own long-standing commitment to the distinction between spiritual and temporal.

Beecher wrestled with the problem of the interaction of religious forces in society with government in 1823, pointing out that although "Christians have some influence to exert, favorable to religion, through the medium of government," they are nevertheless perplexed by the "new state of things" which included uniform federal law, and the multiplication of sects "entitled to impartial protection and excluding . . . governmental favoritism." Beecher then revealed the results of his own reflections. "Christians are not to attempt to control the administration of civil government, in the things merely secular." Of course, "great questions of national morality . . . such as the declaration of war; or, as in England, the abolition of the slave trade; or the permission to introduce Christianity into India by missionaries" are another matter; it "becomes Christians to lift up their voice and exert their united influence." This does not constitute, however, an "injudicious association of religion with politics." [55]

Christians should not become implicated in party disputes nor make any attempt to "hinder the prosperity of other denominations by any monopoly of governmental influence and favor." At one time the infant church of Massachusetts needed civil aid, but in the new circumstances a contest for the favor of government would break out. In fact, the interest of the denominations lay in watching lest any one of them seek the "adventitious favor" of

55. Lyman Beecher, *The Faith as Delivered to the Saints* (Boston: Crocker & Brewster, 1823), p. 28.

government—"by rendering their own sentiments as a passport to places of honor and trust," for example. Churches would rise up without delay to end such abuse of civil and religious liberty.

Beecher repeatedly urged that Christians vote only for candidates holding correct views on dueling,[56] intemperance, Sabbath law, and other causes, but this did not mean that "churches are bound . . . to confine their suffrages exclusively to persons of their own denomination; or to regulate them, exclusively, with reference to piety or doctrinal opinions." There are minima, to be sure, without which no public official can play his role in the moral government of God: belief in oaths, belief in reward and punishment, respect for religion, etc. But religion is cheapened when it is imposed as a qualification for office. "It was this mistake of our pious fathers, in making the terms of communion and civil trust the same, which produced the lax mode of admission to the churches of New England, followed by the long and dreadful declension from evangelical doctrine and piety." Here one perceives the massive foundation of theocratic support for separation of church and state: the union of religion and law brings piety to ruin—all American history proves it. But this was also the cleft: society itself—particularly republican America—cannot survive unless it honors the moral government of God, and this demands an effective impact of organized religion on public opinion; on the other hand, freedom is the essence of the moral and must be honored by the laws of the nation and the actions of the sects toward one another and toward the whole public.[57] The latter dictum did not require government to withhold its favor to religion in a general way. Public law should foster a climate of positive friendliness to religion, simply because "civil laws cannot reach the spring of action and prevent social evils. . . . It is only the influence . . . maintained by religious institutions, breathing their benign influence into system of legislation" that can secure

56. Lyman Beecher, *The Remedy for Duelling: A Sermon . . . April 16, 1806* (Sag-Harbor: Spooner, 1807).
57. Beecher. "The Faith Once Delivered to the Saints." in *Sermons Delivered on Various Occasions* (Boston: T. R. Marvin, 1828), pp. 244–51.

the whole intent of law.[58] The function of civil government was not confined to checking wrongdoing: "the formation and establishment of knowledge and virtue in the citizens of a community is the first business of Legislation," wrote Dwight.[59]

When the theocrats adopted, in addition, the ancient Christian precept that "the first duty of a ruler . . . is the support of religion" they complicated their problem. Their acceptance of disestablishment excluded laws that were preferential; their activity, however, brought their sincerity into question among many Americans who saw vigorous public propaganda and support societies as little more than a loosely knit churchlike organization claiming to articulate the national moral religious commitment. Emmons grumbled that the whole cooperative movement of the churches smelled of Rome. "Self-created union proved a source of the greatest evils to the church which it ever suffered," he wrote. "And notwithstanding this alarming example before their eyes, some of the most pious, most learned and most influential ministers and christians are at this day forming plans to bring about the same unscriptural and unwise union in all the churches in New England." [60] Dwight very early showed himself sensitive to any union of church and state that appeared to resemble the Catholic system, but did not live to grapple with the issue.[61]

The theocrats might have solved their problem by holding more severely to their doctrine that religion alone could appeal effectively to conscience, relying on revivalism and religious educa-

58. Ibid., p. 195. An example of Beecher's conviction of the state's function in true religion is reflected in a deed he had drawn up for the Hanover Street Church, Boston, of which he was pastor. The instrument ensured that only full members of the church (not pewholders as a whole) should share in the selection of the pastor. This reflected, of course, the commitment of the revivalist Calvinists to the position of Edwards and their opposition to Stoddardean inclusiveness. Cf. "A Recent Attempt to Defeat the Constitutional Provisions in Favor of Religious Freedom . . . " by "A Layman" (Boston: Hilliard, Gary 1828).
59. Cf. Lyman Beecher, "The Bible a Code of Laws," in *Sermons*, p. 141.
60. Emmons, *Works*, 2:311; see also 1:36–37. From the Unitarians came bitter charges that the orthodox intended to destroy religious liberty. See William Ellery Channing, *Works*, 10th ed. (Boston: American Unitarian Assn., 1849), p. 180. See also Moses Stuart's reply, *A Letter to Wm. E. Channing, D.D., on Religious Liberty*. 3d ed. (Boston: Perkins & Marvin, 1830).
61. Timothy Dwight, *Virtuous Rulers a National Blessing . . . May 12, 1791* (Hartford: Hudson & Goodwin, 1791), p. 18.

tion to elevate the public spirit. Taylor related conscience and public opinion closely enough to support such a policy.

He who formed and protects us has provided within our own bosoms a check for that injustice which is beyond the restraining power of man. There is a voice within, which gives to moral sanctions an efficacy more powerful than that of a thousand gibbets. In the presence of conscience, man is in the presence of God. . . . I need not say how entirely all this influence on the great mass of the community depends on the soundness of public opinion. It is public opinion . . . which gives to conscience all its power. Were a corrupt public opinion to dispense with the moral and religious instruction of children, with the institution of the Sabbath, with the revelation which God had made of himself, of his law, and of human destiny, with all the appointed vehicles of conveying moral truth to the mind conscience would become extinct in the soul of man. And what, then, would be the power of human edicts?[62]

Actually, however, the theocrats built a massive apparatus for directing moral conviction to specific social and legal ends and provoked the charge that they were themselves violating rights of conscience. "Shall clamors about the rights of conscience induce us to throw away Heaven's richest legacy to earth?" protested Taylor. "Has any man rights of conscience which interfere with a nation's happiness?" His declaration on this matter articulated a broad plank in the theocratic platform. "We only ask for those provisions of law . . . in behalf of a common Christianity, which are its due as a nation's strength and a nation's glory." The alternative was the chaos of the French Revolution.

To save the nation from itself, Beecher organized a "system of means" that became the model for cooperative Christian action down to the present time.[63] Its evolution since his lifetime has con-

62. Nathaniel W. Taylor, *A Sermon Addressed to the Legislature of the State of Connecticut . . . May 7, 1823,* 2d ed. (New Haven: A. H. Maltby, 1823), pp. 12–13.
63. Lyman Beecher, *A Reformation of Morals Practical and Indispensable* (New Haven: Hudson, 1813), p. 8. Classically the word *means* had meant the sacraments of the church, plus, for Protestants, preaching and teaching the Bible. But revivalism had already expanded it to include all the methods by which the Bible was made effective for conversion. The controversy on this subject that racked the revivalist movement—whether, for example, the "anxious bench" was just an "artifice to excite mere human feeling" (as Beecher called it in his *Autobiography,* vol. 2, chap. 12) that could only abort a truly spiritual conversion—is not pertinent to this study. Dwight did not regard the law as a "means of grace" in the strict theological sense (*Theology Explained and Defended,* 4:49–74).

sisted mainly in a strengthening of denominational organizations and a federal form of church cooperation rather than independent societies outside the churches; but insofar as the general term *Protestant* has acquired historical meaning in the United States, it refers to religious groups that learned the lessons of consensus and collaboration from Lyman Beecher.

The origin and history of this network of organizations and movements has been recounted by several authors [64] and is tangential to the purposes of this study. But the role of the clergy in relation to civil law illuminates the thought of the theocrats on the rising religion of the Republic sufficiently to require treatment.

The minds of both Dwight and Beecher had been furnished by the early Connecticut experience, where the clergy had been a dominant influence. Both extrapolated from this to the national scene. "In Republics which have been most distinguished for virtue, Ministers of the Gospel have had the greatest influence," wrote Dwight. "I speak here, it will be observed, only of protestant ministers of the Gospel. . . . The existence of virtue [in republics] has been exactly proportioned to the influence of Ministers of the Gospel." [65]

"There is a state of society to be formed," wrote Beecher, "by an extensive combination of institutions, religious, civil and literary, which never exist without the cooperation of an educated ministry." [66] Beecher expected the state to foster a class of educated clergy by its "official influence." A celebrated quarrel over a subvention to the purely Congregational Yale College in 1817 had played a role in the defeat of the Connecticut ruling party, but Beecher never abandoned the principle. He made his primary appeal, however, to voluntary effort. "The prevalence of pious,

---

64. See, for example, Clifford S. Griffin, *Their Brothers' Keepers: Moral Stewardship in the United States, 1800–1865* (New Brunswick: Rutgers University Press, 1960); Foster, *An Errand of Mercy;* Sidney E. Mead, *The Lively Experiment: The Shaping of Christianity in America* (New York: Harper & Row, 1963); and Elwyn A. Smith, "The Forming of a Modern American Denomination," *Church History,* vol. 31, no. 1 (1962), pp. 74–99.
65. Timothy Dwight, "Depravity of Man: Remarks," sermon 33 in *Theology Explained and Defended,* 3:494–95.
66. Cf. Purcell, *Connecticut in Transition,* pp. 218–19.

intelligent, enterprising ministers through the nation at a ratio of one for 1000 . . . would produce a sameness of views, and feelings, and interests which would lay the foundation of our empire upon a rock. Religion is the central attraction which must supply the deficiency of political affinity and interest." [67]

Furthermore, the Roman Catholic church was threatening. Against all this Beecher proposed a clerical phalanx. "Principles of civil and religious liberty have always accompanied evangelical religion and made their most desperate resistance to arbitrary power," he wrote. "What possible danger to liberty can arise from clerical influence . . . ?" Fear of a "national religion, to be reared by clerical intrigue and pecuniary influence," he scorned as "the most chimerical and laughable imagination that ever danced in the brain of a lunatic." The real danger was "the tendency . . . of political atheism to prostrate our republican institutions . . . to suspend the restraining action of the divine government until self-government becomes impossible." [68]

In connection with a stubborn campaign against the Sunday mails, the question was raised whether church-supported legislation prohibiting transportation and classification of mail on Sunday did not encroach on the First Amendment. Beecher responded: "Let God be praised that there is at length one nation . . . where church and state are not united and where reason and conscience are free. But the petitions are, not that Congress will do anything *for* religion, but, simply, that by legislation they will do nothing *against* religion," namely, keep mail-carriers, etc. away from church on Sunday. "We ask for no union of church and state; but simply, that the moral influence of the Sabbath may not be thus bartered away for secular gain." A "national act of Sabbath violation" intruded upon his rights of conscience as a citizen and taxpayer, Beecher argued. The largest issue, however, remained the risk to the nation itself. "The American character, and

67. Lyman Beecher, *On the Importance of Assisting Young Men of Piety and Talents in Obtaining an Education for the Gospel Ministry* (Andover: Flagg & Gould, 1815), p. 16.
68. Beecher, *Republican Elements in the Old Testament*, p. 95. Cf. Emmons, *Works*, 2:139 ff.

our glorious institutions, will go down into the same grave that entombs the Sabbath; and our epitaph will stand forth a warning to the world—THUS ENDETH THE NATION THAT DESPISED THE LORD AND GLORIED IN WISDOM, WEALTH, AND POWER." [69]

Taylor made more analytic distinctions than either of his senior colleagues. The civil magistrate has no higher function "than that of the guardian and promoter of the highest happiness of [the] temporal community." To such a state, the Christian owes the duty of "disinterested benevolence." But the obligation of man to God is a "higher principle . . . the sum of all virtue or moral excellence" and is "in no respect the subject of civil legislation. . . . It is no part of the function of the civil ruler to make . . . his subjects *religious* by law. He has . . . no concern with claiming or enforcing benevolence to God or to the sentient universe."

Taylor came as close to Jefferson as a Connecticut theocrat could when he acknowledged that the law "takes cognizance of overt action" alone, and even then "no subject who cannot by overt action be proved to be actuated by [hostility to the state] can be considered and treated as a disobedient subject." [70] Such a definition of civil authority marked it off sharply from the divine government.

The systematic reformulation of the conception of the moral government of God presented, to a culture in which the Puritan stream still ran powerfully, a rationale and policy for a single religion of the Republic. If the republican theocrats would not sanction public support of denominations or sects, it was because legal churchmanship had already failed to do justice to the moral government of God, which of its nature called for voluntary response. Nine years after the dissolution of the Connecticut establishment, Lyman Beecher declared: "[Christianity] has survived the deadly embrace of establishments nominally Christian and now, bursting from their alliance, finds in them the most

69. Lyman Beecher, "Preeminent Importance of the Christian Sabbath," in *Sermons*, pp. 159–60. On the role of the clergy, cf. idem, *The Reformation of Morals*, p. 16.
70. Taylor, *Lectures on Moral Government*, 2:368–69.

bitter opposition to evangelical doctrine and vital godliness. . . . There is no substitute but the voluntary energies of the nation itself." [71]

If the theocrats did not come to these views quickly or happily, their full acceptance of disestablishment is attested by the significant reordering of priorities in their theology and the enormous energy they poured into social reform movements. Turning from metaphysical theology to a facultative psychology, they put personal accountability and the human potential for change at the heart of their exposition of God's government.[72] It was natural that Beecher should regard theology and politics as "next of kin" and the government of God as a model of human government.[73]

One question they left for later generations to answer, of course, was the extent to which a free people, persuaded by religious influences that sumptuary laws were vital to the national interest, might end by enforcing practices deemed by dissenters prejudicial to their own rights and freedoms. The tendency of later constitutional development to regard much sumptuary law as tending toward an establishment of religion would have been incomprehensible to the early republican theocrats. Legislation inevitably had a moral content, and legislatures were responsible for the health of the whole society. Sumptuary law, therefore, was not a matter of church and state at all.

Calvinists who recognized prosperity as a reward for virtue and a sign of the divine blessing inveighed against prodigality and irresponsible use of money and goods. These "open and gross immoralities . . . are in the strictest sense land-defiling and God-provoking iniquities, which threaten to destroy our highest and best interests, both for time and eternity," wrote Emmons—and he spoke for all.[74] To render a national social and political catastrophe impossible was the clear duty of public authority. Sump-

---

71. Beecher, *The Memory of Our Fathers*, pp. 11, 28.
72. Cf. Mead, *Nathaniel William Taylor*, pp. 110 ff.
73. Beecher, *Autobiography*, 1:323.
74. Cf. ibid., 2:254.

tuary legislation came to be regarded as an expression of religion later in the century and therefore was questioned among the heirs of Beecher;[75] but the principle did not vary: a free and democratic people possesses every right to establish its society through the cultivation of public virtue and the nurture of the religion of the people.

75. Moses Stuart, "Civil Government," *Princeton Review,* January 1851, p. 26.

8

The Republic and the Millennium

J. F. MACLEAR

In May 1777 the historian Jeremy Belknap, described by a modern historiographer as "rationalist" and "close in spirit to the modern historian," excitedly turned to Scripture to uncover the true meaning of the American Revolution. Using the best writers on prophecy, he found assurance in Daniel and Revelation that no "rotten toe of Nebuchadnezzar's image" or "proud horn of the seven-headed beast" should ever "exercise dominion over this country."

Neither in method nor in patriotic conclusion was Belknap unique. Other spokesmen of the Revolutionary age also hastened to locate the new American nation in a grand apocalyptic interpretation of universal history, the only conceptual framework acceptable to a people still rooted in the providential assumptions of the English Reformation. In most evangelical minds this conviction rapidly became part of a complex of religious-political assumptions which long influenced American Protestantism and which helped shape the common national myths of the American people. The nation was an elect people, a new Israel, providentially prepared for a redemptive historical role, bound in covenant with God faithfully to perform his will, and summoned to lead all the nations to a millennial fulfillment. Viewed thus, the American vocation inspired a conjoined patriotic and theocratic emotion. "This country," stressed Samuel Worcester, "which, with such an emphasis of grateful significance we may call *our own,* is still *not our own.*

God owns it all. And it is ours only in the covenant of his gracious Providence, that it may be beautified with holiness." [1]

These motifs have long been recognized as central nineteenth century concepts of American self-consciousness and mission. But historians have recently given much greater emphasis to the power of millennial ideas in the Awakening, their role in the Revolution, and their continuing importance in the evolution of American nationhood. Hence it may be appropriate in a volume on the religion of the Republic to survey the relation between the mythology of a national redemptive and millennial mission and the shaping of American religion. [2]

1

The destiny of the American Republic to lead the world to millennial glory was claimed immediately on the birth of the new nation. For men who, under the sway of the Great Awakening, had expected God to bring forth some new stage of universal history in the Western world, the Revolution could be no mere political convulsion. Within a few months of the clash at Lexington, an interpretative literature, chiefly sermons and histories, began to develop, arguing that the Revolution was "big with such consequences of glory or terror" for the whole Christian world that the apocalyptic prophecies might, "not unaptly, be applied to our

1. Michael Kraus, *The Writing of American History* (Norman: University of Oklahoma Press, 1953), pp. 73–74. Jeremy Belknap, *A Sermon Delivered on the Ninth of May, 1798* (Boston, 1798), pp. 17–19. However, Belknap did not identify Christ's kingdom with the American state. Samuel M. Worcester, *Our Country and Our Work* (Salem, 1843), pp. 7–8.
2. This essay surveys only one strand of the incredibly rich postmillennial tradition in America. I have made no effort to view the place of millennial thinking in the various utopian and communitarian experiments or in such enduring churches as the Mormons, the Campbellites, or the Jehovah's Witnesses. This sketch principally treats articulate spokesmen of middle-class Protestant denominations—often ministers, professors, or college presidents of Presbyterian, Congregational, Episcopal, Methodist, or Baptist backgrounds. Because of the Puritan heritage of mission and the New England predominance in much of the life and thought of these denominations, representatives from this area have figured more prominently. Lastly, it should not be supposed that all enthusiasts for the millennium reserved distinction therein for the United States. Yet the views described in this essay were so common as to be almost canonical.

case, and receive their fulfillment in such providences as are passing over us." [3] With independence, the establishment of the Republic, and victory, the conviction became irresistible that a final and American stage preparatory to the millennium had now commenced. To all these interpreters, the Revolution was the greatest revealing moment since the Reformation, illuminating the past and pointing to a future in which the nations would increasingly adopt "our wisdom, liberty, and happiness," knowledge and religion would be diffused throughout the earth, and mankind would be prepared "for the universal REIGN of the SON OF GOD in the glories of the latter day." [4]

These claims were most commonly presented from pulpits in New England, where they served to revitalize the province's ancient and deep sense of vocation, but they were heard in every section, particularly where the Reformed tradition was strong. Always the same elements were present: the new grasp of divine providences; the conjunction of freedom and religion, twin ideals

3. See, e.g., Samuel Sherwood, *The Church's Flight into the Wilderness* (New York, 1776), p. 18. This sermon was preached on January 17, 1776. Even earlier was Ebenezer Baldwin, *The Duty of Rejoicing under Calamities and Afflictions* (1776), preached November 16, 1775, with its soaring prophecy: "I would suppose these Colonies to be the Foundation of a great and mighty Empire; the largest the world ever saw, to be founded on such Principles of Liberty and Freedom, both civil and religious, as never before took place in the World; which shall be the principal Seat of that glorious Kingdom, which Christ shall erect upon Earth in the latter Days. And that these Calamities are remotely preparing the Way for this glorious Event" (pp. 38–39).
4. Benjamin Trumbull, *A Sermon Delivered at North-Haven December 11, 1783* (New Haven, 1784), p. 22. The most familiar example of this literature is probably Ezra Stiles, *The United States Elevated to Glory and Honour* (Worcester, 1783). Stiles tended to identify Reformed Protestantism with the American mission: "And when GOD in his Providence shalt convert the world, should the newly Christianized nations assume our form of religion; should American missionaries be blessed to succeed in the work of Christianizing the heathen . . . , it would be an unexpected wonder, and a great honour to the United States. And thus the American republick, by illuminating the world with TRUTH and LIBERTY, would be exalted and made high among the nations . . . ." (pp. 118–19; see also pp. 96–100). See also Timothy Dwight's warning against a vainglorious interpretation of Yorktown in *A Sermon Preached at Northampton, on the Twenty-eighth of November, 1781* (Hartford, n.d.): "These events . . . are to be viewed only as a preparation for others of higher importance . . . They were . . . accomplished . . . that the work of Divine providence might be carried on, and a way opened for the arrival of scenes, which shall respect happier ages, and influence in their consequences the events of eternity" (p. 27).

which America was to preserve, perfect, and propagate through the world; and the assurance of national greatness beyond worldly glory and secular patriotism. Thus, at a time when national consciousness was still half formed, some patriotic divines were advancing a focused historical perspective on the past and a vital and coherent interpretation of national purpose for the future. But despite the rooting of these hopes in the piety of the Awakening, a fundamental change had here passed over the millennial conception itself. An earlier evangelical hope that God's people in America might be granted the spiritual power to prepare the world for Christ's kingdom now passed, in some of these statements, into a conviction of the high destiny of the United States. The millennium was to be related not only to contemporary American history but to the particular political and national structure which American patriots were now erecting.

Despite its importance, the tradition born here has only recently begun to receive serious historical analysis. It is now more than thirty years since Richard Niebuhr published *The Kingdom of God in America* with its brilliant elucidation of one central conception in the development of American religion. But while Niebuhr's work has not been superseded, neither did it attempt detailed treatment of the history and scope of the millennial argument nor deeply examine its political implications. Since then, most of the students of American identity have touched on religious backgrounds, but their interest has been given principally to national destiny and vocation in terms of republican and democratic ideals, and they have seldom been drawn to eschatological literature.[5] In-

5. H. Richard Niebuhr, *The Kingdom of God in America* (Chicago: Willett, Clark, & Co., 1937). Of the extensive literature on the forming national consciousness, see such standard treatments as Merle Eugene Curti, *The Roots of American Loyalty* (New York: Columbia University Press, 1946); Ralph H. Gabriel, *The Course of American Democratic Thought: An Intellectual History since 1815*, Ronald Series in History (New York: Ronald Press Co., 1940); Hans Kohn, *American Nationalism: An Interpretative Essay* (New York: Macmillan Co., 1957); Russel B. Nye, *This Almost Chosen People: Essays on the History of American Ideas* (East Lansing: Michigan State University Press, 1966); and Max Savelle, *Seeds of Liberty: The Genesis of the American Mind* (New York: Alfred A. Knopf, 1948), chap. 10. Historians of "manifest destiny" have given little heed to religious ideas. See Albert K. Weinberg, *Manifest Destiny* (Baltimore: Johns Hopkins Press, 1935); and Frederick Merk, *Manifest Destiny and Mission in American History: A Reinterpretation* (New York: Alfred A. Knopf, 1963).

creasingly, however, religious historians studying diverse problems have found it necessary to come to terms with American Protestantism's fascination with the millennium—in colonial thought, in the Awakening and Revolution, and in the evangelism and reforms of the nineteenth century. Finally, E. L. Tuveson, building on his earlier study *Millennium and Utopia,* has most recently sought to evaluate the ideology of the *Redeemer Nation* and place it in the total context of the millennial tradition.[6] From these developing critical accounts, as well as from the vast primary literature, it is now possible to summarize the several factors which contributed importantly to the formation and popularization of this version of the American purpose.

6. Some older historians recognized the prevalence of millennial belief but were little heeded; see, for example, Oliver Wendell Elsbree, *The Rise of the Missionary Spirit, 1790–1815* (Williamsport, Pa., 1928), pp. 122–45. Significant modern works which have dealt with the millennial element in American religion are the several Puritan studies of Perry Miller, especially "The End of the World," in his *Errand into the Wilderness* (Cambridge, Mass.: Harvard University Press, 1956), pp. 212–39, and *The Life of the Mind in America, from the Revolution to the Civil War* (New York: Harcourt, Brace, & World, 1965), pp. 3–95 and passim; Alan E. Heimert, *Religion and the American Mind: From the Great Awakening to the Revolution* (Cambridge, Mass.: Harvard University Press, 1966); Whitney Rogers Cross *The Burned-Over District: The Social and Intellectual History of Enthusiastic Religion in Western New York* (Ithaca: Cornell University Press, 1950); Timothy L. Smith, *Revivalism and Social Reform in Mid-Nineteenth-Century America* (Nashville: Abingdon Press, 1957). Briefer discussion is found in John Rainer Bodo, *The Protestant Clergy and Public Issues, 1812–1848* (Princeton: Princeton University Press, 1954), pp. 251–52; and Charles Chester Cole, Jr., *The Social Ideas of the Northern Evangelists, 1826–1860,* Columbia Studies in the Social Sciences (New York: Columbia University Press, 1954), pp. 231 ff. Suggestive also are Charles L. Sanford, *The Quest for Paradise: Europe and the American Moral Imagination* (Urbana: University of Illinois Press, 1961); and George H. Williams, *Wilderness and Paradise in Christian Thought* (New York: Harper & Row, 1962). LeRoy Edwin Froom, *The Prophetic Faith of Our Fathers,* 4 vols. (Washington, 1946–54) is an uncritical Adventist account, but encyclopedic and indispensable for study of the history of millennial ideas. Useful articles are the survey by Ira Brown, "Watchers for the Second Coming: The Millennial Tradition in America," *Mississippi Valley Historical Review,* vol. 39. no. 3 (1952), pp. 441–58; and the bibliographical study by David E. Smith, "Millenarian Scholarship in America," *American Quarterly,* vol. 17, no. 3 (1965), pp. 535–49. Ernest Lee Tuveson's *Millennium and Utopia: A Study in the Background of the Idea of Progress* (Berkeley: University of California Press. 1949) and *Redeemer Nation: The Idea of America's Millennial Role* (Chicago: University of Chicago Press, 1968) provide the best guide to the evolution of the millennial tradition. However, these works are brief interpretations, and a comprehensive examination of millennial literature and argument still awaits an author.

First, throughout the American states, though most definitely in New England, a particular Protestant view of history had long been widespread. This view rested partly on the usual Protestant interpretation of papist apostasy and Reformation renewal of the church and partly on English and Scottish convictions that the British kingdoms harbored a people chosen by God for unusual service in advancing his providential plan.[7] American settlers made their peculiar appropriation of this tradition by impregnating the idea of providential guidance with their own sense of historic mission. Evident even in southern colonial rhetoric, this claim was raised to high art in the New England historical style. Histories of New England were never fundamentally parochial because they were ruled by the conviction that the church in the New World was joined in a historic continuum with the Old Testament patriarchs and the apostles and was leading the people of God in their modern pilgrimage. These assumptions, broadened, amalgamated, invigorated, and politicized by the Revolution, stood behind the popular image of the American Israel, with all its implications of special election, vocation, and guidance. Hence Christian patriots saw nothing incongruous in linking Moses and Winthrop with Washington, who "with his worthy companions and valiant band, were instrumental in the hand of JESUS, the King of Kings, to deliver this American Israel from their troubles."[8]

Second, this self-consciousness was given new dimension by the growing importance and changing meaning of the millennial scheme of history in the eighteenth century. Expectation of a glorious consummation to history, a thousand-year reign of Christ and the

7. See William Haller, ed., *The Book of Martyrs and the Elect Nation* (New York: Fernhill House, 1963). Transfer of the millennial role from Britain to the new American state may be observed in Stiles: "Oh England! how did I once love thee? how did I once glory in thee! . . . In the rapturous anticipation of thine enlargement and reflourishing in this western world, how have I been wont to glory in the future honour of having thee for the head of the *Britannico-American* empire, for the many ages until the Millennium—when thy great national glory should have been advanced in then becoming a member of the universal empire of the Prince of Peace . . . . But now farewell—a long farewell—to all this greatness!" (p. 53). Yet, from Dwight to Josiah Strong, Christian patriots generally gave a secondary millennial vocation to Britain.
8. Seth Stetson, *The Substance of a Discourse Preached in the Second Parish, Plymouth, December 22, 1806* (Boston, 1807), p. 7.

saints, was, in orthodox Reformed tradition, primarily a seventeenth century addition to the apocalyptic story.[9] Though capable of causing upheaval, this millennial doctrine had more often served as consolation, promising that though God's people might have to wander until the far-off end of history, Christ's second advent would ultimately banish oppression and suffering and inaugurate the blessed millennium antecedent to the final judgment. But by the end of the eighteenth century, millennial thought was not only more central in theology but had altered in structure, most significantly in the tendency to expect Christ's coming after rather than before the millennial age. Thus the genuine eschatological states did not commence until after the church's enjoyment of the millennial blessing, which was expected within history and which was to be realized by the ordinary means of propagating the gospel in the power of the Spirit. By the same shift the future marked by tribulation, expected by tradition, was transformed into a future of hope, overcoming psychological obstacles to prayers for the swift completion of history. "Postmillennial" exegesis, usually traced to the Anglican scholar Daniel Whitby, was widely disseminated in America through the influence of the great Edwards and his disciples, but even without their recommendations it would have become widespread through such popular English works as those of Moses Lowman, Thomas Scott, Adam Clarke, and David Bogue.[10] Such millennial interpretation had the effect of teaching

9. Its entry into the English orthodox Reformed tradition may be the Savoy Declaration's promise that "in the later days . . . the Churches of Christ being inlarged, and edified through a free and plentiful communication of light and grace, shall enjoy in this world a more quiet, peaceable, and glorious condition than they have enjoyed." See chapter 26, "Of the Church," in Williston Walker, *The Creeds and Platforms of Congregationalism* (New York, 1893), p. 396. The Westminster Confession does not so hint at a millennium.
10. This statement of the alteration of millennial doctrine in the eighteenth century is much simplified. For fuller accounts of changing interpretation with reference to biblical commentary, see Miller, "The End of the World," in *Errand into the Wilderness*, Tuveson, *Redeemer Nation*, pp. 26–73; Froom, *The Prophetic Faith*, 2:640–796, 3:9–259; C. C. Goen, "Jonathan Edwards: A New Departure in Eschatology," *Church History*, vol. 28, no. 1 (1959), pp. 25–40. What the change essentially meant for later Americans was apparent in the succinct definition quoted from Bogue by William Cogswell in *The Harbinger of the Millennium* (Boston, 1833): "The Millennarians, or Chilianists, believe the saints will reign on earth with Christ a thousand years. These views are not embraced by Christians generally in the

many Americans to expect some coming perfection of history, achieved by progressive stages, to which contemporary events, first the Awakening and later the Revolution, must be the prelude.

Third, the evangelical impulse, both in colonial and later revivals, worked a change of emphasis whereby the millennium ceased to be primarily a stage in formal eschatology and instead became the object of intense speculation, anticipation, and longing. Many besides Samuel Hopkins lived "in a region of imagination, feeding on visions of a holiness and happiness which are to make earth all but heaven." [11] This shift from doctrine to popular piety was fundamental in preparing the millennial hope to serve as a dynamic ideology. Further, this very ardor and the visible evidence of the Spirit's work in America suggested both an American location for the millennial dawn and its imminent appearance. That Edwards and others perceived the hoped-for signs in New England conversions is well known. And this perspective gave to all succeeding American events a continuing cosmic importance. Thomas Prince saw the French and Indian War as "opening a way to enlighten the utmost regions of America" preparatory to the millennial reign.[12] Revolutionary preachers in their turn found the prophecies unfolding in the triumph of independence and lib-

present day. Most of them believe that the Millennium is that time in which there will be far more eminent measures of divine knowledge, of holiness of heart and life; and of spiritual consolation and joy, in the souls of the disciples of Christ, than the world has yet seen: and these will not be the attainments of a few Christians, but the general mass. This delightful internal state of the church will be accompanied with such a portion of external prosperity and peace, and abundance of all temporal blessings, as men never knew before. The boundaries of the kingdom of Christ will be extended from the rising to the going down of the sun; and Antichristianism, Deism, Mahometanism, Paganism, and Judaism, shall all be destroyed, and give place to the Redeemer's throne. . . . Religion will then be the grand business of mankind. The generality will be truly pious; and those who are not, will be inconsiderable in number, and most probably be anxious to conceal their real character" (p. 361).

11. The characterization was that of William Ellery Channing, in his *Works*, 10th ed. (Boston: American Unitarian Assn., 1849), p. 427. For Hopkin's "Treatise on the Millennium," see *The Works of Samuel Hopkins, D.D.*, 3 vols. (Boston, 1852), 2:223–364. The work was dedicated "TO THE PEOPLE WHO SHALL LIVE IN THE DAYS OF THE MILLENNIUM."

12. Thomas Prince, *Six Sermons* (Edinburgh, 1785), p. 28. Prince's sweeping prophecy is not well known: "I cannot but expect, that not only all the southern, western, and north-western parts of this new world, and Calefornia [*sic*], will, in their times, be full of pure and pious churches, rejoicing in the great Redeemer, but even all that further western continent, extending from America to Asia."

erty; their successors discovered them in the growth and perfection of the American Republic.

By the time the age of reform and benevolence dawned, the millennial role of America was becoming a commonplace in pulpit eloquence, though its triumph was still recent enough for Lyman Beecher to confess that "when I first encountered this opinion I thought it chimerical. . . . But," he added, "all providential developments since, and all the existing signs of the times lend corroboration to it." [13] Doctrinal historicization of the millennium combined with revivalistic yearning for its realization to foster confidence in man's ability to reach the glorious historical state. Gospel preaching, mass conversions, and prayers for the millennium passed quickly into the reform crusades designed to achieve the ultimate perfection of men and institutions. If we only pray and wait upon the Lord, said Beecher, he will not come. The cry of President Eliphalet Nott of Union College before the Presbyterian General Assembly was unequivocal: the millennium was at the door and would "be introduced by HUMAN EXERTIONS."[14]

Finally, the Revolution turned much millennial speculation in the direction of justifying the nation's existence. This development, though immediately appearing, as we have seen, was also powerfully reinforced by a more gradual perception of the full significance of independence. The new nationality, attained in the cultural context of the Enlightenment, presented a double challenge to conservative Protestants and at length evoked a determined and sustained reaction. By the turn of the century a new republican nationalism was becoming defined, and religious leaders were concerned lest this spirit be separated from older religious ideologies, which were often burdened with a narrowly provincial outlook.

To take the most obvious example, what did the Puritan errand into the wilderness mean to the United States? In time, New England as a discrete society and civilization would pass away, just

13. See Heimert, *Religion and the American Mind*, esp. chaps. 7–10; Lyman Beecher, *A Plea for the West* (Cincinnati, 1835), pp. 9–11.
14. Lyman Beecher, *Works* (Boston: John P. Jewett & Co., 1852–53), 2: 80–81; Eliphalet Nott, *A Sermon Preached before the General Assembly of the Presbyterian Church . . . May 19, 1806*, quoted in Froom, *The Prophetic Faith*, 4:89–90.

as particular New England values would be submerged in ideals common to the entire American community.[15] Second, the danger appeared to be far more acute when account was taken of the rationalist environment in which the United States had indeed been established. The founding fathers had been little concerned with divine providences and had entrusted no religious role to the Republic. Instead, their utterances had implied a self-created union, invoked by social compact, venerating the rights of man, and following the "simple principles of nature." Yet this Republic claimed a universal appeal in offering a gospel of liberty for all mankind. Religious leaders of the Jeffersonian era were well aware that the natural rights philosophy, originally aristocratic, was now advancing into a popular liberal version of the American purpose. Even without the vulgarizations of the school of Thomas Paine, this version was bound to develop because expositors such as Franklin and Jefferson and revered texts such as the Declaration of Independence stood at the center of the national myth. To sharpen anxiety, the dread example of the infidel nationalism of revolutionary France hovered always in the background. "The crisis, then, has come," said Lyman Beecher in 1812. "By the

15. The attempt to broaden the New England tradition to embrace the United States is apparent in Stetson, *The Substance of a Discourse:* "It is probable that no nation under heaven resembles God's chosen Israel, more than the United States of America; especially New England" (p. 4). See also James Flint, *A Discourse Delivered at Plymouth, December 22, 1815* (Boston, 1816), p. 20. Copious illustration for this transition is found in Nathanael Emmons's sermons. An uncompromising conservative, Emmons argued that the Revolution brought independence but did not justify change of the internal religious or political systems of the colonies. Beginning about 1800 Emmons dwelt on the identity of the Hebrews with the American nation. Americans had no explicit convenant with God (as had the Hebrews), but "God's taking our fathers from their native country, and bringing them . . . to this then dreary wilderness, was practically setting them apart for himself and making them his peculiar people." Indeed, the success of God's great plan depended on the Republic, for "unless it please God to continue us his peculiar people, its seems that the light of the gospel and the means of religion may be, in a few years, entirely lost." Other nations "may glorify God by pulling down the kingdom of Satan, and we, by building up the kingdom of Christ." By the end of the century the United States, populated bv ninety-six millions, would be powerful and religious, suited for inaugurating Christ's kingdom in the century next to follow. See Jacob Ide, ed., *The Works of Nathanael Emmons* (Boston, 1871), 5:177–79, 322.

people of this generation—by ourselves, probably—the amazing question is to be decided, whether the inheritance of our fathers shall be preserved, or thrown away."

In this atmosphere of continuing crisis the older themes of providential creation, covenanted relationship with God, and theocratic mission terminating in millennial glory were elaborately restated and made relevant to the new nation's destiny. The work was aided by the reaction against European rationalism, the powerful evangelical renewal, and the great though gradual realignment of interests whereby sectarian religion abandoned an earlier alliance with rationalists and gravitated toward stronger ties with the conservative churches.[16] The success achieved was only partial, for millennial vocation remained only one explanation of the national role. But it was also enduring. Reverence for the Christian Republic commanding the advance of history toward prophesied millennial blessings won a lasting place beside other American dreams of destiny which were less informed by religious ideals. The millennial version was assured prominence, not only because it reconciled the Republic with revered historic and religious values, but because it was spread by clergymen, authors, and educators possessing a disproportionate influence on cultural life.

Thus, from the very beginning of the nation's existence, providential and millennial themes in American religion offered some check to whatever dangers lay in republican ideology and successfully accommodated the United States in the grand design of religious history. Yet it was ironic that, this having been done, American churches were henceforth bound to regard the nation as

---

16. Beecher, *Works*, 2:99–102. Timothy Dwight provided leadership in this campaign. See *President Dwight's Decisions of Questions Discussed by the Senior Class in Yale College in 1813 and 1814* (New York, 1833), pp. 111–14 for his attack on natural origins to civil government. For his vision of the American roles, see Timothy Dwight, *The Duty of Americans at the Present Crisis* (New Haven, 1798); and *A Discourse on Some Events of the Last Century* (New Haven, 1801). For Baptist dissent from this pattern, indicting the "Protestant Beast" and affirming the persistence of "the spiritual tyranny which came from Rome and England . . . in several of the United States of America," see Isaac Backus, *The Infinite Importance of the Obedience of Faith* (Boston, 1791), p. 26, and *The Testimony of the Two Witnesses* (Boston, 1793), p. 22.

having extraordinary religious significance. The American achievement was peculiarly God's handiwork, and American history was evolving into the millennium of Christ. Accordingly, from its inception, the religion of the Republic was unusually open to the American experience.

2

What was the effect of this relation on the course of American religion? Probably the most successful years of postmillennialism in the concept of national mission were those between 1815 and the Civil War. During this era the idea of the redemptive nation may be observed conferring some unity and identity on the pluralistic American religious tradition and reinforcing its activism and optimism. At the same time it is apparent that the millennial hope was itself adjusted and acculturated by common ideas and values. Hence the history of millennial doctrine reflected the broader story of Protestantism's endeavor to penetrate American culture and its reverse penetration by that culture.

The concept of an American Christianity emerged in these years, and to a large degree it rested on the belief in national religious mission. At the Revolution the religious complexion of the colonies was already diversified; it became even more so with the decline of the conservative churches, sectarian expansion, and renewed immigration. The apparent confusion of traditions, polities, and doctrines never failed to perplex foreign observers. But common participation in the American enterprise and common conviction of its millennial denouement gave American churchmen an opportunity for greater unity than that implied in the mutual recognitions of denominational theory. Like the tribes of Israel, the American churches shared a special relation with God and a special destiny on earth which conferred on them a singularity eclipsing their disparate origins, histories, and confessions. It was this common mission which dominated countless Independence Day sermons, inspired the great interdenominational societies, and informed the principal American church histories from Benjamin Trumbull to Leonard Woolsey Bacon.[17]

It seems clear also that commitment to the vision of America as a redemptive instrument strengthened the public activism of evangelical Protestantism. As the bearer of history's promise, the Republic and its political life could never be consigned to a secular sphere free from religious direction. Rather, they were to be progressively perfected and spiritualized, and the religious resources for this task were to be mobilized by expectations of imminent victory. This vision intensified the theocratic determination to keep the United States a Christian republic even though legal ties between church and state were soon broken. The state, though no longer explicitly Christian by confession, would remain so by vocation. In practical terms, this outlook helped preserve religious influence in the ecclesiastically neutral state. The prospect of a millennial perfection to be won through human exertions reinforced, stabilized, and sustained the evangelical impulse, especially during those periods when revival fervor was temporarily on the wane. In the West the millennial dream of filling the continent with true religion and exemplary piety provided the impetus for organized support of the gospel, the Sabbath, the school, and religious and moral associations. "How great will be your happiness," the Connecticut General Assembly told western emigrants, "should you be permitted, after the lapse of one or two centuries, to look down from heaven upon the fertile regions which you now inhabit . . . to behold [your descendants] every where enlightened and pious and happy, under the mild reign of the PRINCE of peace . . . and to behold the whole earth, rejoicing in the unclouded radiance of that bright sun, which will not set for a thousand years!" [18] And all these crusades were spurred on by the assurance

17. Benjamin Trumbull's *General History of the United States of America* (Boston, 1810) bore the subtitle, *Sketches of the Divine Agency, in Their Settlement, Growth, and Protection, and Especially in the Late Revolution;* Leonard Woolsey Bacon, *A History of American Christianity* (New York, 1895), p. 2.
18. The Connecticut General Assembly, *An Address to the Emigrants from Connecticut, and from New England Generally, in the New Settlements in the United States* (Hartford, 1817), p. 18.

that, as Timothy Dwight said, "our own morning may, and if we be willing and obedient, it is presumed will, lose itself in the Millennial dawn." By stressing the continuity of the millennium with the present, Dwight was even able to perceive the actual beginnings of the millennial epoch in 1812! "The dawn may shine bright long before the perfect day," he argued, and "there is no improbability in the opinion . . . that this happy period has, in the sense which I have already specified, already begun." [19] Expressed thus, the prospect before Americans was that of *finishing* the millennial order, fired by the certainty of impending and glorious reward.

Yet as the Civil War approached some observers also noted that the millennium itself had begun to lose religious definition as it had become more entangled in America `e. Loss of focus was perhaps inevitable for another reason. Evangelicalism inclined toward emphasis on the conversion of souls as the sufficient basis for the kingdom's coming, and accordingly it less clearly envisioned social structures appropriate for millennial society. While generating reforms, it also tended to accept and then to sanctify basic American institutions and social values. In any case by 1850 Mark Hopkins, weighing the evidence of the coming millennium, significantly joined "the benevolent and reformatory movements" of the time with "the attempt to realize . . . the liberty and rights of the individual man" and "the subjugation of the powers of nature to the use of man." [20] In doing so he confirmed the widespread coalescence of the millennial conception with both the prevailing republican enthusiasm and the cult of progress.

The "republicanism" of American Protestantism, inevitable as the corollary of the idea of the American Israel, rested partly on the ancient assurance that those who covenanted with God covenanted also with one another, and revivalism sought to universalize such covenant membership in the Republic. But after 1815 Protestant republicanism became more rationalized in arguments which

19. Timothy Dwight, *A Discourse, in Two Parts, Delivered July 23, 1812, on the Public Fast, in the Chapel of Yale College* (Boston, 1813), pp. 42–44.
20. See Emerson Davis, *The Half-Century* (Boston, 1851), p. xvi.

attempted to harmonize human and divine sovereignty, natural liberty and Christian dedication. The usual theme was mutual dependence. Just as the hope of a successful experiment in popular government rested on moral restraints that the Bible alone could supply, so also the pure Christianity of the future could thrive only in a republican society where religious freedom and personal decision prevailed. Preachers regularly demonstrated the biblical origins of republican government—Beecher traced the American polity to Moses—and decried the fatal alliance in Europe between authoritarian regimes and degenerate Christianity. These arguments reflected a settled belief that free government was a mark of true religion, while liberty and piety were alike the concerns of the American church.[21]

This fusion can frequently be seen in Lyman Beecher. His 1827 lecture "The Memory of Our Fathers" offers an example. Beecher was convinced that the moral renovation of the earth was imminent, but that for this impending triumph certain political conditions were necessary. These were the popular ownership of the soil (which alone could foster industry, self-reliance, and religion), representative self-government, and freedom of conscience. In contemporary revolutions Beecher saw the old order in collapse and the nations groping toward these reforms. "But to the perfection of this work, a great example is required, of which the world may take knowledge and which shall inspire hope, and rouse and concentrate the energies of man." For this purpose God created a new nation, "itself free . . . to blow the trumpet and hold up the light." [22] Beecher, of course, gave due attention to exemplary benevolence and evangelical instruction through foreign missions in his description of American responsibility, but his conception of the millennium was always strongly colored by the republican

21. Beecher, *Works,* 1: 176, 331; 2: 92–95. The greatest problem was reconciling Puritan tradition with American testimony for liberty. Though easier after disestablishment in New England, it still required explanations. For several, see Heman Humphrey, *Miscellaneous Discourses and Reviews* (Amherst, 1834), p. 103; William B. Sprague, *The Claims of Past and Future Generations on Civil Rulers* (Boston, 1825), p. 9; Leonard Bacon, *An Address before the New England Society* (New York, 1839), pp. 17–22.
22. Lyman Beecher, "The Memory of Our Fathers," in *Works,* 1:176.

ideal. Scores of other works carried the same message, and by the Civil War it was assumed that "our religion becomes our politics—in the good sense—our statesmanship; and our statesmanship becomes our religion. This identity of principle and of its practical application in government, both in church and state, qualify this American people, above all on earth, to bear the Christian religion and the freedom its doctrines engender to all the families of the pagan nations." [23]

Even more broadly, the millennial convergence of American and Christian history committed churchmen to pursue religious meanings in the total national experience. The close inspection of American culture which this logic required was incidentally furthered also by the particular cultural situation of the United States in the first half of the nineteenth century. The time was one of impressive technological advance, literary venture, and humanitarian reform, while Western "barbarism" increasingly forced the church to promote civilizing institutions for a new society. Even at the beginning of the century millennial preachers had spoken hopefully of the providential advantages to the gospel of the new developments in science, transportation, and communication, and by 1818 Joseph Emerson's popular account of the millennium prophesied how "every cottage will be irradiated with science, as well as with religion" and "every peasant will be able not only to read the bible but to read the stars." [24] Albert Barnes furnishes one of the best examples of the absorption of the progress faith into the mid-century understanding of America's responsibility toward the millennium. Throughout his life Barnes was convinced that "human affairs are tending to that state when science, liberty, justice, pure morals, and the Christian religion will pervade the earth." Further, Barnes thought that the accumulative forces of progress "have a close, . . . an *essential* connection with Christianity," and "become incorporated with it." Thus his teaching of America's historic mission embraced the entire progressive thrust:

This land has been preserved that there might be here furnished, in a land of science, and art, and enterprise, and liberty—in the age

23. George Junkin, *Political Fallacies* (New York, 1863), pp. 318–19.
24. Joseph Emerson, *Lectures on the Millennium* (Boston, 1818), p. 18.

of the world that shall usher in the millennial morning—the fairest civilization that the world has ever seen of a pure Christianity; . . . not obsolete . . . but pure and bright, . . . still in advance of all human progress in refinement and the arts, and incorporating itself with everything that is of permanent value to our race.[25]

These various strands were gathered together in the most reasoned and systematic exposition of America's millennial destiny by President Francis Wayland of Brown. In 1830 Wayland, possibly the most influential figure in college education in his time, preached before the American Sunday School Union in Philadelphia. His sermon, "Encouragements to Religious Efforts," has never received the attention given to his 1825 address, *The Duties of an American Citizen,* yet both are essential to his discussion of the American purpose. In his earlier work Wayland had described the American political and religious system—the rule of law and a free Christianity—and contrasted these with European autocracy and Catholic oppression. But revolutions abroad were pressing irresistibly for change, and in the coming reorganization of the world the nations would look to the United States—"the first that taught them to be free; the first that suffered in the contest." [26] The later Philadelphia sermon related the same messianic purpose to a broader analysis of the meaning of the nineteenth century. The physical condition of man, he declared, was undergoing sweeping changes with steam technology, wider distribution of wealth, and increasing leisure for the ordinary man. Similarly, educational reforms were showing how men's minds could be more easily strengthened for rational and moral decision. Together both changes pointed to the coming victory of free government and pure religion in a historic transformation far more important than the Reformation. To the United States fell the glory of leading

25. Albert Barnes, *The Gospel Necessary to Our Country* (Washington, 1852), p. 22. See also Albert Barnes, *Life at Threescore and Ten* (New York, 1871), pp. 121, 130–31; and Laurens P. Hickock, "The Idea of Humanity in Its Progress to Its Consummation," *Biblical Repository and Classical Review,* ser. 3, vol. 3 (1847), pp. 747–48. But both Barnes and Hickock distinguished Christian progress, dependent on God's grace, from natural doctrines of progress.

26. Francis Wayland, *The Duties of an American Citizen* (Boston, 1825), esp. pp. 19–25.

this wondrous upheaval. There the number of "truly religious persons" was greatest. There "perfect civil and religious freedom" reigned. There sound institutions, religious revivals, and moral societies were molding a new public mind. All the evidence yielded but one conclusion: "Never have there been presented so many or so great encouragements for a universal effort to bring the world into cordial subjection to Jesus Christ." Wayland's peroration disclosed the millennial enthusiasm which sprang from this assessment of the American scene. "Why stand we here all the day idle?" he asked, when with sincere effort

> a revival of piety may be witnessed in every neighbourhood throughout the land; the principles of the Gospel may be made to regulate the detail of individual and national intercourse; and high praises of God may be heard from every habitation; and perhaps before the youth of this generation be gathered to their fathers, there may burst forth upon these highly-favored States the light of Millennial Glory. What is to prevent it? . . . I do believe that the option is put into our hands. It is for us . . . to say, whether the present religious movement shall be onward, until it terminate in the universal triumph of the Messiah, or whether all shall go back again. . . . The church has for two thousand years been praying "Thy kingdom come." Jesus Christ is saying unto us, "It shall come if you desire it."[27]

With these words—with all of their activist and optimistic undertones—the Americanization of the millennial tradition was far advanced. To many Americans the rapid development of the United States—moral, political, cultural—was now bringing to pass the era foretold in prophecy. In this expectancy, this presumption that America was both the locus and the instrument of the great consummation, lay some of the seeds of the democracy-and-progress faith of later American Christianity.

3

Beginning about 1840 the millennial ideology relating American Protestantism to the Republic was disturbed by a rapidly mount-

27. Francis Wayland, "Encouragements to Religious Efforts," in *American National Preacher*, vol. 5, no. 3 (1830), esp. pp. 39–46.

ing crisis. The threat was twofold. First, the structure, survival, and identity of the Republic were brought into question as rising sectional animosities threatened an approaching disruption. And, second, the millennial heritage was itself rendered increasingly insecure through theological changes.

The first trend found expression in the note of uncertainty introduced into sermons and orations on America's role and purpose. Even the repeated assurances that God's former providences proved his future intentions toward the Republic masked an insecurity inspired by the political threat to the Union. The disunity had other effects. It fostered the growth of disparate versions of the once-common faith so that while millennial strivings fired Northern abolitionists, Southern churchmen came to see the national mission as the preservation of slavery and to see covenant-loyalty as an exact regard for the limitations of the general government.[28] And while revivals and crusades continued, politics grew more insistent, antislavery eclipsed other reforms, and churches divided.[29]

More significant was the second trend, the intellectual changes which caused some erosion of the traditional postmillennial doctrine itself. This shift is still largely uninvestigated and must be dealt with speculatively. But it is clear that by the end of the Civil War millennial anticipations in religious literature had often separated from former doctrinal and biblical supports. For this, natural science seems to have been only indirectly responsible. Geology, it is true, had already begun to undermine the reliability of the biblical cosmology, but its controversy tended to fix on Creation and the Genesis account (while its speculations on a final destruction of the earth could be regarded as congenial to traditional eschatology).[30] Another possible influence, the debate over the

28. See, e.g., *The Collected Writings of James Henry Thornwell, D. D., LL.D.* (Richmond, 1873), 4: 510–48; and B. M. Palmer, *Slavery a Divine Trust* (New York, 1861), pp. 6–7.
29. Note the dirge of Laurens P. Hickock, *A Nation Saved from Its Prosperity Only by the Gospel* (New York, 1853).
30. See discussion in Arthur Alphonse Ekirch, *The Idea of Progress in America, 1815–1860,* Studies in History, Economics, and Public Law (New York: Columbia University Press, 1944), pp. 120–25; Conrad Wright, "The Religion of Geology," *New England Quarterly* 14 (1941): 335–58.

flamboyant Adventism of the 1840s, has never been properly assessed, but its influence was probably disturbing. That it gave new prominence to premillennial interpretation was perhaps of minor consequence, though some men not otherwise attracted to Millerism were apparently persuaded. Of greater moment may have been the unfavorable publicity which the Adventist movement drew upon the expectation of a millennium. Miller's religious opponents were not skeptics. They equaled him in enthusiasm for the millennium and agreed that the last age had indeed come. Accordingly, they too may have been placed at some disadvantage by prevalent journalistic ridicule.[31] In any case, in the 1840s orthodox references to the millennium tended to become more cautious and defensive, disclaiming sensual delights, precise prediction of times, and "fanaticism." Even the term *millennium* was sometimes replaced by a euphemism.

The most serious undermining of postmillennial eschatology may have been the work of the new biblical critics. American criticism was still in its infancy, but scholars had already provided Daniel and Revelation with historical exposition which related their prophecies to the context of their age. The Adventist sensation compelled critics to write popular explanations asserting, as in the title of Calvin Stowe's tract, "the utter groundlessness of all the millennial arithmetic." Moses Stuart's *Hints on the Interpretation of Prophecy* is the most important example of this literature, since the author's scholarship and orthodoxy were widely respected. Stuart affirmed a millennium continuous with history, but he insisted that the time of its coming was hidden and that all speculative comparison with current events was useless (in view of the fulfillment of the apocalyptic prophecies in the ancient church).

31. See discussion in Froom, *The Prophetic Faith*, 4:738–60; Francis David Nichol, *The Midnight Cry: A Defense of William Miller and the Millerites* (Washington: Review & Herald Pub. Assn., 1944), pp. 427–53. The usual reply to Miller was that though "the leading periods mentioned by Daniel and John, do actually expire about this age of the world," the "signs of the times all indicate—not, according to Mr. Miller, the overthrow of empires, bloody persecutions of the church . . . —but the gradual, though certain approach of the millennium, the spread of religion, and the universal prevalence of peace, good will, and holiness on the earth." (John Dowling, *An Exposition of the Prophecies, Supposed by William Miller to Predict the Second Coming of Christ, in 1843* [New York, 1843], pp. 29–30, 35.)

Further, to know the time of the millennium would destroy endeavor; if its coming were far distant, men would regard labor as vain, and, conversely, if it were divinely ordained for the present age, men would complacently await the miracle. Only through a benevolent ignorance of the time would Christian effort be fruitful. Last, Stuart warned against enthusiastic representations of the millennium induced by biblical imagery. Sin, pain, civil government, ecclesiastical institutions—all would continue, though divine compassion would be shed abroad to an extraordinary degree as well.[32] The effect of this interpretation from the foremost biblical critic in America was further to historicize the millennium, remove it from meaningful relation to biblical apocalyptic, and center attention on the march of progress rather than on the glorious termination.

Finally, the decline of traditional postmillennialism was probably related to the appearance of a nascent theological liberalism in the very quarter of the American ministry which had been most articulate in promoting a theocratic patriotism. Though patriotic and optimistic, this liberalism also sought to escape the confinement of biblical or credal literalism. Horace Bushnell, its most notable pioneer, was an enthusiastic believer in America's summons to lead the earth to a final era of righteousness, but he could not accept conventional ideas of Christ's ultimate return, either before or after the millennium. "Nothing could be more INEXPEDIENT, OR A PROFOUNDER AFFLICTION THAN A LOCALLY DESCENDED,

32. Calvin Stowe, *Letter to R. D. Mussey, M.D., on the Utter Groundlessness of All the Millennial Arithmetic* (Cincinnati, 1843); Moses Stuart, *Hints on the Interpretation of Prophecy* (Andover, 1842), pp. 140–42. See also Moses Stuart, *Sermon at the Ordination of the Rev. William G. Schauffler, as Missionary to the Jews* (Andover, 1831), pp. 14–16; and idem, *A Commentary of the Apocalypse* (London, 1845), 1:iv. Among others, Edward Beecher objected that "now, just as this great battle is coming to a crisis, and the united energies and wills of the papal world are concentrated against Great Britain and the United States, the great strongholds of spiritual Protestant Christianity and missionary enterprise, a new system of prophetic interpretation arises to strip the people of God of their arms." (Edward Beecher, "Remarks on Stuart's Commentary on the Apocalypse," *Biblical Repository and Classical Review*, ser. 3, vol. 3. [1847], p. 273.) For background to changing scriptural interpretation, see Jerry Wayne Brown, *The Rise of Biblical Criticism in America, 1800–1870: The New England Scholars* (Middletown: Wesleyan University Press, 1969).

PERMANENTLY VISIBLE SAVIOUR," he exclaimed during the Adventist excitement. "What is wanted now is an *unlocalized, invisible, spiritual presence, everywhere present Saviour,* such as we all may know and receive, being consciously known and received by him, AND THIS WILL BE HIS COMING AGAIN, OR HIS SECOND COMING."[33] Not yet of primary importance in the 1840s, this trend was soon to quicken the evaporation of the older postmillennialism, and just after the Civil War a Congregational study of the millennium discarded eschatology altogether. All "the subsequent events of Christ's personal coming, and a material resurrection, and the final judgment" were "unquestionably incorrect," it held. Instead "the Millennial era will be the last period of earth's duration . . . a period long almost beyond comparison with the prior ages—and . . . the sequences of the Millennium are the ending of earthly history and the entering upon the heavenly state, in the spiritual heaven." [34]

As a consequence of these factors, the millennial function of the United States seemed to be losing adequate religious basis just at the time when doubts about its secure nationhood and confusion about its role began to perplex. Yet so fundamental were the millennial assumptions of religious people in America that no real breakdown of consensus was evident. The basic concepts continued to receive ritual expression in the 1850s on every appropriate occasion. Then by the 1860s this millennial nationalism was immeasurably deepened by two profound experiences which bestowed new and poignant meaning on God's commission to his American people. In 1858 began the powerful evangelical renewal which enveloped American cities and produced anew a passionate longing for perfection, reform, and the millennial dawn. And second, the American Civil War re-created an intense emotional commitment to the Union and to its responsibility for the renovation of the world. In the vast sermon literature of the war all the earlier themes were once again heard, charged with new

33. Horace Bushnell, quoted in Froom, *The Prophetic Faith,* 4:755.
34. "A Congregational Minister," *The Coming of Christ in His Kingdom* (New York, n.d.), pp. 10–12. This anonymous work appears to have emerged from Illinois Congregationalism. There is no publishing date, but testimonials printed at the beginning of the work are dated 1869.

sincerity and conviction. God's judgment on his people was truly righteous, cleansing and purging were necessary for his future service, but the baptism by blood was also a reanointing for the task of fulfilling his will in history. When men heard Lincoln invoke "this last, best hope of earth" and armies sang "Mine eyes have seen the glory of the coming of the Lord," the two experiences merged into a single faith.[35]

Thus it is not possible to dismiss this consecration of the Republic with the passing of the older, antebellum America. Just after the war Henry Ward Beecher—patriot, liberal, progressive—gave expression to the persistent millennialism (coupled with indifference to doctrine) of Protestants of the new age: "We must believe . . . that somehow 'in the ages to come' when there is a new heaven and a new earth, righteousness will dwell in them. By what road we are coming to it, by what process the work shall be done, we cannot say. . . . If it be not the literal millennial glory which men have counted upon, it will be in some form the substance of which that is a sign and symbol." [36] A long epilogue was beginning in which attenuated but modernized millennial patterns would continue to invest the Republic with religious meaning.

4

Discrete millennial themes in the national culture are more difficult to trace in the modern period. On the one hand, American nationalism finally was rendered pervasive and secure by the Civil War. Just as the older Federalism disappeared in a new and unprecedented assertion of central power, the former dedication to the Union gave way to a novel but irresistible sense of organic unity. This nationalism no longer had the same need for the older mythic unity supported by religious sanctions. Henceforth patterns of religious patriotism might still prove comfortable embel-

35. See William A. Clebsch, *Christian Interpretations of the Civil War*, Facet Books, Historical Series, 14 (Philadelphia: Fortress Press, 1969); William John Wolf, *The Almost Chosen People: A Study of the Religion of Abraham Lincoln* (Garden City: Doubleday & Co., 1959); and Smith, *Revivalism and Social Reform*, pp. 63 ff.
36. Henry Ward Beecher, "The Ages to Come" (preached April 30, 1871), in *The Sermons of Henry Ward Beecher, in Plymouth Church, Brooklyn*, Sixth Series (New York, 1872), pp. 160–61.

lishments to nationalism, but they would not again serve as a resource of critical importance. Moreover, the sweeping transformations in America's society and world position in the later nineteenth century independently assured the prominence of "progressive" motifs in any national self-appraisal. Mastery of machine technology, the rise of northern wealth, population increase, the great-power role in global politics—all these made inevitable the expectation of an advancing triumph even without the aid of the religious tradition. On the other hand, while faith in a coming era of the Lord remained fervent in large areas of the Protestant community, such faith generally ceased to rely on the language, doctrine, or exegesis of Scripture prophecy. While some persons professed confusion or indifference concerning the means of the kingdom's advent, others tended to reclothe the millennial faith in organic imagery, relying on such appropriate biblical allusions as the parable of the mustard seed. This change had decided apologetic advantages. Friction with science and biblical criticism was avoided, and religious faith was brought closer to the idiom of the prevailing Darwinism. But in the process Protestant liberalism tended to draw even closer to culture, lose independent religious insight, and become preoccupied with progress of every kind—biological, technological, and cultural, as well as spiritual and moral. Hence its persistent millennial motif could not readily be distinguished from progressive assumptions arising from Darwin or Spencer.

Because of these conditions, the primary characteristic of a millennial ingredient in the American sense of mission in the modern era was its diffuseness. And this very diffuseness facilitated its adaptability and ready integration with other modern trends in American Christianity. While the various modifications comprehended much of the history of liberal theology, it is possible here only to select for brief emphasis three features of this modernization of the tradition.

First, though the religious impetus after the Civil War stemmed from the evangelical revival, the dominant theological course in the middle-class churches was set by the "New Theology" which developed under the leadership of such nationally known preachers as Henry Ward Beecher and Phillips Brooks. Sensitive to the religious problems raised by recent scholarship, this school was eager to state a Protestant view of history in terms that were modern, "philosophical," and congenial to the age. This they attempted to do by stressing such ideas as divine immanence, the fruition of the divine purpose in the natural order, and the redemptive character of the cultural process. When they appropriated the millennial inheritance, they found its affirmation of "progress" appealing, but often inclined to place it in a natural context rather than preserve or reconstruct its scriptural basis. In doing so they achieved the ultimate historicization of the millennium. The millennial blessing was no longer beckoning at the end of the human story but was located in the inexorably progressive tendencies of history itself. Furthermore, in relying on a universal redemptive process, this restatement tended to become vague about the role of Christianity and the church. All humanity, rather than the people of God, was pressing toward a perfection that was more than spiritual. In this work the nation, representing the entire community, could be a more appropriate redemptive organ than the church.[37]

Consequently, Protestant liberals were ready to embrace and expand the idea of American leadership in the total cultural ascent of mankind, an idea which had been heard even before the war. Impressed by the triumphs of nineteenth century progress, they also sensed that the United States was now destined to become the master and leader of modern civilization. Hence they expressed

---

37. Winthrop Still Hudson provides useful summaries of "New Theology" in *The Great Tradition of the American Churches* (New York: Harper & Bros., 1953), pp. 157–94, and in *Religion in America* (New York: Charles Scribner's Sons, 1965), pp. 263–76. Sidney E. Mead, *The Lively Experiment: The Shaping of Christianity in America* (New York: Harper & Row, 1963), esp. pp. 134–55, analyzes theological directions after the war and Protestant ideas of destiny. On the development of modern theological liberalism see Daniel Day Williams. *The Andover Liberals* (New York: Columbia University Press, 1941); and Kenneth Cauthen, *The Impact of American Religious Liberalism* (New York: Harper & Row, 1962).

enthusiasm for all aspects of the new America—its machines and wealth, its democracy, its popular culture, and its religion. The trend was transparent in Henry Ward Beecher. By the 1870s Beecher's practical millennialism was cast in the language of development, and long before *Evolution and Religion* (1885) he was seeking the adjustment of Christianity and Darwinism. Consistent with this view, Beecher attributed significance to the entire achievement of man just as his millennial projections went beyond the triumph of Christianity to the development of the superman.[38] Correspondingly, his appraisal of America's readiness to undertake the salvation of the world dwelt on the progress of her civilization. In his 1870 sermon "The Tendencies of American Progress," Beecher devoted two-thirds of his text to technological and cultural advance. While he omitted reference to education (for want of time) and concluded with only a hasty salute to American religious vitality, he found the basis for both in widening prosperity, social amelioration, and popular refinement.

> While upon almost a whole continent [Europe] labor is suspended, or works only at the forge and the foundry, for purposes of destruction, throughout the length and breadth of this great land labor whistles, and sings, and is happy. . . .
>
> You shall hear the sound of the piano in every cluster of three houses throughout the land, almost, from ocean to ocean. . . .
>
> It is not strange to find a man who works at the forge all day, grim and grizzly, going home at night to pursue historical reading.

And on to the triumphant conclusion, linking technology with the highest spiritual life:

> And so, in the train of industry comes wealth, and of wealth, taste, and of taste, beneficence; and refinement flashes throughout the

38. "It has been thought that in the millennium . . . when Christ shall come again on earth, he then, as some seem to think by physical force, by authority, will change things. . . . But now we are taught that that process of change has been going on from the beginning slowly, slowly; that we are on the eve of a day in which that development is to come much more rapidly, and that it is to be an unfolding that is to affect every process of human thought—our notion of dogma, doctrine, government, laws, institutions, philosophies, theologies, everything. These are all growing to a future blossom and future fruit." (Henry Ward Beecher, *Evolution and Religion* [New York, 1885], p. 14.) "We have not come to it yet . . . but before the great ripeness comes the race will be regenerated in physical birth. Generation will in ripe age supersede Regeneration." (Ibid., p. 215.) Beecher expressed the same idea in "The World's Growth" (preached November 26, 1874), in *Sermons*, Third Series, p. 285.

land. . . . And nowhere else does wealth so directly point towards virtue in morality, and spirituality in religion, as in America.[39]

Beecher's enthusiasm reflected some of the naïve vulgarity of the Great Barbecue, but the concept of America's religious mission to lead the world to a perfection of humanity and culture long continued. In an address concerned with "how we can press forward that which moves forward already, and hasten the chariot wheels of the kingdom of God which has come, which is more and more coming, upon the earth," Phillips Brooks found the American nation doing God's work: "I do not know how a man can be an American, even if he is not a Christian, and not catch something with regard to God's purpose as to this great land." Though more theological than either Beecher or Brooks, George Gordon, their younger colleague at the Old South Church, Boston, concluded a long review of history at the opening of the new century with comparable demonstrations that "the United States has been, in this century, the foremost servant of the idea of humanity." Sixteen years later he was still showing how American inventions, science, education, government, and religion had outstripped those of Europe and were creating a new world. "The hope of the Catholic faith is here; the future of essential religion is here; the forward look is here, and it is great with high expectation." And it would be possible to discuss this same American "cultural millennialism" well into the twentieth century (with Newell Dwight Hillis providing an especially suitable example).[40]

Second, late nineteenth century Protestants, no less than their antebellum predecessors, were preoccupied with the quest for a Christian America. The modernization of this pursuit which led,

39. Henry Ward Beecher, "The Tendencies of American Progress," in *Sermons,* Fifth Series, pp. 210–15.
40. Phillips Brooks, *National Needs and Remedies* (New York, 1890), pp. 311, 301. George A. Gordon, *The New Epoch for Faith* (Boston, 1901), pp. 92–100. Idem, *The Appeal of the Nation* (Boston, 1917), p. 65. Hillis frequently preached that "laws are becoming just, rulers humane, music is becoming sweeter, and books are growing wiser," etc. The United States was "divinely ordained to be the teacher of the world in free institutions," for "our nation in its origin, in all its history, in its laws, is not only religious but Christian. Our political system is only a form of applied Christianity. It is a Sermon on the Mount, taking on political form." (Newell Dwight Hillis, *All the Year Round* [New York, 1912], pp. 207–8, 162–63, 73.)

practically, to such experiments as the institutional church or the YMCA also led, theoretically, to urgent redefinitions of the Republic's redemptive work in the contemporary world. These versions owed much to the profoundly evangelical backgrounds of many Protestant liberals and to the new focus in religious thought on the kingdom of God as a comprehensive biblical concept adequate to ground undiminished "postmillennial" expectations. They attained prominence because they attempted to make traditional beliefs relevant to the new American conundrum—the paradoxical fulfillment of national strength and vitality for remaking the world at the very time when a new industrial and pluralistic society jeopardized the old Protestant America. Past testimony about the nation's universal role had included both the foreign missions emphasis on world crusade and a more isolationist but equally evangelical stress on America as a providential refuge and example of true Christianity. So it was again. Classic modern expressions of these versions were supplied by Josiah Strong and Washington Gladden.

Strong wrote partly in response to the expansionist mood of the late nineteenth century, when the country had begun to take seriously its global role and opinion had became more cosmopolitan, aware of the conflict of cultures and the "competition of races." But his rise to prominence was also closely related to conservative America's confrontation with the alien cultures of the "new immigration," neither Anglo-Saxon nor Protestant in composition. Once again inherited values were likely to be lost, and once again Protestant America was ready to respond to an enthusiastic portrayal of the religious mission of the Republic.

Strong's *Our Country* (1885) has been analyzed many times. What has not always been recognized is its skill in blending traditional and modern thought. In the main the message was the ritual one: evangelize both the (urban) frontier at home and foreign lands with the twin gospel that would perfect the world—free government and pure Christianity. God's providential care, the chosen race, the world mission, the critical hour, the appeal for action—all were part of the established antebellum pattern. What was new was the modern intellectual context in which these were placed by his fresh assessment of America's contemporary situation, more "scientific" social survey, and notorious adoption of fashionable Darwinian language concerning the competitive struggle of races. Strong's hope for the future rested on Protestant Saxondom, of which the United States was the effective instrument. Soon this race, led by a divinely prepared Republic, "with all the majesty of numbers and the might of wealth behind it—the representative, . . . of the largest liberty, the purest Christianity, the highest civilization—having developed peculiarly aggressive traits calculated to impress its institutions upon mankind will spread itself over the earth." Some peoples and cultures would suffer extinction, but the ultimate effect would be admirable as well as inevitable. Indeed, "our plea is not America for America's sake; but America for the world's sake." And though Strong addressed his appeal to Christians of the United States, he saw the American nation as the chief means to this end. "For, if this generation is faithful to its trust, America is to become God's right arm in his battle with the world's ignorance and oppression and sin." [41]

In obscuring the distinction between church and world, glorifying American humanity, and trusting in the ascending impulse of history, Strong revealed his debt to newer theological fashions. When in a much later volume he presented a bill of particulars against premillennialism, he made his own modernized millennialism even clearer. That unworthy creed, he complained, was "hostile to the scientific spirit" and to biblical criticism, unsympathetic to "modern culture and the new civilization," "skeptical of all progress," and "hopeless as to the success of God's moral government of the world." Instead, Strong taught, "the coming of Christ is progressive, and is hastened by all true progress in the world." [42]

41. Josiah Strong, *Our Country* (New York, 1885), pp. 213–18, 253–54; Henry Farnham May, *Protestant Churches and Industrial America* (New York: Harper & Bros., 1949), pp. 113–16.
42. Josiah Strong, *The New World-Religion* (New York, 1915), pp. 284–85, 299.

Gladden, like Strong, was a pioneer in the social gospel, but his emphasis fell more on the revival of another millennial theme, that of the exemplary nation. Though basically optimistic, many Protestant liberals were troubled by the evidence of social injustice and distress accompanying the adolescent industrial capitalism of the United States. Hence they returned to the plea for national righteousness, seeking now the perfection of the American community through moderation of competition and adherence to justice, service, and brotherhood. In achieving this harmony, the nation would enlighten all mankind. They, like their forebears, still expected the United States to conduct all peoples to the kingdom.[43]

One reasoned expression of this "nationalism" of the social gospel was Gladden's foreign missions address, "The Nation and the Kingdom" (1909). Gladden looked for an imminent realization of the kingdom of God in history through the adoption of Christ's law of love, which was seen not only as a possible goal for society but as its practical and even inevitable basis. For, untroubled by past failures, he expected men of the future to live by the Golden Rule. Furthermore, in setting up his kingdom, God used national structures. "All these glowing promises made by the old prophets, of the triumphs yet to be won for the kingdom of God in the world, are made to the nation and not to the church." Since theocracy was "God's plan for every nation," America must lead the way in banishing injustice and establishing social harmony. Then will the example of "the holy nation, the socialized nation" result in "the transformation of the other nations into the same type of national life, with righteousness reigning and plenty and peace prevailing." Rejoicing in the "vital relation" between contemporary spiritual and national movements, Gladden even discerned the rise of the City of God, the New Jerusalem, taking place in the United States:

43. The postmillennial fervor of the social gospel is apparent in James Dombrowski, *Early Days of Christian Socialism in America* (New York: Columbia University Press, 1936), pp. 22 ff.; and Charles Howard Hopkins, *The Rise of the Social Gospel in American Protestantism, 1865–1915,* Studies in Religious Education, 14 (New Haven: Yale University Press, 1940).

God has commissioned this nation, within the last few years, in some unwonted and impressive ways, to show the non-Christian nations what Christianity means; and in that call is a mighty summons to the Christians of this country to illuminate and enforce the message of the nation, to clothe it with crowning light and constraining love.

And at last all nations were "beginning to discern something of the loftiness of our national ideals, and to turn with wistful hope to America for leadership." [44]

Last, modern versions of the nation's millennial destiny were no longer exclusively, nor—in time—even predominantly, the property of Protestant heirs of the tradition. By its very diffuseness modern "millennialism" had been readily absorbed by Americans of every creed or none in the increasingly pluralistic post–Civil War society. It mattered little that thousands were Catholic or Jewish, unchurched "Protestants" or premillennial fundamentalists. All could share the inchoate conviction that the Republic constituted a divinely favored nation, fundamentally honest in a guilty world, doing God's will and fulfilling a worthy mission in directing all peoples to democracy, progress, and civilization. While a long succession of clerical and rabbinical patriots voiced these ideas, the real beneficiary was the "fourth faith," the growing phenomenon of generalized religion clustering about American democracy. Though certainly not new, this democratic faith had become more visible in the twentieth century as a genuinely catholic confession for Americans troubled by religious pluralism, the decline of the churches, and finally the subsidence of the older Protestant nationalism. [45]

Here statesmen and journalists, guardians of the public faith, were the appropriate evangelists. Always present in patriotic editorial and public ritual, this faith became most explicit when

44. Washington Gladden, "The Nation and the Kingdom: Annual Sermon before the American Board of Commissioners for Foreign Missions" (orig. pub. Boston, 1909), in *The Social Gospel in America, 1870–1920: Gladden, Ely, and Rauschenbusch,* ed. Robert T. Handy (New York: Oxford University Press, 1966), pp. 135–53.
45. See Martin E. Marty, *The New Shape of American Religion* (New York: Harper & Row, 1959), pp. 67 ff. for analysis. A sophisticated plea for democratic religion is in J. Paul Williams, *What Americans Believe and How They Worship* (New York: Harper & Bros., 1952), pp. 363–75.

threatened. During World War II, in the only sermon ever composed by federal bureaucracy, clergy of all faith were instructed to show how "free men in the excellent fellowship of faith, we can go forward not only to create a nation dedicated to liberty but to build a world of brotherhood fit to be called the Kingdom of God."[46] The subsequent cold war contest with "godless communism" offered further opportunities for recital of America's mission to advance God's will for democracy, civil and religious freedom, and international harmony. "You know what makes America great?" asked Richard Nixon in 1960.

> What makes her great is not our military strength, nor our economic richness, but the fact that we believe in the right things—our faith—our faith in God, our faith in the rights of man; that those rights to freedom, to independence, don't come from men, but come from God, and, therefore, can never be taken away by any man; our belief that America came into the world 180 years ago not just to have freedom for ourselves, but carry it to the whole world. . . . Strengthen the faith of America. See that our young people grow up with faith in God, recognizing that this is a great country, recognizing that the ideals that we have belong not just to us, but to the world, recognizing that America has a mission, and that mission is to keep the peace. That mission is to stand for freedom for ourselves and for others as well. That mission is to lead the world to a world in which all men can live together in friendship, in which all men can have the right to worship God, in which all men can have freedom.

And Nixon, fresh from travels across the country, claimed universality for "this belief, this idealism of the American people, . . . a shining idealism that I see . . . on the faces of millions throughout America." [47]

46. The sermon outline, entitled "Religion and Democracy," was issued by the U.S. Office of Civilian Defense, November 3, 1941. It sought to demonstrate that (1) religion is the source of democracy; (2) democracy gives religion its best opportunities; and (3) democracy and religion can together build the good society. The text is printed in Anson Phelps Stokes, *Church and State in the United States*, 3 vols. (New York: Harper & Bros., 1950), 3:893 ff.
47. Richard M. Nixon, in a speech at Wheaton College Field, Illinois, on October 29, 1960, published in *The Final Report of the Committee on Commerce, United States Senate . . . , Part II: The Speeches, Remarks, Press Conferences, and Study Papers of Vice-President Richard M. Nixon, August 1 through November 7, 1960* (Washington: Government Printing Office, 1961), p. 878.

"American religion is distinctive . . . precisely for the fact that the aspirations it nurtured have found profane embodiments." [48] This thesis may find fresh support in the career of the millennial idea. Today, faith in America's world-redemptive mission is largely a secularized confidence, without sense of grace or judgment alike, while religious opinion, distrustful of the earlier easy nationalism and utopianism, has all but abandoned the theme. Yet for over a century the idea of the elect Republic played a significant role in imparting a distinctive quality to American religion.

Its success in winning this consensus was in large measure related to its breadth and utility. To the novelty and rootlessness of American history it brought a compensating historical grandeur. On diverse peoples and churches it conferred a unifying trust. By it the dynamic of theocratic reform and the conservative instinct were held together. Men labored zealously for the coming kingdom, yet the coming kingdom also affirmed the worth of existing institutions as acceptable bases for the growth to perfection. Most importantly, it seemed to balance and join divergent aspects of national experience—convictions of divine and human sovereignty, theocracy and liberty, providence and nature, reverence for the Pilgrim fathers and for the founding fathers.

In substance, that career underscores an essential continuity in American religion throughout the nineteenth century. Recent reinterpretation of church history has stressed the integrity of the period between the Second Awakening and the Great Depression, despite the "great divide" of the Civil War. [49] Here was the search for a Christian America, and the vision of the nation as "proto-millennium" gave verve and confidence to the quest. At length, however, the great change came. Religious recession in the 1920s signaled a coming transformation, prevailing liberal assumptions

---

48. William A. Clebsch, *From Sacred to Profane America: The Role of Religion in American History* (New York: Harper & Row, 1968), p. 14.
49. See Robert T. Handy, *The Protestant Quest for a Christian America, 1830–1930*, Facet Books, Historical Series, 5 (Philadelphia: Fortress Press, 1967); and Winthrop Still Hudson, *American Protestantism*, Chicago History of American Civilization (Chicago: University of Chicago Press, 1961).

fell victim to the disastrous succession of twentieth century calamities and a new theological realism, and America passed into the post-Protestant decades.[50]

By the 1960s the relation of American Christianity to a partially deconsecrated Republic was not yet clear, nor had credible new forms of national or religious self-identification been established. Although religious testimony varied, it seemed that the churches generally expressed a new critical and theological awareness fatal to visions of worldly millennia or national innocence and were more genuinely sensitive to the limits of history and the failures of men and institutions. Correspondingly, there appeared to be some growing recognition that the passing of the older myth offered fresh opportunities for recovering a sense of the integrity of the Christian community and redefining the church's relation to the general culture. From that vantage point Americans could look back with some detachment, wonder, and perhaps nostalgia on the deep sense of special vocation and promise long confessed in their churches:

> BEHOLD the expected time draw near,
> The shades disperse, the dawn appear;
> Behold the wilderness assume
> The beauteous tints of Eden's bloom.[51]

50. Paul A. Carter, *The Idea of Progress in Most Recent American Protestant Thought, 1930–1960,* Facet Books, Historical Series, 11 (Philadelphia: Fortress Press, 1969).
51. *Psalms and Hymns Adapted to Social, Private, and Public Worship in the Presbyterian Church in the United States of America* (Philadelphia, 1843), hymn 561.

9

The Voluntary Principle in the Forming
of American Religion

JAMES LUTHER ADAMS

THE DEFINITION OF VOLUNTARYISM

Several years ago at the annual meeting in Boston of the American Philosophical Association three philosophers from Russia were guest lecturers on the program. One afternoon during the conference I joined several other Americans for a closeted discussion with these Russian philosophers. Inevitably, questions regarding freedom of speech in Soviet Russia and in the United States were introduced into the discussion. The guest philosophers were quick to assert that in Russia today the citizen is allowed this freedom. Accordingly, they claimed that Soviet Russia is fundamentally democratic. At this juncture one of the Americans responded that freedom of speech is scarcely sufficient to meet the criteria of democracy, that the crucial question is whether there is freedom of association, the freedom of citizens to organize a group to promote an idea or a cause and particularly to promote a cause that may be in conflict with the policies of the establishment, in short, the freedom to organize dissent. The interpreters, however, were unable successfully to communicate this question to the guests, even though they made a persistent attempt. The Russians insisted that they could not see the significance of this question about freedom of association.

After the discussion came to an end and when we Americans were out in the corridor, a British Marxist philosopher who had

217

served as one of the interpreters assured us that the guests from Russia simply could not afford to understand the question. Actually, the Russians might well have pointed to certain limited forms of freedom of association which obtain today in Russia. On the other hand, they could have pointed to the infringements upon freedom of association in the United States which were characteristic of the Joseph McCarthy period, and today they could point to the recent report that about three-fourths of the 1,136 people interviewed under the auspices of the Columbia Broadcasting System said that "extremist" groups should not be permitted to organize demonstrations against government policy, even if there appeared to be no clear danger of violence. In the midst of a war in which over forty thousand Americans have been killed, the government, according to this view, may draft men into a war they oppose, yet these men should not be permitted to exercise their First Amendment right to demonstrate nonviolently against such action. Here we see the disposition on the part of many Americans to limit severely the freedom of association. At the same time those Americans no doubt would claim that the United States is "the land of the free."

Why do we in entering upon a discussion of voluntaryism introduce this issue regarding freedom of association? Precisely because it impinges in a crucial way upon the definition of the term *voluntaryism*. One frequently encounters the definition of "the voluntary principle" as simply the freedom of the individual— for example, freedom of belief or of speech or of self-determination. At other times voluntaryism is defined as the rule of persuasion instead of coercion. These features, to be sure, belong to voluntaryism, but definitions of this sort fall short of grasping its essential social meaning, for they center attention too much upon the individual as an isolated entity; thus they fail to take explicitly into account the institutional ingredient, namely, the freedom to form, or to belong to, voluntary associations that can bring about innovation or criticism in the society. Voluntaryism in this institutional sense distinguishes the democratic society from any other.

Yet, as we have observed, it is by no means exempt from attack in our society. The reason is that freedom of association, viewed as a social function in the open society, represents a dynamic institutional force for social change or for resistance to it. As such, the voluntary association brings about differentiation in the community, a separation of powers.

Voluntaryism, then, involves more than an attitude in favor of freedom of choice. Many people entertain *attitudes* in favor of freedom, but socially effective freedom requires participation in associations that define or redefine freedom and that attempt to articulate or implement that freedom in a specific social milieu. Voluntaryism is an associational, institutional concept. It refers to a principal way in which the individual through association with others "gets a piece of the action." In its actual articulation it involves an exercise of power through organization. It is the means whereby the individual participates in the process of making social decisions. This process, particularly when it affects public policy, requires struggle, for in some fashion it generally entails a re-shaping, and perhaps even a redistribution, of power. This means that it demands a special commitment and expenditure of directed energy in the institutional context of the society.

All of these features—the institutional articulation, the strong commitment, the expenditure of energy, the redistribution of power, the separation of powers—are to be seen in the social phenomena that belong under the rubric of voluntaryism in the modern period. These phenomena include the separation of church and state, the creation of the voluntary church, the invention of other voluntary associations for social reform or for the revitalization of the church, the missionary movement, the anti-slavery movement, the woman-suffrage movement, the emergence of the denomination as a new form of the church, the ecumenical movement, the demand for the welfare state and then for its re-form, the civil rights movement, the struggle of the blacks for a "piece of the action," and hundreds of other group formations—

including groups to oppose such movements. The "table of contents" of the history of voluntaryism and its associations would itself require a large volume, for the number of associations is legion.

Obviously, the institutional dimensions of existence do not exhaust the human condition. The individual is by no means enclosed in the institutional associations. Forms of privacy remain and play an indispensable role. In this realm of privacy the individual's inner life takes shape, as well as the intimate interpersonal relations of his daily existence. There are three dimensions in this realm of privacy: the individual's relation to the creative and redemptive forces available, his relation to himself (his inner dialogue); and his immediate relations to other persons. So understood, however, the realm of privacy cannot properly be separated from the institutional associations of which we have spoken. The inwardness and integrity of privacy affect, and are affected by, the institutional associations.

The family is of course the most important of these associations, particularly by reason of the nurture received by the child in infancy and childhood and also by reason of the normally stabilizing power of the family throughout life. It is therefore impossible to separate privacy from life in the family and in the primary groups of friendship and neighborhood. But the inwardness and integrity of the individual impinge also upon the other associations, that is, upon the political order and upon the various voluntary associations, including the church. Moreover, one's conception of privacy will itself be affected by these associations in the society. From participation in these associations the individual learns to assess the significance of the inner life, and from this participation he also comes to define the forms of privacy which give depth and richness of quality to all of life. Of equal significance is the fact that the formal associations depend for their health and integrity upon the inwardness and independence of individual existence, in short, upon that dynamic substance of the self which transcends all associations. On the other hand, if privacy is itself to achieve order and openness and creative integrity, it requires the disciplines of the inner life which may be defined and nurtured by associations that exist for this purpose. This whole dimension of existence is presupposed by the formal associations of the political and social order. We say that it is presupposed, for only from the subsoil of privacy do the deeper motivations of human existence emerge, and from this subsoil the formal associations receive much of their vitalizing, integrating energy.

THE HISTORICAL ORIGINS OF VOLUNTARYISM

Voluntaryism did not come into history, ancient, medieval, or modern, without dust and heat. We cannot here trace this thrust into the dark backward and abysm of time. But we should observe that in the history of Christianity the first expression of voluntaryism appears in the primitive church, a voluntary association. In referring to the voluntaryism of the primitive church, however, we should not overlook the fact that the concept of voluntary association is not wholly adequate, for the Christian viewed the church in its origin and development as the work of divine grace, and thus its ultimate orientation was transcendent. Yet on the human side the church was a voluntary association. The church appealed to the individual for a voluntary decision to join the movement. It rejected civic religion, the rule of Caesar and of territoriality in the sphere of religious commitment and faith; it transcended the ethnic bonds of traditional Judaism; it gave to the individual certain responsibilities in the new organization; it was open to people of all classes and races; it gave new status to the common man, to the slave, and to women; and it soon developed forms of responsibility with respect to charity and philanthropy; it even formed credit unions. But the institutional aspects of the early church included also other features. In order to become viable this primitive church had to develop new skills of communication and of organization. Primitive Christianity, then, did not only promote new attitudes; nor is it to be understood merely in terms of its message, its kerygma. It gave institutional incarnation to a new covenant, a new commitment, a new community. Indeed, in order to continue to exist it formed an institution that could bear its message to the world—an institution that in important respects adumbrated or illustrated the meaning of the message in its social consequences. Here we see one of the great innovations in the history of the West. More than that, the ethos and organization of the early church again and again served as a stimulus or model for new forms of voluntaryism.

In modern history the first crucial affirmation of voluntaryism as an institutional phenomenon appeared in the demand of the sects for the separation of church and state. In England, for example, and then later in America, the intention was to do away with direct state control of the church and also to remove official ecclesiastical influence from the political realm—toward the end of creating a voluntary church. In the voluntary church, religious faith as well as membership was to be a matter of individual choice. The individual was no longer automatically to become a member of the church simply by reason of his being born in the territory. Moreover, he could choose not to be a member of a church. Nor was rejection of the established confession any longer to be considered a political offense or to deprive the unbeliever of the civil franchise. In rejecting state control, the church (and the theological seminary) were no longer to be supported by taxation. The objection to taxation in support of the church was twofold: tax support, it was held, not only gave the state some right of control; it also represented a way of coercing the nonmember or the unbeliever to give financial support to the church. Freedom of choice for the individual brought with it another freedom, namely, the freedom to participate in the shaping of the policies of the church group of his choice. The rationale for this voluntaryism was worked out theologically by the sectarians of the sixteenth and seventeenth centuries, and more in terms of social and political theory by John Locke in the next century.

From the point of view of a theory of associations, the demand for the separation of church and state and the emergence of the voluntary church represent the end of an old era and the beginning of a new one. The earlier era had been dominated by the ideal of "Christendom," a unified structure of society in a church-state. In the new era the voluntary church, the free church, no longer supported by taxation, was to be self-sustaining; and it was to manage its own affairs. In the earlier era, kinship, caste, and restricted community groups had determined most of the interests and the forms of participation. In the new era these interests became segregated. In this respect the freedom of choice was increased. The divorce of church and state and the advent of freedom of religious association illustrate this type of increase in freedom of choice.

In accord with this new conception of religious freedom and responsibility one must view the collection plate in the church service on Sunday as a symbol of the meaning of disestablishment and of voluntaryism. The collection plate symbolizes—indeed it in part also actualizes and institutionalizes—the view that the church as a corporate body is a self-determinative group and that in giving financial support to the church the members affirm responsibility to participate in the shaping of the policies of the church. Thus the voluntary principle amounts to the principle of consent. One must add, however, that although the struggle for voluntaryism on a large scale in the church began over two hundred and fifty years ago, it was not achieved generally and officially in the United States until the nineteenth century—that is, apart from the colonies that from the beginning had had no establishment.

The thrust toward the separation of church and state could succeed only by carrying through a severe struggle for freedom of association. Initially, the authorities who opposed it asserted that the health of society was threatened by the voluntary principle. They held that uniformity of belief was a prerequisite of a viable social order. As a separation of powers, voluntaryism was viewed as a wedge for chaos. In order to defend the unrestricted sovereignty of the commonwealth, Thomas Hobbes published in 1651 *Leviathan,* the most cogent attack of the times upon the voluntary principle. In his view the church should be only an arm of the sovereign.[1] Indeed, no association of any sort was to exist apart

1. See "Hobbes's Theory of Associations in the Seventeenth-Century Milieu," by D. B. Robertson, in the volume edited by him, *Voluntary Associations* (Richmond: John Knox Press, 1966).

from state control. Therefore he spoke of voluntary associations, religious or secular, as "worms in the entrails of the natural man" (the integrated social whole). Analogous attacks upon the voluntary church came also from conservatives in the American colonies where establishment prevailed.

Hobbes recognized that freedom of religious association would bring in its train the demand for other freedoms of association. His fears were fully justified. Indeed, with the emergence of this multiple conception of freedom of association a new conception of society came to birth—that of the pluralistic, the multigroup, society.

THE THEORY OF ASSOCIATIONS

The pluralistic conception of society entails a modern view of the relations between the community and the state and other associations.[2] According to this view, the institutional system is made up of a complex of involuntary and voluntary associations. The state and the family are involuntary in the sense that one cannot choose whether or not he will belong to a state or to a family; nor can he ordinarily choose his state or his family. Other associations are voluntary in the sense that one may choose to belong or not to belong. Of central significance for voluntaryism within the context of these associations is the claim that the community at large is the embracing association within which the other associations live. The state is one of these associations. It is the creature and the servant of the community, not its creator. The state therefore is not omnipotent or omnicompetent. Between the individual and the involuntary associations of state and family stand the voluntary associations that provide forms of freedom which transcend both the family and the state and which may also exercise some influence upon both of these institutions. The plural-

2. A more elaborate, and more subtle, conceptual framework than the one chosen here would enable one to identify aspects of society which our scheme does not directly delineate. For example, the differentiation between communal and associational types of group, drawn from Ferdinand Tönnies, has been widely used, as in Gerhard Lenski, *The Religious Factor* (Garden City: Doubleday & Co., 1961). Each of these frameworks has its characteristic advantages and disadvantages.

ist society, then, is not a mere aggregate of individuals. It is a group of groups that in turn are made up of individuals.

The individual is not viewed here as wholly comprehended in the community or the state or the family or the other associations. He possesses an integrity and freedom of his own. Luther hints at this idea of privacy when he says that everyone must do his own believing. For him and for other Protestants the individual has direct access to the divine in and through and beyond all institutions and all human mediators. Yet in the developed theory and practice of pluralism the individual's freedom is articulated in the choices he confronts or contrives in the context of these associations. The dependence of the individual upon these intermediary associations for freedom is succinctly stated by the British historian J. N. Figgis: "More and more is it clear that the mere individual's freedom against an omnipotent state may be no better than slavery; more and more is it evident that the real question of freedom in our day is the freedom of smaller unions to live within the whole." [3] In this view of man and his associations, we have the rudiments of a doctrine of man and also the framework for a philosophy of history. Man is an associational being, and his history is the history of his associations. The history of any open society is the history of the changing character of the associations, and of the changing relations between the individual and the associations, and of the changing relations between the various associations.

In the light of this conception of man and history we may see the historical significance of the advent of voluntaryism wherever it appears, and especially its significance for the formation and the expression of the religious mentality. These features became evident in the colonies of the New World.

Voluntaryism in the New World

In its initial stages the development of voluntaryism in the New World varied considerably in the different colonies, though

3. J. N. Figgis, *Churches and the Modern State*, 2d ed. (New York: Longmans, Green & Co. 1914), p. 52.

in the course of time essentially the same dominant tendencies appeared. These tendencies exhibited voluntaryism as the burgeoning characteristic feature of the religious mentality in this part of the world.

In New England and the South the old conception of establishment had been transported from England. The colonists in the middle region, on the other hand, were committed to disestablishment. Here as well as in New England variants on covenant theory played a large role. Given the absence of any establishment in the middle colonies, the churches there could affirm and implement their voluntaryism without any significant struggle with proponents of establishment, and therefore without the necessity for compromise with establishment. From the start, then, these were voluntary, "gathered" churches; so it was unnecessary for them to carry on a struggle for freedom of association. That struggle had been ended by their leaving the Old World. So strong was the spirit of independence that for well over a century these churches held out against any strong centralized organization. This spirit of independence appeared also in the colonies where an establishment prevailed. Indeed, long before disestablishment was officially legitimated, the laity had asserted itself in the management of the congregation. Moreover, by reason of geographical factors local autonomy was practically unavoidable. Here voluntaryism and localism worked hand in hand.

But in all of the colonies a deterioration of energy—we might call it the law of entropy—served to alter the development of voluntaryism. Whereas there was a great release of energy in religious circles in early days, this energy became less readily available as the temperature of commitment diminished. Through adoption of the halfway covenant, for example, the New England churches recognized a changing identity in the succession of the generations. With the increasing number of the unchurched in all of the colonies, the problem of maintaining church commitment became all the more acute. This commitment could not be automatically transmitted from generation to generation. What initially had been a voluntary self-sustaining church gradually became a church seeking to elicit commitment and voluntary support. A new voluntaryism had to be promoted. Faced with this change, the churches in all regions found it necessary to employ the techniques of persuasion "in order to win support and gain recruits by voluntary means." [4] The Great Awakening and the subsequent revivals are to be understood in part in these terms. The law of entropy could be countered only by the attempt to activate the voluntary principle in new ways.

This attempt involved the adoption of new means and forms of communication—the itinerant preacher, the psychic excitement of revivals, the dissemination of tracts, the distribution of Bibles, and even a new rhetoric. In this effort the churches, themselves voluntary associations, began at the end of the eighteenth century to form new, specialized voluntary organizations as instrumentalities to carry out the task of persuasion. Some of these new associations were supported by several denominations in cooperation. This sort of cooperation became even more widespread in the nineteenth century. A full roster of voluntary associations founded before the end of the first quarter of the century would be long. We name only a few of them: The Missionary Society of Connecticut (1798), the Massachusetts Missionary Society (1779), the New Hampshire Missionary Society (1801), the Massachusetts Baptist Domestic Missionary Society (1802), the American Board of Commissioners of Foreign Missions (1810), the American Bible Society (1816), The American Sunday School Union (1824), the American Tract Society (1825), the American Home Mission Society (1826), and so on. By the 1830s many of these "benevolent societies" met every May in New York so that the interlocking directorates could be in ready communication with each other.

The formation of some of these missionary associations brought about severe conflict when they were autonomous and sought to raise funds outside the denominational organizations, thus avoiding accountability to these organizations. In this connection Elwyn

4. Winthrop S. Hudson. *Religion in America* (New York: Charles Scribner's Sons, 1965), pp. 16, 105.

Smith has shown that the willingness of the church groups to enter into cooperation in the formation of intergroup associations may be taken as a sign of the emergence of a new church form. The sect became a denomination, a type of association that combined "the separative and the unitive spirit of American Christianity" and which became "the fundamental church structure of the country." [5]

It should be noted here that this proliferation of associations not only provided a means for concentration upon special purposes; it also offered new definitions of vocation and even of self-identity; accordingly, it gave occasion for the release of new energies in new directions of voluntaryism.

A new stage of development is marked by the rise of non-ecclesiastical associations concerned with specific problems, social and political. In the eighteenth century these associations began to appear with variety of purpose. In the developing frontier all sorts of land development companies were formed. Later, the mounting opposition to British colonial policies gave rise to a multitude of associations both local and interprovincial. In the 1740s the Masonic Order appeared on the stage—though, to be sure, encountering continuous opposition. For a time Benjamin Franklin served as provincial grand master of the Masons. He also formed or belonged to several international societies concerned with learning and with politics. Not without knowledge of Cotton Mather's earlier proposals for the formation of associations "to do good," Franklin showed himself to be one of the major initiators of local and national voluntary organizations concerned with educational, philanthropic, and civic purposes. He also instituted the American Philosophical Society, America's oldest learned society.

After the Revolution, freewheeling political activities issued in local associations concerned with opposing views on public policy. For example, associations disseminating pro-French propaganda elicited countervailing associations. So vigorous were these associations and so intense were the disagreements that President

5. Elwyn Smith, "The Forming of a Modern American Denomination," *Church History* 31 (1962):97.

Washington in his Farewell Address warned against "all combinations and associations, under whatever plausible character, with the real design to direct, control, counteract, or awe the regular deliberation and action of the constituted authorities." This formulation approximates the kind of statement that had become familiar in the opposition to freedom of religious association. It is perhaps significant that although the First Amendment to the Constitution protects freedom of speech and assembly and rules out the establishment of religion, it makes no explicit mention of freedom of association. Nevertheless, by the end of the first quarter of the nineteenth century the country was alive with associations, religious, quasi-religious, and secular.[6] During the nineteenth century thousands of these associations were formed. Already in the 1830s religious periodicals were saying that the benevolent societies had grown beyond the most sanguine expectations of their founders; the revenues were "such as kings might envy; together they formed a benevolent empire," "a gigantic religious power . . . systematized, compact in its organization, with a polity and a government entirely its own, and independent of all control."[7] Yet most of the societies here referred to were less than ten years old.

THREE AMERICAN PROTESTANT THEORIES OF ASSOCIATION

Starting early in the nineteenth century, a Protestant literature on "the principle of association" began to appear. Testimony regarding the ways in which this voluntaryism was giving shape to American religion in its moral and social outreach is found in the writings of three of the principal theorists, Lyman Beecher, Francis Wayland, and William Ellery Channing—a Presbyterian, a Baptist, and a Unitarian—men who differed from each other as much in theology as they agreed with each other on the significance of associations.

6. A classical, compact study of this development appears in Arthur M. Schlesinger, Sr., "Biography of a Nation of Joiners," in *Paths to the Present* (New York: Macmillan Co., 1949).
7. These quotations are cited from religious journals of the 1830s. See G. H. Barnes, *The Antislavery Impulse 1830–1844* (Gloucester, Mass.: Peter Smith, 1957), p. 17.

Continuing an interest acquired in 1797 as a student under the influence of a religious revival at Yale, Beecher preached in favor of the formation of societies for the suppression of vice and "the promotion of morality." He viewed these societies as watchdogs and aides in support of the magistrates' efforts to enforce the laws. The vices mentioned for correction were swearing, drinking, gambling, playing cards, and dueling. Moreover, the laws of several of the states prohibited blasphemy, atheism, Sabbath breaking, and other gross violations of general Christian morality. The societies were to "constitute a sort of disciplined moral militia, prepared to act upon every emergency and repel every encroachment upon the liberties and morals of the state." [8] They were also to promote the careful selection of law enforcers and to lend them "support requisite to the full discharge of their official trust." [9] These efforts were calculated also to "prepare the way for the acceptance of such offices by men who will be faithful." [10] The branch societies were to scrutinize the character of schoolteachers and tavern keepers; they could also encourage boycotts of businesses run by those who violated the moral law as set forth in the Bible. In these efforts the clergy and the laity were to cooperate.

The rationale for the formation of voluntary societies Beecher coupled with a defense of the establishment (in Connecticut). Soon after disestablishment in 1818, he came to approve the fact that it "cut the churches loose from dependence on state support. It threw them wholly on their own resources and on God." [11] In 1826 he preached a sermon to praise the effectiveness of voluntary associations. "Now we are blessed," he says, "with societies to aid in the support of the Gospel at home, to extend it to the

8. Lyman Beecher, "Sermons, Delivered on Various Occasions," in *Works,* 3 vols. (Boston: John P. Jewett & Co., 1852), 2:94.
9. Lyman Beecher, *Address of the Connecticut Society for the Promotion of Good Morals to the Respective Branch Societies* (New Haven: no publisher named, 1814), p. 4.
10. Ibid.
11. Lyman Beecher, *The Autobiography of Lyman Beecher,* ed. Barbara M. Cross, 2 vols. (Cambridge, Mass.: Harvard University Press, Belknap Press, 1961), 1:253.

new settlements, and through the earth." [12] In these societies, he pointed out, the evangelicals of different types could unite in opposing rationalism and "infidelity." In association he saw strength. During his six-year pastorate in Boston, Beecher extended the range of purposes for associations by organizing or sponsoring at least a dozen societies, ranging in character and purpose from the Boston Lyceum to the Franklin Debating Society to the Young Men's Temperance Society to the Young Men's Christian Association. He supported the antislavery societies, and at the same time belonged to the American Colonization Society.

Beecher went beyond the confines of the parish and also beyond the boundaries of the "denominations," toward the end of promoting societies concerned with public policies as well as with private morals. This was, in effect, an extension of the voluntary principle to the sphere of public affairs. One can see in Beecher, however, a strong element of elitism, or what Sidney Mead has called paternalism.[13] A Federalist, he intended his voluntaryism mainly for the middle-class protectors of private and public morals rather than for underlings or "delinquents"—these were supposed to be under scrutiny and guidance. Indeed, he injected a vigorous spirit of intolerance into his crusading efforts. Beecher's attack on the Roman Catholics was probably a contributing cause for the burning of the Ursuline convent in Charleston, Massachusetts. Moreover, he apparently did not conceive of a voluntary association that could legitimately promote a cause fundamentally incompatible with his conception of Christian private or public morals. In any case, he was the head and fount of associational theory in American church life, though he did not work out a systematic theory regarding the relations between the voluntary and the involuntary associations.

The Reverend Francis Wayland (1796–1865), at one time president of Brown University, wrote extensively on associations both voluntary and involuntary. He was the author of *The Ele-*

12. Lyman Beecher, "Lectures on Political Atheism and Kindred Subjects, Together with Six Lectures on Temperance," in *Works*, 1:325.
13. Sidney E. Mead, *The Lively Experiment: The Shaping of Christianity in America* (New York: Harper & Row, 1963), pp. 97–98.

ments of Political Economy (1837), a popularization of Adam Smith's views and one of the most widely used textbooks of the period. As a Baptist, Wayland was a promoter of radically congregational polity. He opposed every kind of denominational centralization. He rejected also every attempt of the congregation to coerce the believer or the unbeliever, including any attempt of the congregation directly to regulate the behavior of members; the congregation was simply to "withdraw" from the recalcitrant deviant.

Unlike Beecher, Wayland attempted to work out a theory of associations which would relate the Christian to universal mental and moral "sensitivity" and also to natural religion. In the spirit of Bishop Joseph Butler he adopted an antiutilitarian system of conscience and duty. Natural religion and conscience, properly understood, together with Baptist voluntaryism, were viewed as conducive to the establishment of a coercion-free society. Mutual edification and education rather than compulsion, he surmised, would one day direct men's affairs. He viewed teaching as the counterpart of the church's preaching.

Wayland assigned to voluntary associations a crucial role, conceiving of them in contractual terms. The association was an instrumentality of conscience based upon contract. Just as commitment to Jesus Christ was the basis of the Christian voluntary church, and just as the autonomy of the individual believer must be protected there, so the voluntary association was a contractual arrangement, and the autonomous individual might not properly be coerced into any obligations he had not assumed freely upon entering the association. Since conscience was the basis of social order and also of authentic associations, the voluntary association was to serve to enhance individual conscience and responsibility. "Autonomy" was Wayland's watchword. Therefore voluntary associations of great size were to be viewed with skepticism and caution. They threatened always to pervert individual conscience and to dislocate responsibility.[14]

14. Francis Wayland, *The Limitations of Human Responsibility* (Boston: Gould, Kendall & Lincoln, 1838), pp. 103 ff. I am indebted for most of the citations here to a paper by Ronald M. Green on "The Social Philosophy of Francis Wayland," presented in a course at Harvard Divinity School on voluntary associations.

In the guidelines that Wayland set up for associations one can see the rudiments of a philosophy of voluntaryism which gives central place to the principle of consent. The purpose of an association and the manner of pursuing it should be clear, and they should be agreed to by all members. Moreover, they "should be perfectly and entirely innocent; that is, they must be such as are incapable of violating the rights of any human being." [15] Accordingly, he opposed abolition societies that demanded forced emancipation. He held that in face of the slaveholders the conscience-bound citizen should set an example "of the most delicate regard to their rights." Anyone "whose first act is an act of injustice" violates the dominion of right.[16]

In practice, however, the dominion of right would at times be egregiously violated not only by voluntary associations but also by "the civil society." In this situation neither passive obedience to the state nor resistance to it by force was ethically justifiable. Here the conscientious citizen might find the only recourse to be "suffering in the cause of right." Wayland's view of "righteous suffering" approximates what we today call civil disobedience; it presents, he said, "the best prospect of ultimate correction of abuse by appealing to the reason and conscience of men . . . , a more fit tribunal to which to refer moral questions than the tribunal of force." [17]

It is worth noting that whereas Beecher's theory of associations was engendered initially in the milieu and spirit of an established church and of a firm authoritarianism, Wayland's conception derived primarily from his Baptist ecclesiology and from a sectarian heritage that had suffered from persecution at the hands of the establishment. Another contrast with Beecher is to be observed in Wayland's search for a universal religious-ethical basis, a sort of doctrine of natural law, in terms of which the Christian might cooperate with the unchurched. Most noticeable, however, is Way-

---

15. Ibid., p. 109.
16. Ibid., p. 182.
17. Francis Wayland, *The Elements of Moral Science,* ed. Joseph Blau (Cambridge, Mass.: Harvard University Press, Belknap Press, 1963), p. 337. For a discussion of the significance of the voluntary association in contemporary civil disobedience, see James L. Adams, "Civil Disobedience: Its Occasions and Limits," in *Political and Legal Obligation,* eds. J. Roland Pennock and John W. Chapman (New York: Atherton Press, 1970).

land's intention to develop with complete consistency the ramifications of the voluntary principle, the principles of persuasion and consent, not only giving special emphasis to the methods appropriate in associations but also stressing the rights and sensitivities of others in face of voluntary associations bent on persuasion. Nothing of Beecher's paternalism is to be found here. Fearful of the dangers of the crusading mentality, Wayland would have sympathized with the aphorism that was current in England during the period of the Restoration: "Nothing is more dangerous than a Presbyterian just off his knees." On the other hand, with his irenic temper he would scarcely have understood Nietzsche's claim that some things must be loved for more than they are worth if they are to make an impact on history. Moreover, with his stress on autonomy, he seems to have been little aware that autonomy is often the cloak for a hidden heteronomy. Such are the dilemmas of voluntaryism in an imperfect world.

William Ellery Channing's "Remarks on Associations" (1830) is the first systematic essay in American literature on voluntary associations. For this reason it is surprising that more attention has not been given to this treatise. By reason of his stress on freedom and autonomy, Channing stands much nearer to Wayland than to Beecher. Likewise, he recognizes the threats to autonomy provided by associations. Channing's essay reads very much like a document written today. He is aware of the relation between voluntary association and the modern technology of transportation, communications, and coalition. He even speaks of "the principle of association" as "a mighty engine."[18] "An impulse may be given in a month to the whole country, whole states may be deluged with tracts and other publications, and a voice like that of many waters, be called forth from immense and widely separated multitudes."

This essay is replete with psychological as well as sociological, ethical, theological, and political observations and analyses. Recognizing that man is an associational being, Channing takes a view

18. William Ellery Channing, *The Works of William E. Channing* (Boston: James Munroe & Co., 1848), 1:233.

quite different from that held, for example, by sociologist Ferdinand Tönnies, who a generation later in Germany wrote that voluntary associations represent a force of depersonalization in modern society issuing from rationalism and contractualism. "Men not only accumulate power by union, but gain warmth and earnestness. The heart is kindled," says Channing. Moreover, he sees the principle of association as a great releaser of energy. "By the feeling and interest which it arouses" union "becomes a creative principle, calls forth new forces, and gives the mind a consciousness of powers, which would otherwise have been unknown." [19]

Channing does not overestimate the significance and value of voluntary associations. He gives priority to what we have called the involuntary associations and to what he calls "those associations formed by our Creator, which spring from our very constitution, and are inseparable from our being." These associations are "the connections of family, of neighborhood, of country, and the great bond of humanity, uniting us with our whole kind." He clearly distinguishes these associations from "those of which we are now treating, which man invents for particular times and exigencies"—"missionary societies, peace societies, or charitable societies, which men have contrived."[20] He then proceeds to "illustrate the inferiority of human associations," by contrasting the pervasive and perduring benefits of the family "among the masses of men" with the limited number of people served by "asylums for children." Since he places the churches among the associations created by God he does not consider them under the rubric of the voluntary association (though he does of course favor the ecclesiology of the voluntary church—considered as established by God through Christ); and he contrasts the church with missionary societies, whose work he does not aim to discourage. The latter are not to be preferred to the church with its concern for "the common daily duties of Christians in their families, neighborhoods, and business." He notes that "the surest way of spreading Christianity is to improve Christian communities; and accordingly, he who

19. Ibid., pp. 283–84.
20. Ibid., p. 297.

frees this religion from corruption, and makes it a powerful instrument of virtue where it is already professed, is the most effectual contributor to the great work of its diffusion through the world." [21]

In the midst of the Great Awakening Jonathan Edwards wrote his *Treatise on the Religious Affections.* In an age when voluntary associations have become "a mighty engine," Channing presents in his "Remarks on Associations" a treatise on associations. Whereas Edwards deals only with individual behavior, Channing, with a moral social concern, deals also with institutional behavior. In his treatise he aims to suggest "a principle by which the claims of different associations may be estimated." In doing so, however, he gives primary status to the individual. In his explication of a criterion for the voluntary principle one finds a formulation of the essential intention of voluntaryism which Wayland could readily have approved. He states his major premise succinctly:

> The value of associations is to be measured by the energy, the freedom, the activity, the moral power, which they encourage and diffuse. In truth, the great object of all benevolence is to give power, activity, and freedom to others. We cannot, in the strict sense of the world, *make* any being happy. We can give others the *means* of happiness, together with motives to the faithful use of them; but on this faithfulness, on the free and full exercise of their own powers, their happiness depends. There is thus a fixed, impassible limit to human benevolence. It can only make men happy through themselves, through their own freedom, and energy. We go further. We believe that God has set the same limit to his own benevolence.[22]

The rest of Channing's essay is dedicated to the task of applying this criterion by examining typical associations in order to show that "associations which in any degree impair or repress the free and full action of men's powers, are thus far hurtful." He then

---

21. Ibid., pp. 298–302.
22. Ibid., pp. 302–3. Whereas motivations in the associational theories of Beecher and Wayland are related primarily to Congregationalist ecclesiology, we see in Channing's outlook motifs drawn in part from the Enlightenment and in part from Romanticism. For a systematic discussion of analogous changes in milieu and motif in the history of philanthropy from the colonial period to the present, see William G. McLoughlin, "Changing Patterns of Protestant Philanthropy, 1607–1969," in *The Religious Situation, 1969,* ed. Donald R. Cutler (Boston: Beacon Press, 1969).

proceeds to illustrate the ways in which certain associations repress human energy, stultify the intellect, pervert the moral powers, disseminate false information, and inflame public opinion to irrational and instinctual attitudes and behavior. Channing's warning that spurious voluntary associations will only create or entrench a sense of dependency is strikingly similar to current criticisms of undemocratically organized associations and also of the social agencies of the welfare state.

One of the principal ways in which voluntary associations "injure the free action of individuals and society" is through the accumulation of power in a few hands. There are two principal ways in which this centralization of power perverts human energies. First, voluntary associations may exercise inordinate influence on the public mind in the direction of encroaching on freedom of thought, of speech, and of the press. By artful manipulation "as cruel a persecution may be carried on in a free country as in a despotism . . . as if an inquisition were open before us." He does not spare the tract societies.

> Now, by means of Tract societies, spread over a whole community, and acting under a central body, a few individuals, perhaps not more than twenty, may determine the chief reading for a great part of the children of the community, and for a majority of the adults, and may deluge our country with worthless sectarian writings, fitted only to pervert its taste, degrade its intellect, and madden it with intolerance.[23]

Channing devotes pages to illustrating the ways in which associations can function to promote in the public at large "a servile, tame, dependent spirit" or can through internal oligarchic control exercise tyranny over the members of the association. Voluntary associations may disseminate narrow sectarianism, half-baked ideas, petty legalism, prying encroachments upon private life, and blatant chauvinism. It should be added here that Channing recurrently appeals to the example of Jesus, "that brightest manifestation of God," in order to emphasize the decisive significance of moral independence and integrity of motive for "resisting and

23. Ibid., p. 305.

overcoming the world." He also avers that "in no department of life has the social principle been perverted more into an instrument of intellectual thraldom, than in religion." [24]

At the same time, Channing views participation in voluntary associations as an indispensable means of exercising moral and citizenship responsibilities. He vindicates this claim by his own participation and by his voluminous writings on public issues. At least five highly significant associations were formed in his living room, including the Massachusetts Peace Society. Indeed, he ends his essay rather abruptly, saying that he had intended to "add some remarks on some other associations, particularly on the Peace Society." He then says of the "spirit of association": "We have done what we could to secure this powerful instrument against perversion." In setting forth the criteria of authentic association—or, we may say, of voluntaryism—his major presupposition, we have seen, is that "our connection with society, as it is our greatest aid, so it is our greatest peril." [25]

STRENGTHS AND WEAKNESSES OF VOLUNTARISM

If we now take a bird's-eye view of the development we have traced, we must speak of it as an organizational revolution. As such it represents the creation of space in modern society for associations, loyalties, and activities the like of which have not appeared anywhere to the same extent in previous history. These voluntary associations are significant not only in themselves but also by virtue of their influence on each other and upon the involuntary associations—for good or for ill. In the context of the present essay, however, their principal significance is their import for the shaping of American religion. As Channing suggests, the

24. Ibid., p. 295.
25. Ibid., p. 291. We have devoted these pages to the exposition of the ideas of Beecher, Wayland, and Channing, not only because one encounters in current literature only summary statements of their views, but also because their formulations provide *loci classici* of the voluntary principle. A more complete account, to be sure, would include an analysis of secular writings of the period which, like *The Federalist Papers,* set forth the dangers and values of voluntary associations. Especially instructive in these papers is the argument that pluralistic democracy would be seriously threatened if all the churches together were able to achieve one compact organization.

voluntary principle is "a creative principle." It functions as a creative principle by making way for free interaction and innovation in the spirit of community. Thus the church may remain open to influence from its members, from outside the church, and from the Holy Spirit; at the same time it assumes the responsibility of exercising influence in the community. The organizational prerequisite for this kind of interaction is the separation of powers, a separation that combines independence and interdependence and which looks toward the achievement of unity in variety. When, however, the voluntary principle is the sole principle, the question remains as to the source and character of the unity. To this question we shall return.

Not all of the churches adopted the voluntary principle without reservation. The Presbyterians and the Reformed, the Anglicans and the Lutherans in the nineteenth century rejected or severely criticized the principle insofar as it left the churches open to development in any direction that historical accident or the will of the members determined. Their resistance expressed itself in a variety of formulations. The voluntary principle, it was said, militated against any structured continuity within the rich organism of historical Christianity. For one thing, the heavy reliance, in the nineteenth century, of many of the voluntary churches on revivalism was a mixed blessing. Even where revivalism is now largely a thing of the past it has left a residue of subjectivity, erratic spontaneity, a mere sense of immediacy—with the consequence that many of these churches have shown little concern for theology or for history, for liturgical substance and form or for denominational structures.[26]

These old-line churches, however, were not alone in adversely criticizing this kind of voluntaryism. Channing, as we have already observed, criticized the bad taste, the irrationalities, the highly organized forms of ignorance, which were perpetrated by the voluntary societies set up by some of the churches. Thus one can

26. Cf. H. Shelton Smith, Robert T. Handy, and Lefferts A. Loetscher, *American Christianity: An Historical Interpretation with Representative Documents*. 2 vols. (New York: Charles Scribner's Sons, 1963), vol. 2, chap. 13.

say that the bulwark of bad taste, invincible ignorance, and wild "varieties of religious experience" is to be found in many of these voluntary churches. We shall return to this point later, in another connection.

Nevertheless, the churches that have opposed these vagaries have not been able to remain immune to the voluntary principle, as is evident especially in the similarity of the structures which obtains in the local parishes of these denominations and in those of the churches of pronounced voluntaryism. On the other hand, some of the "free churches," skeptical of the spontaneities and disruptions of revivalism, have been sensitive to the need for continuity and structure. Witness Horace Bushnell's critique a century ago of "the thunderclaps of grace" (the phrase comes from Jonathan Edwards), and his preference for "Christian nurture." Witness also his highly original analysis of language.

It would be exceedingly difficult to trace the influences back and forth in order to explain these varieties of, and changes in, religious consciousness and perception. Yet one can affirm that among the various types of churches, and in general in the pluralistic society, mutuality of influence obtains. This mutuality of influence appears not only between churches of different types but also between the churches and other associations.

The variety of voluntary associations, as we have already hinted, is almost beyond the power of unaided imagination to conceive. Their purposes have included prison reform, the prevention of cruelty to children and to animals, the establishment of schools and colleges, the conservation of natural resources, the protection of civil liberties, the attack on poverty, the improvement of race relations, the emancipation of women, church lobbies in Washington and at state capitals, the promotion of world peace, and so on. We have already mentioned the missionary societies, antislavery societies, and tract societies. Through participation in voluntary societies, members of many churches have been able to extend their perception of the social realities. Indeed, one can say that associations such as these provide the means whereby the churches achieve a knowledge of "the world." They are media through which the churches promote a vital relation between religion and culture. Like the voluntary churches, they serve also as the means for the achievement of skills of discussion and organization, and even the skills of listening. Consider, for example, the variety of knowledge and skills learned by church members, and especially by the women, in the missionary societies of the nineteenth century. In terms of skills these women might well be thought of as the spiritual ancestors of the League of Women Voters. The skills of which we speak were required initially by the men and women who were struggling for the right of freedom of association, the right to form a voluntary church. In the eighteenth century the Friends were conspicuous for their ingenuity in registering dissent and in bringing about changes in legislation.[27] These expressions of the voluntary principle have provided the occasions for the churches not only to influence other associations (including the state) but also to gain new perceptions from them, and even to gain broader conceptions of Christian responsibility.

This whole development, including the emergence of the voluntary church, probably would not have been possible without the tremendous expansion of economic resources in the modern period. Indeed, one can argue that the voluntary churches in their emergence and growth accompanied the emergence into modern history of the middle class. If we view the long historical perspective that embraces the development of the voluntary principle in Anglo-American history, however, we must see more than the emergence of the middle class. The voluntary principle was in some degree taken over into the political realm to confirm the demand for the extension of the franchise (for "government by consent") and even to promote the idea of the loyal opposition an an extension of the protection, instead of the persecution, of minority views.[28] From there the voluntary principle moved into the realm of private education; next, to the initiation of the labor

27. Norman Hunt, Exeter College, Oxford, has shown in convincing detail that the Friends in the early eighteenth century had already contrived all the essential methods we today associate with pressure groups. See his *Two Early Political Associations* (Oxford: Clarendon Press, 1961).
28. Cf. George H. Williams, "The Religious Background of the Idea of a Loyal Opposition," in Robertson, ed., *Voluntary Associations.*

movement; then, to the franchise for women, and in our day to the civil rights movement and the beginnings of a movement to promote black-empowerment. The voluntary principle has operated also in the transformation of the authoritarian family into the consensus family. All of these movements were, to be sure, opposed as well as supported by the voluntary churches.

We have spoken of the voluntary principle as the dimension in which the churches have been able with some concreteness to move in the direction of a theology of culture and to attempt to fulfill the mission of the church in a new age. This process could not take place without cooperation between church members and nonmembers. In this process the voluntary churches have learned to some degree that social order and social justice require them to cooperate even with those who do not agree with them regarding theological presuppositions or specifically Christian norms. At the same time this cooperation again and again has served to prevent the churches from making absolute claims; indeed, it has promoted the recognition that God can work through secular people and even through "infidels." Equally significant is the fact that in the twentieth century, cooperation (in voluntary associations) between Protestants and Roman Catholics became possible. Indeed, one of the documents (not yet published) of Vatican Council II proclaims it to be the responsibility of the Catholic to work with others in voluntary associations concerned with the common good. The cooperation in voluntary associations between members of different churches, Protestant and Roman Catholic, and between church members and nonmembers, is of such long standing that we may claim that it represents the oldest ecumenical movement. Possibly the existence of this sort of ecumenism explains the relative absence of significantly organized anticlerical movements in regions where the voluntary church has prevailed.

On the other hand, many of the voluntary churches and many voluntary associations as well have exhibited something less than democratic principles, not to speak of Christian perspectives. We think here not only of the Know-Nothing movement but also of the ways in which the voluntary churches have accommodated themselves to the segregations of our society—in terms of race, of class, of education, of occupation, and of neighborhood.

It is therefore reasonably fair to say that, whereas historically the voluntary churches revolted against the establishment of centralized ecclesiastical-political power, today, particularly in the middle and upper-middle classes, they represent the establishment. This observation becomes all the more pertinent if we take into account the fact that the views that obtain in the business community are almost normative for the churches.

In the light of these ambiguities in the attitudes and behavior of the churches one must conclude that the voluntary principle, taken alone, provides no guarantees with respect to the ends pursued or with regard to theological presuppositions. It does not guarantee even that there will be any interest in theology.[29] Accordingly, the spectrum of the voluntary churches reaches all the way from fundamentalism with its racism and nationalism to the churches that at least ostensibly adhere to more universal principles. The voluntary churches, however, have no monopoly on particularism and idolatry. It would be instructive to compare the performance of the voluntary churches with either that of the Old World state-churches or that of the American churches that stand in closer continuity with those state-churches with respect to theology or ecclesiology.

Actually, these ambiguities arise from the human condition itself. John Robert Godley, a British High Churchman who visited the United States in 1844, spoke to the point when he wrote regarding the American churches: "The reception by a people of any religious system will (humanly speaking) depend chiefly upon the prevalent habits of thought and feeling which exist among them; for our reason is biassed by our affections."[30] Religious

29. Cf. Robert T. Handy, "The Voluntary Principle in Religion and Religious Freedom in America," in Robertson, ed., *Voluntary Associations.*
30. John Robert Godley's essay appears in *The Voluntary Church: American Religious Life (1740–1865) Seen through the Eyes of European Visitors,* ed. Milton B. Powell (New York: Macmillan Co., 1967).

faith, as Augustine would say, is itself biased by the affections. Man becomes what he loves. And so with the church, voluntary or not.

THE REFORMATION OF REFORMATION

Since the time of its birth three or more centuries ago the voluntary church has moved more and more from nonconformity and dissent to conformity (and deformity). In the framework of associations the churches, by reason of the multiple institutional segregations of our society and by reason of the preferences nourished by these segregations, are today part and parcel of the poverty, the racism, and the nationalism of the social system. This must be said despite the large number of reformist associations that have been spawned. They simply have not been sufficient for the evil of the century. Actually, the proportion of the church membership which has participated in these associations has not been and today is not impressive. And even if the reader holds that it is so impressive as to give reason for pride, he must recognize that the racial segregation and the segregation and deprivation of the poor (of various colors) are today greater than they were two or three generations ago.

Many a churchman, to be sure, is concerned and is stricken in conscience. But we live in a society in which the most powerful associations are those which function in collusion with each other to make the involuntary association of the state serve primarily the interests of those who "have," to the detriment of those who "have not." We seem to be caught in a vise produced by the organizational and technological revolution.

In face of this situation one can bravely and rightly work for the creation of a more inclusive church,[31] and for the engendering of a piety and commitment that can serve as an effective, prophetic, nonconformist thrust. This is no mean task. It calls not only for theological reformation but also for associational reformation.

31. James M. Gustafson, "The Voluntary Church: A Moral Appraisal," in Robertson, ed., *Voluntary Associations*.

Tocqueville once suggested that a perennial temptation in a democracy, where liberty may be sought to the neglect of equality, is "lethargic somnolence." Unfortunately, the voluntary principle can serve as a sleeping pill as well as a stimulant. It may be the servant of ends and of binding attachments which in a time of somnolence are hidden assumptions.[32]

What, then, is the remedy? Certainly not the scuttling of the principle. That way lies tyranny. If the voluntary principle is to serve nourishing and prophetic purposes, the demand is for an understanding of the authentic ends of Christian piety and for the costly sacrifices that at least exhibit seriousness of commitment.

A special demand confronting the churches, then, is the demand for the reformation of reformation—the reformation of the voluntary principle. In the history of the church this function has been performed by a special kind of association, the *ecclesiola in ecclesia,* the small church in the large, which redefines Christian vocation in the changing historical situation. In the Middle Ages and also in the so-called Dark Ages monasticism functioned as an *ecclesiola.* In the modern period the *ecclesiola* has been the small group of firm dedication, which sometimes promotes the disciplines of the inner life, sometimes bends its energies to sensitize the church afflicted with ecclesiastical somnolence, sometimes cooperates with members of the latent church in the world to bring about reform in government or school or industry, or even to call for radical structural transformation.

To be sure, catastrophe can accelerate the process of reappraisal, but even then the commonwealth or the church cannot rise above the level of actual or latent spiritual integrity and power. The voluntary principle came to birth at the end of an era. In some quarters today it is held that we are approaching the end of an era. If we are, the increase in membership of the churches characteristic of our period gives little reason for encouragement, for it would appear in large part to bespeak the attractiveness of somnolence, that is, of devotion to self-serving and "religion" of privacy.

32. W. Alvin Pitcher, " 'The Politics of Mass Society': Significance for the Churches," in Robertson, ed., *Voluntary Associations.*

In any event, the voluntary principle, insofar as it pursues worthy ends, requires sharp critical judgment of the actualities and vigorous, though serene, commitments that can make freedom of association, religious or secular, the salt that has not lost its savor. These are issues that are forced upon us when we consider ways in which the voluntary spirit may contribute to an American or a Christian or a Jewish or any other kind of religion in a time of turmoil.

10

The Fact of Pluralism and the
Persistence of Sectarianism

SIDNEY E. MEAD

Any attempt to understand the religious situation in America must begin with recognition of the fact of pluralism. Philip Schaff, seeing this fact in historical perspective, declared in 1855 that the United States presented "a motley sampler of all church history, and the results it has thus far attained." [1] During the century since Schaff wrote, the pluralism has been augmented until, as Mr. Justice Brennan noted in the Murray-Schempp decision, religiously we are

> a vastly more diverse people than were our forefathers. They knew differences chiefly among Protestant sects. Today the Nation is far more heterogeneous religiously, including as it does substantial minorities not only of Catholics and Jews but as well of those who worship according to no version of the Bible and those who worship no God at all.[2]

In this essay I have attempted, first, to analyze some of the implications of this basic fact and, second, to note the persistence of "sectarian" reactions to it.

Traditionally in Christendom, and clearly after the Reformation and the emergence of nations, it was almost universally assumed that the being and continued well-being of a civil commonwealth

1. Philip Schaff, *America: A Sketch of Its Political, Social, and Religious Character,* ed. Perry Miller (Cambridge, Mass.: Harvard University Press, Belknap Press, 1961), p. 80.
2. Justice Brennan, concurring opinion in the Murray-Schempp decision of June 17, 1963, in *The Bible and the Public Schools . . . the Full Text of the Majority Concurring and Dissenting Opinions of the Court . . .* (New York: Liberal Press, 1963), pp. 95–96.

depended upon there being religious uniformity within it. The church was the institution that defined, articulated, and inculcated the common religious beliefs and actualized the proper forms of ecclesiastical structure, discipline, and worship. It was the guardian of the nation's tribal cult. Church and state were separate only in the sense that they had different functions in promoting the common end of both, which was the glory of God. The first charter and early laws for Virginia make this clear. They assert that the king's "principall care" in all his realms is "true religion, and reuerence to God." In keeping with this view, the laws were "declared against what Crimes soeuer, whether against the diuine Majesty of God, or our soueraigne, and Liege Lord, King James."

Here the established church was not abstract and invisible, but an institutionalized authority alongside the civil authority. Together they represented the institutionalized power structure of the *common*wealth. Clergy and magistrates represented two distinct but related authorities in the body politic, and most of the problems of church and state rose out of conflicts between them.

In this context the question of the relationship between church and state, while often puzzling, is at least definable because one is talking about the relation between two institutions, each represented by officials. As the state was the persons vested with the authority of civil government, so the church was the persons vested with the authority of ecclesiastical government.

This situation existed for so long in Christendom that there came to be practically universal intellectual acceptance and justification of "establishment."

With the emergence of a commonwealth with religious pluralism during the seventeenth and eighteenth centuries, something new appeared—or perhaps something as old as the pre-Constantinian Roman Empire reappeared. In any case it appeared to be so new in America that the founders defended it primarily as an experiment worth trying. The American experiment was to find out whether a commonwealth could exist and flourish "with a full liberty in religious concernments" and a plurality of religious groups, each claiming in traditional fashion exclusively to be "the church."

Such religious diversity had become an accepted fact of the experienced order of things without the intention of the nation's civil-ecclesiastical authorities. As Reinhold Niebuhr has put it,

> Most of the proponents of the various religious positions did not really believe in either freedom or toleration. Freedom came to the Western world by the providence of God and the inadvertance of history. Tolerance was an absolute necessity for a community which had lost its religio-cultural unity and could find peace only if toleration and freedom were accepted.[3]

By and large, in America civil authority forced toleration upon reluctant churchmen, most of whom finally saw that the only way they could get freedom for themselves was to grant it to all others.

But it is one thing for a religious group of necessity to accept and adapt outwardly to a radical change in the experienced order of events, and quite another thing to reformulate and accept the change in the conceptual order necessary to make it compatible with the changed experienced order thrust upon it by what A. N. Whitehead called the force of "senseless agencies." My suggestion is that as religious freedom became an inescapable fact of the experienced order—its newness evidenced by a multiplicity of religious groups in a commonwealth—churchmen and theologians were called upon to develop new concepts to enable new ways of explaining and defending what they accepted in practice.

We think by relating concepts. We experience concrete details, but we must think in abstract generalizations. My suggestion implies that the traditional concepts of Christendom ("church" and "state") used to think about the relationship between civil government and religious institutions are not applicable, and likely to be confusing, in attempting to think about the new situation created by the kind of religious freedom actualized in the American experiment.

3. Reinhold Niebuhr, "A Note on Pluralism," in *Religion in America: Original Essays on Religion in a Free Society,* ed. John Cogley (New York: Meridian Books, 1958), p. 43. See also Crane Brinton, *The Shaping of the Modern Mind* (New York: New American Library, 1953 [paperback]), p. 66. (*The Shaping of the Modern Mind* is the concluding half of *Men and Ideas* [orig. pub. Englewood Cliffs: Prentice-Hall, 1950 and 1953].)

In the United States "the church," in the sense that the words conveyed in Christendom for centuries, simply does not exist. "The church" is not an aspect of the American's experienced order. Rather it exists as an abstract concept, a figure of speech, a theological assertion, pointing beyond the actual and confusing diversity of sects to the pious faith that each is a part of the unbroken body of Christ. For this reason alone the old concepts of church and state no longer describe the actuality experienced. The church as such is not a recognized legal entity in the U.S. at all.[4] This is what the American observes and experiences.

What one sees and how he conceives it are of course inseparable. The unit is an observation. Details experienced are "invariably interpreted in terms of the concepts supplied by the conceptual order" which Whitehead describes as "a rough system of ideas in terms of which we do in fact interpret" our experiences.[5] In this context, novel observations ought sooner or later to be reflected in modifications of the conceptual order. But, and especially if the conceptual order of the observer has an aura of sacredness about it rooted in his unreflective acceptance of his religious tradition, he may cling to it, stubbornly thinking he ought to try to make the new experienced order again conform to it.[6]

4. The common legal view seems to be that the "provisions of the code for the incorporation of churches or religious societies, and all powers conferred thereunder, relate alone to their properties or temporalities, and have no reference to the churches or societies as such, which bodies, as spiritual or ecclesiastical organizations, exist independent of their charters." Therefore "wherever there is an incorporated church, there are two entities, the one, the church as such, not owing its ecclesiastical or spiritual existence to the civil law, and the legal corporation, each separate though closely allied." Quoted in John J. McGrath, *Church and State in American Law: Cases and Materials,* 1962), pp. 5–6. See also my "Neither Church nor State: Reflections on James Madison's 'Line of Separation,'" *A Journal of Church and State* 10 1968):349–63.

5. Alfred North Whitehead, *Adventures of Ideas* (New York: A Mentor Book [orig. pub. 1933]), pp. 158–59.

6. This seems to me one way of looking at the difference between the "progressive" and "conservative" church-state views of contemporary Roman Catholics which are so clearly presented by Thomas T. Love, *John Courtney Murray: Contemporary Church-State Theory* (Garden City: Doubleday Co., 1965). Central in Murray's position was his insistence that modern "lay" democracy (limited) was something new and to be distinguished from nineteenth century "laic" democracy (absolutistic). This was what induced him to make his tremendous reexamination of his church's inherited conceptual order.

This, I think, is the point at which theologians often find themselves at odds with Supreme Court justices. Theologians in discussing the relation between civil authority and their religion commonly attempt to make the profane civil matters conform to their sacred conceptual order—for example, the court's attempt to maintain the necessary religious neutrality of the civil authority is interpreted as a thrust toward the establishment of a "secular religion."[7]

We all face a very complex situation. A multiplicity of religious groups implies a great diversity of religious beliefs, each given more or less systematic intellectual structure in theological systems. And because a religious commitment is an all-or-nothing matter for the one who holds it, the builder of a theological system, whether amateur or professional, aspires to delineate a complete conceptual order. Pluralism means that two people may bring quite different conceptual orders to an event both experience. In this sense they live in different worlds, and insofar they simply do not, and cannot, "see" the same thing in it. Therefore, while everyone in the commonwealth may apparently share a commonly experienced order of events, the things seen do not have the same meaning for them. Consequently different people react quite differently to the same event—as witness the emotion-laden reactions to the school Bible reading and prayer decisions, or to the abolition of the Blaine Amendment in New York.

The confusion thus created is compounded because key words and phrases may mean quite different things in the context of different conceptual orders. Two persons may use the same words and phrases and each may think they are talking about the same thing, when actually their minds are not meeting at all. Obvious examples are the words *church, state, establishment, free exercise,* and, most confusing of all, *separation.* All the key words used in the discussion of the relation between civil authority and religion are for this reason ambiguous. Even the word *God* had become so ambiguous long before theologians announced his death that the

---

7. See, e.g., Mr. Justice Clark's opinion of the court in the Murray-Schempp decision, in *The Bible and the Public Schools (1967),* pp. 77–78.

Federal Communications Commission was led to declare in July 1946 that "so diverse are these conceptions that it may be fairly said, even as to professed believers, that the God of one man does not exist for another."[8] This is one of the most obvious results of our basic freedoms and consequent religious pluralism.

But the United States *is* a *common*wealth. We are all, as Thomas Jefferson held and James Baldwin says he discovered in Paris, "American."[9] To think about this sense of common identity as Americans one must, I believe, entertain some such concept as what philosopher A. N. Whitehead called "a general form of the forms of thought"[10] of an age and place; what anthropologist Ruth Benedict refers to as the constellation of "ideas and standards" that define a culture and bind its people together;[11] what economist Adolf A. Berle, Jr., defines as the "public consensus";[12] and what historian Ralph Gabriel calls "social ideas." These "ideas and standards" or the "general form" are of such high generality that they "rarely receive any accurate verbal expression." They are, as Whitehead put it, "hinted at through their special forms appropriate to the age in question," for example, in a cross, a flag, a star—through poetry, the arts, and rituals. For example, the flag

8. Federal Communications Commission, quoted in Anson Phelps Stokes, *Church and State in the United States* (New York: Harper & Bros., 1950), 3:246.
9. James Baldwin, "The Discovery of What It Means to Be an American," in *Nobody Knows My Name* (New York: Dell Publishing Co., 1963). This essay was first published in the *New York Times Book Review,* January 25, 1959.

Baldwin says he discovered in Europe, whither he had fled under "the illusion that I hated America," that "I proved, to my astonishment, to be as American as any Texas GI. And I found my experience was shared by every American writer I knew in Paris. Like me, they had been divorced from their origins, and it turned out to make very little difference that the origins of white Americans were European and mine were African—they were no more at home in Europe than I was" (pp. 23, 17–18).
10. Whitehead, *Adventures of Ideas,* pp. 19–20.
11. Ruth Benedict, *Patterns of Culture* (orig. pub. 1934), with a new preface by Margaret Mead (Boston: Houghton Mifflin Co., 1959), p. 16.
12. Adolf A. Berle, Jr., *Power without Property: A New Development in American Political Economy* (New York: Harcourt, Brace, & World, 1959), pp. 110–16.

is the symbol of the unity of America and what it stands for.[13]

Therefore, although the "ideas and standards" lie at the heart of a culture, usually they are but faintly impressed upon the conscious rational minds of the people in that culture. Yet within a culture the great conversation that makes a civilization possible can go on only because and so long as a significant number of the participants share these high generalities which provide the premises of the dialogue.

However, the participants in the heat of a discussion of controverted issues, speaking as each does out of his own set of specific notions, easily lose sight of the high generalities they share with all the others. Anyone who has lived in an academic community will immediately recognize the phenomenon to which Whitehead refers:

> It is difficult even for acute thinkers to understand the analogies between ideas expressed in diverse phraseologies and illustrated by different sorts of examples. Desperate intellectual battles have been fought by philosophers [and theologians] who have expressed the same idea in different ways.[14]

A striking example of such a battle is provided by the conflict between defenders of New England orthodoxy and the "infidels" during the late eighteenth and early nineteenth centuries. Although they never actually crossed swords, we may take Lyman Beecher of Connecticut and Thomas Jefferson as representatives of the respective parties. The prime premise of Jefferson's *Act for Religious*

13. Whitehead, *Adventures of Ideas,* pp. 19–20. Mr. Justice Frankfurter said (*Minersville School District* v. *Gobitis,* 310 U.S. 568 [1940]), " 'We live by symbols.' The flag is the symbol of our national unity, transcending all internal differences, however large, within the framework of the Constitution. This Court has had occasion to say that '. . . the flag is the symbol of the Nation's power, the emblem of freedom in its truest, best sense . . . it signifies government resting on the consent of the governed; liberty regulated by law; the protection of the weak against the strong; security against the exercise of arbitrary power; and absolute safety for free institutions against foreign aggression.' *Halter* v. *Nebraska.*" (In Joseph Tussman, ed., *The Supreme Court on Church and State* [New York: Oxford University Press, 1962], p. 83.
14. Whitehead, *Adventures of Ideas,* p. 175.

Freedom in Virginia was that the use of coercion in matters of religious belief was "a departure from the plan of the Holy Author of our religion, who being Lord both of body and mind, yet chose not to propagate it by coercions on either, as was in his Almighty power to do." The basic premise of Lyman Beecher's theological model was that God created men as free moral agents and can govern them only as such. For, he argued, "when God has formed moral beings, even he can govern them, as such, only by moral influence, and in accordance with the laws of mind: mere omnipotence being as irrelevant to the government of mind, as moral influence would be to the government of the material universe."[15]

Beecher and Jefferson, although bitter antagonists on the level of "specific notion," seem to me to have been in agreement on the high generality that the essential nature of Deity in his relationships with men is persuasion and not coercion—the intuition respecting "the nature of things" that the thought of Christianity has sought to incarnate in actual practice.

Eventually Beecher came to the same conclusion as did Jefferson respecting religious freedom in a commonwealth—a deduction from the common principle. But for many years—until after disestablishment in Connecticut in 1818—contrary to that principle he defended the standing order, which meant coerced tax support for his type of the public worship of God. Meanwhile Jefferson in his First Inaugural Address had noted that "every difference of opinion is not a difference of principle," and that in the political controversies "we have called by different names brethren of the same principle. We are all Republicans, we are all Federalists," that is, we are all Americans. Forty years later some Protestant evangelical churchmen were proclaiming what to them was their "new" idea that although Protestants were divided into many competing organizations they were all "Christians." And only yesterday did a significant number of Protestants and Catholics begin to refer to each other as brethren of their Christian faith.

15. Lyman Beecher, "Resources of the Adversary and Means of Their Destruction," (1827), in *Sermons Delivered on Various Occasions* (Boston: T. R. Marvin, 1828), p. 268.

I agree with what appears to have been the conclusion reached by Anson Phelps Stokes in his massive three-volume study of *Church and State in the United States*—that the high generality on which religious liberty rests is now an ineradicable part of that constellation of ideas and standards that defines the world view behind the American way of life. But for centuries, although latently ever present in the universality inherent in the Christian tradition, it was certainly not a prominent element among the specific notions that defined the sects and nations of Christendom. It did not, in Herbert Butterfield's words, get into the "majority report" of Christians.

The mainline denominations of the United States, the direct descendants of the national churches of Europe, had been formed in the old national-church crucible, and each elaborated the rationale for its sense of identity and its justification for separate existence in that context. That these national tribal cults were transplanted to what was to become the United States meant that here Christianity—"the all-embracing culture religion of the West"[16]—was poured into "sectarian" molds and hardened in those distinct but now crumbling shapes which we see in our denominations.

Because religious commitment is an all-or-nothing matter, each religious group tended to absolutize the particular tenets of its generally Christian theology and polity that distinguished it from all others. For in these its sense of peculiar and significant identity and its justification for separate existence were rooted. As L. W. Bacon noted in his *History of American Christianity,* published in 1895:

> The presumption is of course implied, if not asserted, in the existence of any Christian sect, that it is holding the absolute right and truth, or at least more nearly that than other sects; and the inference, to a religious mind, is that the right and true must, in the long run, prevail.[17]

16. Wilhelm Pauck, "Our Protestant Heritage," in *Religion and Contemporary Society,* ed. Harold Stahmer (New York: Macmillan Co., 1963), p. 92.
17. Leonard Woolsey Bacon, *A History of American Christianity* (New York: Charles Scribner's Sons, 1895), p. 404.

It is for this reason that every religious group tends to resist emphasis on the tenets it shares with all others—to resist, for example, consistent probing for the high generalities implied in such phrases as "a common core of religion," "Christianity in general," or "religion in general," or the eighteenth century's "the essentials of every religion." Because theology in the grand tradition has to do with the high generalities of Christianity and its culture, this built-in aversion to inclusive or cosmopolitan abstractions helps to explain the often-noted untheological nature of American religious groups.[18]

This innate tendency was accentuated in the United States because religious freedom put each group (now a voluntary association) in a competitive relationship with all the others, not only for the allegiance of the uncommitted in the great free market of souls, but also for those committed to other groups. Christians developed extensive programs for the conversion of Jews; Protestants maintained havens for "converted" priests; Roman Catholics publicized the conversion of prominent people from Orestes Brownson to Luci Johnson; fundamentalists tried to win liberals; liberals tried to enlighten fundamentalists; while the Unitarians almost automatically welcomed any refugee from the disciplinary action of another denomination.

Competitors, whether "selling" cigarettes or religion, are seldom inclined to stress the virtues of their competitors' claims and practices, or to dwell upon the good and valuable elements they share in common with them. Yet in the religiously pluralistic commonwealth inclusive generalities are the only viable concepts of general application. In 1675 the then Lord Baltimore noted that the first Lord Baltimore, in order to establish religious freedom in Maryland, had had to settle for "Christianity in general." And today a reference to religion in the United States cannot mean anything but religion in general, unless one is of the happy sectarian mentality of Parson Thwackum in Henry Fielding's *Tom Jones,* who

18. See, e.g.: Wilhelm Pauck, "Theology in the Life of Contemporary American Protestantism." *Shane Quarterly* 13, (1952): 37–50; Joseph Haroutunian, "Theology and American Experience," *Criterion* 3 (1964): 1–10; and John Tracy Ellis, *American Catholics and the Intellectual Life* (Chicago: Heritage Foundation, 1956).

declared, "When I mention religion I mean the Christian religion; and not only the Christian religion, but the Protestant religion; and not only the Protestant religion, but the Church of England." There are still many Parson Thwackums among the churchmen in the United States today, and some of them are highly sophisticated and very learned.

Pluralism means, then, not only the division into many different ecclesiastical organizations and theological points of view, but also a state of mind instinctively defensive of it. The resulting confusion was described by Professor Wilhelm Pauck in 1963:

> The denominations [in the U.S.] preserve and cling to special religious traditions, creeds (if they have any), liturgies, polities, moral codes, in a stubborn and even self-satisfied way, as if no other forms of Christian faith or order existed or have the right to exist. Think, for example, of the behavior of some Lutherans, Unitarians, Presbyterians, or Episcopalians, to mention only these, who stick to their own particular traditions with a dogged determination. . . . But . . . they grant to members of other denominations the right to hold and practice the same judgment concerning their beliefs, usages and conventions. Denominationalism is thus a curious combination of tolerance and intolerance. On the one hand, it reflects the exclusiveness that was characteristic of the churches when in the era prior to the establishment of religious freedom they had to conform to the requirements of religious uniformity. On the other hand, it exhibits the freedom of religious profession which was made possible when the modern state assumed a neutral attitude toward the religious faith of its members and citizens.[19]

This situation, only slightly changed by the ecumenical movement, exhibits not only the intellectual confusion, but also the continuing tension between the many particularistic and inherited conceptual orders of the sects of Christendom and that new experienced order that came with religious freedom and its consequent religious pluralism in a commonwealth. I take it that concern about this situation and an urge to do something about it provides a strong motivation for ecumenical endeavors.

But the fact that the commonwealth exists implies that at its center must lie a constellation of ideas and standards that bind its

19. Pauck, "Our Protestant Heritage," pp. 108–9.

people together—what Abraham Lincoln referred to as the "bonds of affection; the mystic chords of memory" that constitute the score for "the chorus of the Union." And it seems to me that the "bonds of affection" which bind all the heterogenous people together in such a union must somehow be more cosmopolitan, more universal, more general, than the "bonds of affection" which bind a particular group of these people together in a particular voluntary association, even though it be called a church. Will Herberg should not have been surprised to discover that the girls in that Catholic school thought of themselves as "Americans who happen to be Roman Catholics."[20] For being an American today is for most citizens a matter of providence or a happenstance of birth rooted in a choice made by an immigrant ancestor, while being a Catholic, or Presbyterian, a Baptist, an Episcopalian, or a Lutheran is a matter of voluntary choice.

Finally, then, religious pluralism means that the issue commonly referred to as being between "church" and "state" is for the church member an issue between his outlook as a citizen and his outlook as a member of a religious denomination and, by implication at least, a defender of its particularistic interpretation of the faith and order of Christians. As Loren P. Beth has argued, the "designation of our problem as 'church and state' is incomplete and misleading" because "our conflict is not merely between two institutions, but between two sides of the individual—the political and the religious."[21]

To be sure, Jesus' admonition to "Render therefore to Caesar the things that are Caesar's, and to God the things that are God's" (Matt. 22:21) still suggests an admirable guideline. But in the democratic Republic the citizen, unlike his ancestor in the Roman Empire (whether citizen or not), cannot objectify "Caesar" as the coercive power from without or from above that imposes order on the society. For under what Tocqueville has called the dogma of

20. Will Herberg, "Religion and Culture in Present-Day America," in *Roman Catholicism and the American Way of Life*, ed. Thomas T. McAvoy (Notre Dame: University of Notre Dame Press, 1960), p. 15.
21. Loren P. Beth, *The American Theory of Church and State* (Gainesville: University of Florida Press, 1958), pp. 141–42.

our democracy, that sovereignty resides in the people, the citizen participates in "Caesar" and the struggle between Caesar and God is internalized. As Albert G. Huegli noted, "In his role as a Christian the Christian citizen in a democracy confronts himself in his role as a citizen."[22] This is the main reason why designation of the issue as between "church" and "state," which projects the struggle outward and into two institutions, is misleading and distracts attention from the nature of the real problem.

This, then, to adapt Gunnar Myrdal's observation respecting what he called "the American Negro problem," is another "American dilemma." It is "a problem in the heart of the American," made manifest in the

> ever-raging conflict between, on the one hand, the valuations preserved on the general plane which we shall call the "American Creed," where the American thinks, talks, and acts under the influence of high national and Christian precepts, and, on the other hand, the valuations on the specific planes of individual and group living, where personal and local interests; economic, social, and sexual jealousies; considerations of community prestige and conformity; group prejudice against particular persons or types of people; and all sorts of miscellaneous wants, impulses, and habits dominate his outlook.[23]

It is on the level of what Myrdal calls "specific planes" that we observe the persistence of "sectarianism" which the thrust of the ecumenical and merger movements often brings to the surface.

I think I use the words *sectarian* and *sectarianism* with fair consistency and with a definiteness of meaning that I learned from those evangelical Protestant leaders of Europe and America who at the great meeting in London in August 1846 formed the Evangelical Alliances.

It has been said that next to the grace of God is the ability to see and make distinctions where differences exist. This is an aspect of the intellectual love of God. And those evangelicals saw a real

22. Albert G. Huegli, ed., *Church and State under God* (St. Louis: Concordia Publishing House, 1964), p. 436.
23. Gunnar Myrdal, *An American Dilemma: The Negro Problem and Modern Democracy* (New York: Harper & Bros., 1944), p. xlvii. In the book this passage is italicized.

difference, and made a sharp distinction, between "the church," a "denomination," and a "sect"—and between "denominationalism" and "sectarianism"—all key concepts, in the discussion of the matter before us, which today are often used interchangeably.

The phrase *the church* was recognized, not as a description of what was observed, but as a *theological assertion* of the unity of all believers in the "idea and purpose" of God, in "the mystical union" with Christ, and in "the willing and conscious bond of union" called faith." The church, the body of Christ, is one—this was the primary premise of the inherited conceptual order which they brought to the observation of the new fact of division into numerous independent religious organizations.

The pressing question, then, was, why the divisions? Because, Charles Hodge, professor of theology at Princeton, explained in a classic statement in 1873, it is not promised that "they shall be perfect [and therefore one] in knowledge." It follows that "diversity of doctrine . . . among believers is unavoidable in our imperfect state," and diversity of doctrine has led to disagreements respecting proper forms which are institutionalized in the several separate organizations.[24] From this perspective, division into numerous groups is not a sin, as some ecumenical leaders today would have it.

In this conceptual context a denomination was seen as an organized group that, accepting these premises, recognized itself as a visible but finitely limited part of the church founded upon imperfect knowledge, apprehension, and exemplification of the gospel. A denomination did not make the claim exclusively to be the church. It did not absolutize or universalize any of the particularities that distinguished it from other Christian groups.

A sect was defined by these nineteenth century evangelicals as a group that does make such claims—whether it be as small as 'the society of Sandemanian Baptists [in New York], consisting of seven

24. Charles Hodge, "The Unity of the Church Based on Personal Union with Christ," in . . . *Documents of the Sixth General Conference of the Evangelical Alliance, Held in New York, October 2–12, 1873,* ed. Philip Schaff and S. Irenaeus Prime (New York: Harper & Bros., 1874), pp. 139–44. Hereafter cited as *E. A. Conference, 1873.*

persons, two men and five women, who hold that they constitute the whole church in America,"[25] or as large as the Roman Catholic church with its millions of members. A sect based its exclusivistic claim, not on those elements it shared with all Christians, but upon those peculiarities of emphasis in doctrine and practice which distinguished it from other Christians. It universalized its particularities and viewed observance of them as necessary for salvation. It exhibited, as one evangelical said, the very human tendency of each individual "at least in thought, to hold that Christendom, to be one, must be drawn within the circle of belief in which he dwells, and which he thinks to be the very citadel of the truth of God."[26] This was sectarianism.

Denominationalism, on the other hand, was conceived as that system wherein the church—the body of Christ—was divided into discrete bodies, each denominated by a different name. Recognition of the underlying unity of the church prevented any true denomination from making the absolutistic claim exclusively to be the church. Hence, as Philip Schaff noted in 1855:

> There is a difference between denominationalism and sectarianism. The former is compatible with true catholicity of spirit [and with religious freedom]; the latter is nothing but an extended selfishness, which crops out of human nature everywhere and in all ages and conditions of the church.[27]

Here in this movement, then, we see a vigorous attempt to reconcile an inherited conceptual order of Protestant Christendom with a new and different observed and experienced order, out of which

25. "Theories of the Church," *The Biblical Repertory and Princeton Review* 18 (1846): 148. This article is a clear statement of the evangelical's doctrine of the church as distinguished from the "ritualistic" and the "rationalistic" views.
26. Eliphalet Nott Potter, "The Communion of Saints: Modes of Its Promotion and Manifestation," *E. A. Conference, 1873*, p. 156.
27. Philip Schaff, "Religion in the United States of America," in *The Religious Condition of Christendom Described in a Series of Papers Presented to the Seventh General Conference of the Evangelical Alliance, Held in Basle, 1879*, ed. J. Murray Mitchell (London: Hodder & Stoughton, 1880), p. 90.

was adumbrated a Christian theology in explanation and defense of pluralism.[28]

The denominational stance implies the eventual erosion of belief in the ultimate significance of the particularities of doctrine and practice that distinguish one Christian group from another.[29] A Presbyterian clergyman said as much in summarizing his understanding of the meaning of the organization of the Evangelical Alliances in 1846. A Christian, he said, must join a denomination, "for he is bound to belong to the Church visible, as well as to that which is invisible." But henceforth "let that connexion be on the maxim,—'Preference not exclusion.'" Exclusivistic claims were ruled out on the basis that perhaps "God can see a Christian where we cannot."[30] This is to say that a finite man must entertain the possibility that he and even his "church" may be wrong. This stance is an absolute necessity for real dialogue.

Obviously a revolutionary change in conceptual order is taking place when, for example, the mode of baptism, or the apostolic succession, or Presbyterian polity is not defended on scriptural authority and/or tradition, but adhered to as a matter of preference or taste. For this means that a member's basis for choice between the "churches" is shifted out of the realm of authority and rational deduction into the realm of taste or aesthetics. That Episcopalian felt this who is alleged to have said, in a gross popularization of a profound point, that of course there are other

28. Of course, as Winthrop S. Hudson has made clear, the evangelical stance in the nineteenth century was rooted in the revivalistic movement of the eighteenth, and before that, in the thinking of some of the Independent Divines of the seventeenth century. (*American Protestantism* [Chicago: University of Chicago Press, 1961], chap. 1, sec. 3. Note especially Hudson's quotations from Gilbert Tennent, Samuel Davies, and George Whitefield.)
I have wondered why the evangelical movement with its fine and useful distinctions became an almost forgotten chapter of American church history, and why sectarianism came so largely to prevail.
29. This was implied in both the rationalistic and the pietistic movements of the eighteenth century. This was what enabled them on the issue of religious freedom to combine against the particularistic traditionalists. See my *Lively Experiment: The Shaping of Christianity in America* (New York: Harper & Row, 1963), pp. 38–41.
30. *Evangelical Alliance: Report of the Proceedings of the Conference, Held at Freemasons' Hall, London, from August Nineteenth to September Second, Inclusive, 1846* (London: Partridge & Oakey, 1847), p. 87.

routes to heaven, but no gentleman or lady would take them. The denominational stance implies this shift.

I think that practically all the pressures of the unfolding history-that-happens, the history that can be observed in the development of the United States, have been and are on the side of the denominational stance. This is what was inherent in principle from the beginning of America's "lively experiment." Philip Schaff saw more than a hundred years ago that

> America seems destined to be the Phenix grave not only of all European nationalities, . . . but also of all European churches and sects, of Protestantism and Romanism. I cannot think, that any one of the present confessions and sects . . . will ever become excusively dominant there; but rather, that out of the mutual conflict of all something wholly new will gradually arise. [31]

The thrust of our contemporary ecumenical movement is of the same nature. "The final and terrible difficulty," wrote its outstanding historian with what sounds like an echo of Schaff's view:

> is that Churches cannot unite, unless they are willing to die. In a truly united Church, there would be no more Anglicans or Lutherans or Presbyterians or Methodists. But the disappearance from the world of those great and honoured names is the very thing that many loyal churchmen are not prepared to face. Much has already been achieved. But until Church union clearly takes shape as a better resurrection on the other side of death, the impulse towards it is likely to be weak and half-hearted. [32]

This is to say that the ecumenical movement represents now, as did the evangelical movement of the nineteenth century, a real threat to the sectarian roots of the self-identity which has characterized every Christian group. Therefore resistance to it is commensurate with the sectarianism of a group. And this is why, while on what Myrdal calls the "general plane . . . of high . . . Christian precepts" there is much grand talk of ecumenism and church unity, when representatives of two or more religious groups meet

31. Schaff, *America: A Sketch of Its Political, Social, and Religious Character*, pp. 80–81. *America . . .* was first published in 1855.
32. Ruth Rouse and Stephen Charles Neill, eds., *A History of the Ecumenical Movement 1517–1948*, 2d ed., with rev. bib. (Philadelphia: Westminster Press, 1967), p. 495.

eyeball-to-eyeball on the ecumenical or merger line they often exhibit an extreme sectarianism.[33]

Some examples drawn from a journalistic examination of church unity movements illustrate this. Roman Catholics, it was noted, now join Protestants "in confessing the 'sin' of Christian divisions, . . . and asking God to 'break our heart of stone and give us a heart able to repent.' "[34] It is recognized that "Protestant-Catholic unity can develop . . . only if both sides are receptive." I suppose that "receptivity" means that each must be willing to surrender some of the particularistic forms that distinguish it. Granted that division is sinful, as many seem to assume, this would be tangible evidence of—fruit worthy of—such repentence as is prayed for, because it is their particularities (what some call their "distinctives") that divide the Christian groups one from another.

But *can* these groups give up any of their distinctive peculiarities? In one sense, by definition *they* cannot, because for a group to relinquish what to it is a substantive point would be to lose its historical and present identity and become something different—to lose its life. So "both faiths remain adamant on matters of substance," apparently unmindful that "whoever would save his life will lose it" (Matt. 16:25). Roman Catholic leaders have insisted that their church will not yield on theological issues, for "there can be no compromise on . . . divinely revealed doctrine." A Protestant leader echoes, "We also are not interested in compromises." And W. A. Visser 't Hooft, at the time general secretary of the World Council of Churches, declared that "no serious participant in our movement wants to give up his spiritual integrity and his real convictions."

33. For examples see my "The Post-Protestant Concept and America's Two Religions," *Religion in Life* 33 (1964): 191–208.

For some American churchmen ecumenism and merger have taken their place beside "mother, home, and heaven" as things not to be criticized. It may be salutary for those insiders who believe, rightly, that "ecumenicity is a great and exciting reality in our time" to see themselves as some profane outsiders saw them in 1965 and drew their portrait in the popular journalistic venture from which I have drawn much of what follows.

34. Lee E. Dirks, ed., *Religion in Action: How America's Faiths Are Meeting New Challenges* (Silver Spring, Md.: National Observer, 1965), p. 19. The following eight quotations, i.e., down to n. 35, are taken from this work, pages 14, 16, 19, 25, 22, and 24, in that order.

Perhaps that Methodist bishop spoke with candor what many unityists unconsciously felt, who is reported to have said that "the process . . . moves from acquaintance to acceptance to affiliation and finally to assimiliation." To assimilate means to digest, and while unity is a high and impeccable idea, the fear of being digested seems often to dampen enthusiasm at the crucial point. "I have found," said another Methodist bishop, "that many will shout 'hosanna' to the vision but cry out 'crucify it' when they see what it costs." Episcopalians seem most commonly to have counted the cost in advance and to have frankly stated the price they would not pay. Typically their representatives have entered a six-denomination discussion with the flat declaration that their "delegation was required to insist on its views of the ministry." And one of their bishops blew old embers into flame by saying that "Only a jaundiced Puritan can fail to see the beauty of . . . the chain of hands down through the ages. . . . We must pool our riches," he explained, "and one of the riches we . . . have to offer is the apostolic succession." But to a Methodist this meant "admitting we've been illegitimate for 200 years" and, indicating that Methodists might resist having *their* "riches" dissolved in the Episcopalian's pool, he added, "Our success shows that we need more illegitimacy." Perhaps the layman who suggested that related denominations ought to get together "as fast as they can without waiting . . . [for the clergy to] settle knotty theological problems with remote denominations" did not understand the profound inertia lurking in such clerical jargon as "the chain of hands" and "illegitimacy."

As a layman I would have to admit that the particularities that form the foundation of sectarianism have become practically meaningless to me, and I suspect that my counterparts on the campuses and in the pews are legion. Laymen have been not just sprinkled with an ecumenical shower from above but soaked and agitated in the historical flood of religious pluralism until sectarianism has been washed out. They are ready to believe with Philip Schaff that something "wholly new will gradually arise"—and with Ronald E. Osborn that God "has permitted a common type of faith and life to emerge from the freedom and denominational variegation of

265

American Christianity."[35] For them the pressing question is: "What is that 'common type of faith and life' that God has permitted to emerge out of the American experience of Christianity?" This, I think, is the primary question confronting the denominations today.

35. Ronald E. Osborn, *The Spirit of American Christianity* (New York: Harper & Bros., 1958) pp. 137–38.

11

The Reform of the Racist Religion
of the Republic

J. EARL THOMPSON, JR.

A persistent, powerful religion of the Republic presents a formidable challenge to the administrative, intellectual, and spiritual leaders of the denominations.[1] They have to deal with a sizable proportion of their constituency whose religious loyalties are divided, often unequally, between commitments to the religion of the Republic and to their sect, and they have to reach a large number of people who are increasingly unresponsive to sectarian claims.

The religion of the Republic has generated in denominational communities a range of attitudinal responses varying from enthusiastic approval to scornful rejection. The debate has tended to polarize around two sharply divergent assessments of this religion. Its fervent defenders contend that in the main it is a creative, dynamic, and self-critical national religion that gives transcendent meaning and a high set of moral values to individual Americans and produces just, humane goals for the nation. In the other camp, its detractors condemn it as intrinsically idolatrous. Unwilling to credit the religion of the Republic with constructive moral and

---

1. In our study of the religion of the Republic, we have been helped by the following: Robert N. Bellah, "Civil Religion in America," in *The Religious Situation, 1968*, ed. Donald R. Cutler (Boston: Beacon Press, 1968), pp. 331–93; Ralph Henry Gabriel, *The Course of American Democratic Thought: An Intellectual History since 1815* (New York: Ronald Press Co., 1940); Sidney E. Mead, *The Lively Experiment: The Shaping of Christianity in America* (New York: Harper & Row, 1963); idem, "The 'Nation with the Soul of a Church,'" *Church History* 36 (1967):262–83; and Alice Felt Tyler, *Freedom's Ferment: Phases of American Social History to 1860* (Minneapolis: University of Minnesota Press, 1944).

religious resources, they inveigh against it as a perverted offshoot of the Judeo-Christian tradition with a diluted set of beliefs, an anemic moral code, and a pale conception of transcendence insufficient to give rise to a self-critical religious consciousness. Because of these distortions and deficiencies, the religion of the Republic is denounced as inimical to the proclamations and programs of the denominational religions and to the spiritual vitality and moral integrity of the country.

The argument of this essay is that the proper stance of the denominations toward the religion of the Republic should be that of sympathetic critic. They should steer a middle course between the Scylla of hostile rejection of the religion of the Republic and the Charybdis of unqualified endorsement. Their responsibility should be neither to dismiss it as of no consequence nor to enfold it in a cozy, uncritical embrace but to subject it to thorough analysis and incisive judgment. The task of the sympathetic critic of the religion of the Republic, then, should be to ferret out its commendable and condemnable ideals, values, and practices, and especially to single out the contradictions between its professions and its performances. Taking this posture, we shall offer some critical perspectives and principles on the basis of which the religion of the Republic can be purged of its perversions, disentangled from its distortions, and led back to its highest ideals. This undertaking is prompted in part by the belief that it is only through the process of continually reforming the religion of the Republic that its adherents will acquire transcendent purpose and solid moral values for their lives. Perhaps it is not overly dramatic to suggest that the hope of a just, humane, and inclusive social order in America depends in large part upon the development of a self-critical religion of the Republic; at least, this thought is eminently worth contemplating.

1

The religion of the Republic is the "national religious self-understanding" that embodies and cherishes the ideals, aspirations, and hopes that have been traditionally associated with America.[2]

2. Bellah, "Civil Religion in America," p. 341.

In their purest form the essential beliefs taught by this religion are not intrinsically idolatrous. Originating in two sources, the Enlightenment and evangelical Protestantism, these tenets combined to form the belief system of the religion of the Republic.

Here are the central beliefs that it has inculcated and celebrated. The God this religion reveres is an austere, righteous deity who sits in judgment upon the deformations and wickedness of the nation. Demanding that his people conform to the fundamental moral law of the universe, he expects them to order and conduct themselves in a virtuous, just manner and will reward them with prosperity, wealth, and happiness only if they do. Since they are *"free, rational,* and *responsible,"* they have the wherewithal to attain this level of living.[3] Progress is calculated in terms of individual moral development: "The advance of civilization . . . is the progress of virtue."[4] Americans, furthermore, are a chosen people with a divinely ordained destiny. Having delivered his chosen people from the tyranny and oppression of Europe, the God of the Republic has nurtured and guided their development until they have become the most prosperous, free, and happy people in the history of mankind. There have been national setbacks, disgraces, and tragedies—for example, the Civil War—but despite these detours God has led his people back to the superhighways of the sure fulfillment of their national destiny. While the people have been on these detours their moral fiber has purified and strengthened by sacrifice and suffering. Special privileges impose sacred responsibilities. The adherents of this religion acknowledge their obligation to share their material abundance and political wisdom with their dispossessed countrymen and with the underdeveloped nations of the world. Democracy, the political instrument by which Americans work out their destiny under God, is fair, flexible, and inclusive and can guide people of all races, nationalities, and creeds into the mainstream of American society, assuring them of equal opportunity and an impartial administration of the law. To all her citizens America guarantees the protection of the inalienable free-

3. Ralph Henry Gabriel, *Spiritual Origins of American Culture,* Hazen Pamphlets, 14 (1945), p. 9.
4. Gabriel, *The Course of American Democratic Thought,* p. 19.

doms, especially the freedom of worship and religious belief secured by the separation of church and state.

Unfortunately, the ideology of the religion of the Republic has rarely, if ever, remained free from contamination; nor has it ever been actualized in its purest form. If we were to limit our judgment strictly to the core principles of this religion, we would have to rule that they were not intrinsically idolatrous. But, having been repeatedly and even systematically violated in theory and practice, these ideals have hardly ever stayed unsullied. Alfred North Whitehead once observed that "great ideas enter into reality with evil associates and with disgusting alliances."[5] The religion of the Republic's most evil associate has been racial prejudice, and its most disgusting alliance has been with discrimination. As a result, both in its theoretical combinations and in the ways in which it has functioned in the course of our history, the religion of the Republic has been idolatrous, substituting homage to the god of racial supremacy for loyalty to the one true God. Believing in a humane creed, white Americans have systematically oppressed and brutalized black Americans. Professing an inclusive creed, whites have carefully excluded blacks from full and equal participation in our society. Confessing a just creed, whites have rarely extended equal justice to blacks. Honoring a tolerant creed, whites have denied blacks the decision-making power that could affect the character of our institutions and better their competitive position in society. By undemocratic and unjust actions white Americans have restricted the religion of the Republic almost solely to their own kind, twisting it into a racial religion. By these actions they have perverted the religion of the Republic into an arrogant white Americanism.

2

That the religion of the Republic was defiled even in its earliest formulations by racist ideas is an indisputable historical fact with which neither its defenders nor its detractors have yet come to

5. Alfred North Whitehead, *Adventures of Ideas* (New York: Macmillan Co., 1933), p. 22.

terms. The prototypal sources of this religion, the Enlightenment and evangelical Protestantism, mirror its racial distortions. This contention can be proved by presenting a brief exposition of the racial attitudes of Thomas Jefferson and Lyman Beecher, exemplars of the parent traditions of the religion of the Republic.

"We hold these truths to be self-evident, that all men are created equal, that they are endowed by their Creator with certain unalienable Rights, that among these are Life, Liberty and the pursuit of Happiness."[6] Thomas Jefferson, author of the Declaration of Independence and eloquent spokesman for the natural rights philosophy undergirding them, despised slavery, political and chattel. As a matter of fact, until the end of his life, he held that involuntary servitude is immoral and unjust. The most vigorous statement of this belief took the form of steadfast opposition to the slave trade. In composing his rough draft of the Declaration of Independence, Jefferson included a scathing condemnation of the British monarch for his involvement in the slave trade. "He has waged cruel war against human nature itself, violating it's [*sic*] most sacred rights of life & liberty in the persons of a distant people who never offended him, captivating & carrying them into slavery in another hemisphere, or to incur miserable death in their transportation thither."[7] Jefferson sought to put the American colonies on record as decrying the Crown's "piratical warfare" against and "execrable commerce" in Africans.[8] Afraid that this provision might have dangerous repercussions on chattel slavery in their regions, the delegates to the Continental Congress from South Carolina and Georgia refused to sign the document unless this section was deleted. Jefferson and his cohorts relented before this threat and sacrificed their principles on the altar of colonial unity.[9] This was

6. From the Declaration of Independence, quoted in Carl Becker, *The Declaration of Independence: A Study in the History of Political Ideas* (New York: Alfred A. Knopf, 1953), p. 186.
7. Becker, *The Declaration of Independence*, p. 147.
8. Ibid.
9. Cornel Lengyel, *Four Days in July: The Story behind the Declaration of Independence* (Garden City: Doubleday & Co., 1958).

not the last time that Jefferson temporized about slavery or exploited Negroes in order to gain economic and political benefits.

Despite its espousal of the natural rights of man, the Declaration of Independence was completely silent about the bondage of the blacks and about their future in the "land of the free." This "monstrous inconsistency"[10] has been noted many times since the eighteenth century, but never more movingly than by William Lloyd Garrison in an address to a meeting of the American Colonization Society gathered in Boston on July 4, 1829:

> Every Fourth of July, our Declaration of Independence is produced, with a sublime indignation, to set forth the tyranny of the mother country, and to challenge the admiration of the world. But what a pitiful detail of grievances does this document present, in comparison with the wrongs which our slaves endure! In the one case, it is hardly the plucking of a hair from the head; in the other, it is the crushing of a live body on the wheel—the stings of the wasp contrasted with the tortures of the Inquisition. Before God, I must say, that such a glaring contradiction as exists between our creed and practice the annals of six thousand years cannot parallel. In view of it, I am ashamed of my country. I am sick of our unmeaning declamation in praise of liberty and equality; of our hypocritical cant about the unalienable rights of man.[11]

At the beginning of the revolutionary struggle for political freedom, therefore, the jangling contradiction between the embryonic nation's professed ideals and its racial realities was evident. And it has persisted. Jefferson's attitudes toward the Negro were a faithful representation of the racial outlook of the Enlightenment, especially of the radical ambivalence of this tradition toward blacks. A slaveholder himself, Jefferson deplored slavery nonetheless and hoped that it would soon be uprooted from the soil of American society. In his *Notes on the State of Virginia,* written in 1781–82, he said, "The spirit of the master is abating, that of the slave rising from the dust, his condition mollifying, the way I hope preparing,

10. Winthrop D. Jordan, *White over Black: American Attitudes toward the Negro, 1550–1812* (Baltimore: Penguin Books, 1969), p. 289.
11. William Lloyd Garrison, quoted in Wendell Phillips Garrison and Francis Jackson Garrison, *William Lloyd Garrison* (New York: Century Co., 1885), 1:131–32.

under the auspices of heaven, for a total emancipation."[12] But, as William Cohen has pointed out, "his libertarian views about slavery tended to be mere intellectual abstractions."[13] Owning more than 180 slaves and entirely dependent upon this enforced labor for his high standard of living and social position, Jefferson was never willing to manumit substantial numbers of his slaves, even in his will. According to Winthrop Jordan, "he never doubted that his monetary debts constituted a more immediate obligation than manumission."[14] For reasons of political and economic expediency, then, he remained a slave owner.

Jefferson's intellectual abhorrence of slavery stemmed from several complex sources. In the first place, he could not square slavery with his natural rights philosophy; the theoretical contradiction was simply too obvious to conceal from himself. Even though the Monticello master did not treat his Negroes with the dignity and respect befitting human beings, he never for a moment doubted that they were human beings invested with inalienable rights— liberty among them—by the Creator. To enslave anyone, he admitted, was to deprive him of his natural rights and to engage in a moral and political evil that was contemptible and condemnable.

Another element influencing Jefferson's negative view of slavery was the deleterious effects it seemed to have upon the character of white men. Studying the master-slave relationship, he concluded that a social system in which one class had virtually life-and-death authority over another class fostered despotic attitudes in the former and unmanly submission in the latter. "The whole commerce between master and slave," he bemoaned, "is a perpetual exercise of the most boisterous passions, the most unremitting despotism on the one part, and degrading submissions on the other."[15] These attitudes were transmitted by the propensity of children to imitate their parents. "The parent storms, the child looks on, catches the lineaments of wrath, puts on the same airs in

12. Thomas Jefferson, *Notes on the State of Virginia* (Philadelphia, 1801), p. 322.
13. William Cohen, "Thomas Jefferson and the Problem of Slavery," *Journal of American History* 56 (1969): 506.
14. Jordan, *White over Black*, p. 431.
15. Thomas Jefferson, quoted in ibid., p. 319.

the circle of smaller slaves, gives a loose to the worst of passions, and thus nursed, educated, and daily exercised in tyranny cannot but be stamped by it with odious peculiarities."[16] Jefferson declared, furthermore, that besides despotism slavery bred indolence among slaveholders. "In a warm climate, no man will labour for himself who can make another labour for him. This is so true, that of the proprietors of slaves a very small proportion indeed are ever seen to labour."[17] The moral deterioration of the white community imperiled its liberties, claimed Jefferson. If masters refused to respect the natural rights of their slaves, what would stand in the way of masters' depriving their own kind of their basic rights?

And if white men did not strip other white men of their liberties, there was a strong likelihood that God would. The last reason that Jefferson hated slavery was his belief that the righteous Lord of the world would probably not permit a gross injustice like slavery to go unrequited.

> Indeed I tremble for my country when I reflect that God is just: that his justice cannot sleep for ever: that considering numbers, nature and natural means only, a revolution of the wheel of fortune, an exhange of situation is among possible events: that it may become probable by supernatural interference! The almighty has no attribute which can take side with us in such a contest.[18]

Beneath his aversion to slavery was also a nagging fear that slave rebellions could conceivably decimate segments of the white population and topple the towering achievements of American civilization.

Actually Jefferson's loathing of slavery and admirable opinions of human freedom had very little practical effect upon his conduct as a slave owner; on the contrary, his racial arrogance accounted in great measure for his proslavery behavior. Cohen is correct: "From an intellectual point of view, his strong 'suspicion' that the Negroes were innately inferior is probably of great significance in explaining his ability to ignore his own strictures about their rights."[19] Based upon what he considered were careful observa-

16. Ibid., p. 320.
17. Ibid., p. 321.
18. Ibid.
19. Cohen, "Thomas Jefferson," p. 525.

tions and, indeed, covering his racism with the mantle of scientific objectivity, he conjectured that the white man was by nature far superior to the black man: "I advance it therefore as a suspicion only, that the blacks, whether originally a distinct race, or made distinct by time and circumstances, are inferior to the whites in the endowments both of body and mind."[20] On the physical level he was impressed by the "superior beauty" of the white race, set off by its interesting variety of hues, its long, fine hair, and its "elegant symmetry of form," and by the white race's possession of the passions of grief and affection in a refined form.[21] On the mental level he was convinced that the white man surpassed the black man in reason and imagination but not in memory. These conclusions did not imply that the black man was subhuman, for he was endowed with the fundamental constitutive principle of humanity, the moral sense. Jefferson explained the slaves' penchant for thievery by his oppressive environmental circumstances, not by "any depravity of the moral sense."[22] But he drew back from expounding the blacks' mental underdevelopment according to the same logic. By his canons of judgment, there was nothing physically or intellectually beautiful about the "eternal monotony" of black.[23] And throughout his career he held firmly to the view that, as regards the blacks' inferiority, "it is not their condition . . . but nature" which is responsible.[24]

For Jefferson, furthermore, the Negro—slave or free—was a malevolent influence upon America. Jefferson's overriding concern was the welfare of white America. "With slavery's effect on black men he simply was not overly concerned." [25] Since he was sure that "slavery was a blight on the white community," he worried that keeping blacks in bondage would only endanger the moral and political integrity of the nation.[26] But he was no more enthusiastic about freeing his or anyone's slaves. Instead, he reckoned

20. Jefferson, *Notes*, p. 281.
21. Ibid., pp. 270–71.
22. Ibid., p. 279.
23. Ibid., p. 270.
24. Ibid., p. 278.
25. Jordan, *White over Black*, p. 433.
26. Ibid.

that the "unfortunate difference of colour, and perhaps of faculty, is a powerful obstacle to the emancipation of these people. Many of their advocates, while they wish to vindicate the liberty of human nature are anxious also to preserve its dignity and beauty." [27]

Jefferson's assumption was "that Negroes were members of a race so alien and inferior that there was no hope that whites and blacks could coexist side by side on terms of equality." [28] In fact, the possibility that, once free, the black man might claim a fair share of the American birthright of equality of opportunity repelled him. Believing that emancipated blacks had no place in the unfolding destiny of America, Jefferson could hardly entertain the notion of freedmen's aspiring to social and political equality with the whites. The history of American slavery, he rationalized, stood in the way.

> Deep rooted prejudices entertained by the whites; ten thousand recollections, by the blacks, of the injuries they have sustained; new provocations; the real distinctions which nature has made; and many other circumstances, will divide us into parties, and produce convulsions, which will probably never end but in the extermination of the one or the other race.[29]

The promises of American freedoms, therefore, could not safely be offered to the blacks. Jefferson succored his conscience by taking refuge in proposing various colonization schemes designed to remove freedmen to some distant region in North America or Africa far away from the lure of establishing social relations with whites and of intermarrying with them. "When freed," he wrote, "he is to be removed beyond the reach of mixture." [30] Until that new day, however, Jefferson, the apostle of freedom, chose to keep his slaves imprisoned in involuntary servitude at Monticello and to reap the fruits of their labors.

3

Jefferson was not alone in imputing an inferiority and baseness to the Negro and in desiring to withhold from him full and fair participation in American society.

27. Jefferson, *Notes,* p. 282.
28. Cohen, "Thomas Jefferson," p. 514.
29. Jefferson, *Notes,* p. 269.
30. Ibid., p. 282.

Jefferson's opinion of the Negro was widely shared by the church-men of his generation, who in general displayed more concern for the sensitivity of the slaveholders than for the condition of the slaves. They agreed with Jeffersonian humanitarians that the Negro was totally unfit for democratic society and feared lest an ignorant and vicious colored population destroy white freedom.[31]

This is a fairly accurate description of the racial outlook of Lyman Beecher, Congregational and Presbyterian preacher, theological seminary president, and moral crusader. He shared many of Jefferson's racial viewpoints, including some untidy ambivalences.

Beecher's earliest racial ideas surfaced in connection with his interest in and support of the American Colonization Society. This voluntary benevolent organization was started in 1817 for the purpose of expatriating free Negroes to Africa. The society's overly optimistic hope was that their movement would encourage slave owners to manumit their slaves to be returned to their home-land. Beecher was active in the foundational stages of this move-ment as a consultant to Samuel J. Mills, one of its architects and martyrs. Always a devoted believer in and forthright exponent of the cause of colonization, Beecher gave it invaluable public en-dorsement. Addressing a gathering of colonizationists in Pittsburgh in 1836, he summarized his abiding faith in their mission. "In its commencement it was God's Society; in its progress it has been God's Society; and the station it now occupies in the midst of all the difficulties which have grown out of inexperience, and the peculiar nature of the subject, shows it to be God's Society; and so does its success in Africa." [32]

Committed to colonization, Beecher was no friend of slavery. He assailed it as "wrong, and a great national sin and national calamity." [33] Unequivocal about the fact that involuntary servitude was a violation of the blacks' natural rights, he was equivocal about whether or not slaveholding was a personal sin. By refrain-ing from labeling slavery a personal sin, he infuriated abolitionists.

31. John L. Thomas, *The Liberator: William Lloyd Garrison* (Boston: Little, Brown, & Co., 1963), p. 94.
32. Lyman Beecher, in *African Repository and Colonial Journal* 12 (1836): 205–6.
33. Ibid., 10 (1834): 281.

They sensed that he was not nearly as zealous in his advocacy of the cause of the slave as he was in his support of the temperance movement and the Sabbath observance. This tepid commitment to the liberation of the blacks is partly understandable in terms of his belief that many complex forces were combining to bring a quick end to slavery.

> In our own country, it is manifest that slavery must terminate quickly; and we trust that before the close of the present century, the reproach will be wiped away. Our free institutions, public sentiment, the climate, and the depreciation of slave labor in some states,—in others, the exhaustion of the soil, and in all, the growing knowledge, impatience, inutility and peril of the slave population—the increase of emigration, from considerations of conscience or fear or necessity, and the existing or fast approaching emancipation of the colored race in the Islands, in Mexico, and in many of the non-slaveholding states, all declare the termination of the relations of master and slave to be near.[34]

Meanwhile, Beecher was constantly hunting for the most expedient and expeditious way to assist this process, and he deplored any strategy or organization that jeopardized the society's methods of liberating the slaves. He had in mind, of course, the abolitionists.

Wishing to live in peace with abolitionists and to safeguard evangelical unity, he proposed that the two groups cooperate in their respective tasks of emancipating and expatriating the blacks: "Let the abolitionist press abolition, not seek to destroy the colonizationist; and the colonizationist, let him press still harder colonization, since that is what he is engaged in. Let each do his own work, as a coadjutor of the other in a common cause." [35] In his judgment colonization, not abolition, was the most practicable means of freeing the slaves from their degrading bondage and of furnishing them with the "blessings and privileges of honorable citizenship and Christianity." [36] These blessings were to be enjoyed, however, not in America but in Africa. Beecher was nearly

34. Ibid., p. 279.
35. Lyman Beecher, "Union of Colonizationists and Abolitionists," *Spirit of the Pilgrims* 6 (1833):400.
36. Ibid., p. 396.

ecstatic about the prospect of having freedmen—educated, civilized, and Christianized—extricate Africa from the quagmire of ignorance, barbarism, and paganism. He envisaged this mission to Africa as a crucial campaign against political and religious oppression that would soon end in the final triumph of Christianity and the inauguration of the millennial age.

> The emancipation of them [Africans] is connected with the emancipation of all nations—with their emancipation too from religious and political delusion, from ignorance, degradation, vice, immorality and debasement; it is a part of that grand achievement by which the world is to be regenerated, and in the accomplishment of which, the whole human family is to be carried forward to the acme of perfection.[37]

Lurking in the shadows of Beecher's sanguine expectations for colonization was his dread of the precarious consequences for emancipated blacks themselves and for America if they were not returned to Africa. The common assumption of the colonizationists was that the only alternative to expatriation was an amalgamation of the races. This possibility both horrified and revolted Beecher.

> I know it is said the slave may remain in this country, although emancipated, and so we have no need of colonization; but the idea of their remaining and amalgamating with the whites, is a wild chimera, fit only for the brain of a zealot or an enthusiast of the most visionary character.[38]

Realistic in his appraisal of the pervasiveness and tenacity of racial prejudice in America, he doubted that it could ever be conquered, and he warned that it was not expedient even to try. The blacks had been held down so long in moral and intellectual deprivation that herculean efforts to uplift them would result in their attaining only a level of "doubtful mediocrity." [39] "Ought they to be satisfied with an elevation so low and privileges so meager and doubtful, compared with the blessings of a distinct nationality [in Africa]?" [40] From the airy heights of his paternalism, Beecher was

37. Ibid., p. 398.
38. Ibid.
39. Beecher, in *African Repository* 10:282.
40. Ibid.

confident that they would not be content with anything less than a new life in Africa for their children and themselves.

The champion of colonization thought that the blacks had no worthwhile future in America as long as racial prejudice prevailed and that America would have no security as long as blacks made the futile attempt to come up to the cultural level of the white society. Absolutely certain that the successful outcome of the American experiment of republicanism pivoted upon the development of an informed, virtuous electorate, Beecher doubted that the foundations of the national freedoms could withstand an influx of benighted freedmen. As far as Beecher was concerned, the Republic was already threatened by the onslaught of white immigrant Roman Catholics, who were allegedly antipathetic to democracy, and by the drift of white pioneers to the western frontiers, which were supposedly perilously close to reverting to barbarism. If blacks were allowed to claim the privileges of American citizenship, they would probably tip the scales against the nation's religious and political liberties. National security necessitated, therefore, that they be shipped back to Africa. In short, reasoned Beecher, they were not wanted in America; they could not be accommodated by the nation's civil and religious institutions; and they had to be denied the blessings of the American way of life for their own good and the preservation and prosperity of God's American Israel.

These insights into Beecher's racial notions clarify certain dimensions of his ambiguous relationship with the abolitionist students at the infant Lane Seminary, of which Beecher was president, in 1834. This important incident in the history of abolition further underscored Beecher's ambivalent attitude toward the Negro. Led by Theodore Weld, the Lane students, against the faculty's recommendation to postpone it indefinitely, engaged in a protracted discussion of the principles and programs of colonization and abolition. Before the debate began, few students were abolitionists. Yet this inquiry meeting, stretching over seventeen evenings, culminated in an almost unanimous decision of the students in favor of immediate emancipation without expatriation.

Dialogue gave way to practical involvement. Soon many of the Lane abolitionists began to tackle the religious and intellectual problems of the free Negroes of Cincinnati. Going into the black community, they started Sunday schools, Bible classes, a debating society, and a lyceum. In the course of their work, the students had frequent social contacts with the freedmen, visiting, eating, and even boarding with them. Weld remembered, "If I slept in the City it was in their homes. If I attended parties, it was *theirs—weddings — theirs — Funerals — theirs — Religious meetings — theirs —* Sabbath schools — Bible classes — theirs."[41] This social intercourse was prompted as much by solid conviction as by expediency. The students declared:

> It is fundamental to our principles to treat men according to their character without respect to condition or complexion. Thus we have learned the law of love. Thus we would act against the pride of caste.[42]

The respectable white citizens of this "Southern city on free soil" reacted in anger.[43] Rumors began to fly about moral indiscretions of the Lane students. It soon became apparent to the faculty and trustees that the labors of the students had "rendered the institution an object of intolerable odium and indignation." [44] During the summer vacation while Beecher was in the East raising funds, the Lane trustees, without consulting him, suppressed the seminary's Abolition Society and caused the students to withdraw from Lane.

Beecher's response to this heavyhanded treatment of the Lane abolitionists is puzzling. There is evidence that he purposely avoided returning to Lane, at Weld's request, to head off the trustees, but there is also evidence to confirm that when he came back in the fall he tried to mediate between the contending factions and pull off a rapprochement that would have kept the students in seminary. His belated attempt at reconciliation was ineffective,

41. Theodore Weld, quoted in Benjamin P. Thomas, *Theodore Weld: Crusader for Freedom* (New Brunswick: Rutgers University Press, 1950), p. 73.
42. "Statement of the Faculty Concerning the Late Differences at Lane Seminary," *Liberator,* January 17, 1835.
43. Thomas, *Theodore Weld,* p. 44.
44. "Statement of the Faculty" (see n. 42 above).

and he lost a group of unusually mature, creative, and fervent students.

Many factors converged to form the matrix of Beecher's decision: his ambivalent attitude toward abolition; his thinly disguised resentment of Weld's popularity and power among the students, mixed with a genuine respect for his ability; his impatience with student insubordination; and his natural reluctance to alienate generous benefactors. But looming above these was what the students called "the great stone of stumbling to the community," [45] namely, "the doctrine and practice of immediate [social] intercourse irrespective of color." [46] Beecher and Lane's authorities simply would not tolerate whites fraternizing with blacks because it would inevitably lead to "promiscuity and mongrelization." [47] Social intercourse prescribed by the abolitionists paved the way to social equality, and social equality was the end of the road for republican liberties. The degree of Beecher's hostility toward the abolitionists became apparent in 1838.

> I regard the whole abolition movement, under its most influential leaders, with its distinctive maxims and modes of feeling, . . . as [a] signal instance of infatuation permitted by Heaven for purposes of national retribution. God never raised up such men as [William Lloyd] Garrison, and others like him, as the ministers of his mercy for purposes of peaceful reform, but only as the fit and fearful ministers of his vengeance upon a people incorrigibly wicked.[48]

Beecher, therefore, set his face against any danger to the holy mission of democratic America, even if to do so involved closing the blacks off from participating in that democratic experiment—as it did.

Thomas Jefferson and Lyman Beecher typified the *dominant* ethos of the two primary sources of the religion of the Republic. Both the Enlightenment and evangelical Protestantism were equiv-

---

45. Ibid.
46. Ibid.
47. Bertram Wyatt-Brown, *Lewis Tappan and the Evangelical War against Slavery* (Cleveland: Press of Case-Western Reserve University, 1969), p. 177.
48. Lyman Beecher, *The Autobiography of Lyman Beecher*, ed. Barbara M. Cross (Cambridge, Mass.: Harvard University Press, Belknap Press, 1961). 2:321.

ocal about slavery and about the role of the freedmen in America. While abhorring civil and religious oppression bent on preventing people from determining their own destinies, both traditions actually excluded the blacks from the rights and responsibilities of American citizenship. While denouncing tyrannical government, both deprived the Negroes of economic and political power, the most effective means of redressing their grievances. While deploring ignorance and immorality as inimical to the peace and prosperity of the nation, both failed to supply the blacks with education and religious instruction. While regretting divisive racial prejudice, neither did very much to combat it. While giving lip service to the natural rights of all men, both rejected the notion that the blacks had the right to enjoy social equality with the whites. While proclaiming America as mankind's last, best hope, both were certain that America held out little hope for Negroes. These two traditions, therefore, shaped American republicanism as a government of whites, by whites, and for whites.

4

If the religion of the Republic is to be reformed, it will have to be freed from the idolatry of racial supremacy. One way of beginning this process is by the instrumentality of black studies. The standard line is that these disciplines will assist blacks to overcome their inferiority complex and attain a secure sense of racial identity,[49] but this argument can be inverted and applied quite as legitimately to whites. The country's racist heritage has deadened the moral sensitivities of whites, dulled their intellectual acumen, and distorted their racial self-image to such a degree that they have been unable to face squarely their racial arrogance. In re-

49. For examples, consult Eugene D. Genovese, "Black Studies: Trouble Ahead," *Atlantic* 223 (1969): 37–41; W. Arthur Lewis, "Black Power and the American University," *University: A Princeton Quarterly* 40 (1969): 8–12; Henry Pachter, "Teaching Negro History," *Dissent*, March-April 1969, pp. 151–55; DeVere E. Pentony, "The Case for Black Studies," *Atlantic* 223 (1969): 81–82, 87–89; Armstead L. Robinson, Craig C. Foster, and Donald H. Ogilvie, eds., *Black Studies in the University: A Symposium* (New Haven: Yale University Press, 1969); and Peter Schrag, "The New Black Myths," *Harper's Magazine* 238 (1969): 37–42.

spect to their overbearing racial pride, therefore, whites need to reconsider their own identity. Surprisingly, very few commentators have mentioned the values of black studies for whites even though whites have a much more desperate need for the incorporation of black studies in formal and informal educational programs than blacks and stand to gain more than blacks. Plagued by a swollen conception of the supremacy of the white race and by a sordid tradition of shaping their racial dignity by inflicting indignities upon other races, whites stand to gain a more wholesome racial identity and integrity.

Pregnant with creative possibilities, then, black studies can certainly contribute to halting the degeneration of the religion of the Republic, to the renewing of the prophetic spirit of this religion, and to the rekindling of the commitment of its supporters to its lofty ideals. They can exert this reforming influence in several interrelated ways. White Americans' ignorance of black history, black culture, and black social psychology is as inexcusable as it is appalling. Black studies can fill up this knowledge void. Forcing whites to come to grips with the hard, often painful details of this history, black studies can lessen the propensity of whites to view the past according to their desires and fantasies. I. A. Newby is right in his assertion that

> the white American needs a more balanced view of racial history, of racial differences, of race itself. He sorely needs a better understanding of racism, the mechanics of racial discrimination, and how these have operated historically to elevate white and repress blacks. He needs, in other words, a generous dose of racial realism and modesty.[50]

Satisfying these needs, black studies can open whites to the ugly truth about themselves as haughty oppressors of the black minority in the country. If imagination buckles under the weight of comprehending the whites' brutalization of blacks, black studies can aid whites to begin to perceive the enormity of their crimes. The main reason for exposing the extent of whites' exploitation of blacks is not to indulge in morbid curiosity or to engage in self-

50. I. A. Newby, "Historians and Negroes," *The Journal of Negro History* 54 (1969):33.

flagellation but to engender in the religion of the Republic what Saint Paul calls "godly grief" which "produces a repentance that leads to salvation and brings no regret" (2 Cor. 7:10*a*). The pursuit of black studies, therefore, can guide whites to the altar of repentance of their personal and corporate sin against the blacks.

By no means is it fanciful to ponder whether or not black studies represent the great black hope for the religion of the Republic in a society that is being broken apart on the rack of racism, poverty, and militarism, for the way to national reconciliation and unity may very well be hidden in the history of Negroes. Martin Luther King, Jr., declared that precisely because of the black condition of agelong exploitation, blacks "bring a special spiritual and moral contribution to American life—a contribution without which America cannot survive." [51] And Vincent Harding has suggested that by their suffering and humiliation blacks have elucidated the true meaning of being a chosen people.[52] Perhaps, being instructed by a common past, Americans will soon realize that even as blacks and whites have been "bound together in a single garment of destiny," even so they have been chosen together to usher in a reign of peace and justice for all.[53]

51. Martin Luther King, Jr., quoted in *Playboy* 16 (1969):231
52. Vincent Harding, "The Uses of the Afro-American Past," *Negro Digest* 17 (1968): 83–84.
53. Martin Luther King, Jr., *Where Do We Go from Here: Chaos or Community?* (New York: Harper & Row, 1967) p. 61.

Contributors

JOHN F. WILSON is associate professor of religion at Princeton University. He contributed to *Church and State in American History* (Boston: D. C. Heath & Co., 1965), a volume for which he also served as editor.

ROBERT MICHAELSEN is professor of religious studies at the University of California, Santa Barbara. Most recent among his publications is *Piety in the Public School: Trends and Issues in the Relationship between Religion and the Public School in the United States* (New York: Macmillan Co., 1970).

THOMAS T. MCAVOY, C.S.C. died in 1969 after nearly forty years' study of American Catholic history. Among his books are *The Great Crisis in American Catholic History, 1895–1900* (Chicago: Henry Regnery Co., 1957) and *The Formation of the American Catholic Minority, 1820–1860* (Philadelphia: Fortress Press, 1967).

DOROTHY DOHEN is associate professor of sociology at Fordham University. She is the editor of *Sociological Analysis: A Journal in the Sociology of Religion* and the author of *Nationalism and American Catholicism* (New York: Sheed & Ward, 1967).

JACOB B. AGUS is professor of rabbinic Judaism at the Reconstructionist Rabbinical College, Philadelphia, and visiting professor of religion at Temple University. He is also a rabbi in Baltimore, Maryland, and the author of *The Evolution of Jewish Thought: From Biblical Times to the Opening of the Nineteenth Century* (New York: Abelard-Schuman, 1960) and the two-volume *Meaning of Jewish History* (New York: Abelard-Schuman, 1964).

JAMES H. SMYLIE is professor of American church history at Union Theological Seminary in Richmond, Virginia. His doctoral dissertation at Princeton Theological Seminary dealt with "American Clergymen and the Constitution of the United States of America, 1780–1796."

ELWYN A. SMITH is professor of religious studies and vice president for student affairs of Temple University. Co-editor of *Journal of Ecumenical Studies,* he is also the author of *The Presbyterian Ministry in American Culture: A Study in Changing Concepts, 1700–1900* (Philadelphia: Westminster Press, 1962) and *Church and State in Your Community* (Philadelphia: Westminster Press, 1963).

J. F. MACLEAR is professor of history at the University of Minnesota in Duluth. Two of his published essays relate directly to the concern of this present book: " 'The Heart of New England Rent,' " *Mississippi Valley Historical Review,* March 1956, and " 'The True American Union' of Church and State," *Church History,* March 1959.

JAMES LUTHER ADAMS is professor at the Andover Newton Theological School. Among his many publications is *Paul Tillich's Philosophy of Culture, Science, and Religion* (New York: Harper & Row, 1965).

SIDNEY E. MEAD is professor of religion in American history at the University of Iowa. He is the author of *Nathaniel William Taylor, 1786–1858: A Connecticut Liberal* (Chicago: University of Chicago Press, 1942) and *The Lively Experiment: The Shaping of Christianity in America* (New York: Harper & Row, 1963).

J. EARL THOMPSON, JR., is associate professor of church history at the Andover Newton Theological School. He is the author of "Black Studies and White Americanism," *Andover Newton Quarterly,* November 1969.

Index of Names

Index of Names

291

Index of Subjects

Index of Subjects

Lamentabile, 70
Lane Seminary, 280
La Verité, 64
League of Women Voters, 241
Lincoln's Birthday, 4
Lithuanians, 99
Little Rock, Arkansas, 53
Liubavich Hasidic Judaism, 107
Longinqua Oceani, 61
L' Osservatore Romano, 84
Lutherans, 78, 118, 121, 124, 239, 258

Manhattan College, 80
Marxism, 108
Maryland, 45, 117, 119, 129, 131
Massachusetts, 22, 31, 117, 119–121, 123, 124, 127, 128, 130, 154–157, 162, 167, 174
Massachusetts Baptist Domestic Missionary Society, 227
Massachusetts Missionary Society, 227
Massachusetts Peace Society, 238
Memorial Day, 2, 3, 4
Methodists, 31, 134, 135, 138, 141, 156, 184, 265
Metropolitan, 49
Mexicans, 99
Millenialism, 178–216
Milwaukee, Wisconsin, 55
Minnesota, 59
Missionary Society of Connecticut, 227
Modernism, 70, 73
Mormonism, viii, 33, 184

Nancy, France, 64
Nashville, Tennessee, 36
National Catholic War Council, 69
National Catholic Welfare Conference, 71, 74
National Catholic Welfare Council, 71
National Education Association, 23, 24, 36
Negroes, 52, 99, 272, 274, 275, 276, 281, 283, 285
New Amsterdam, 100
New England, 18, 126, 127, 129, 130, 135, 140, 141, 154, 155, 158, 160–162, 167, 168, 175, 176, 188, 226
New Hampshire, 117, 128, 156
New Hampshire Missionary Society, 227
New Jersey, 117
New Scholasticism, 73
New York, 78, 117, 119
New York Christian Union, 32
New York Herald, 58
New York, New York, 106, 143
New York Review, 68, 70
Niagara River, 100
North American Review, 66
North Carolina, 117
Notre Dame University, 75
Nuns, 78, 84

Ohio, 27, 28
Oregon, 30, 41
Orthodox Judaism, 77, 102, 103, 105–107, 109, 110

Quanta Cura, 50

Palestine, 101
Papal infallibility, 52, 53
Paris, France, 61
Parochial schools, 36, 37, 38, 50, 53, 59, 60, 67, 72
Pascendi, 70, 73
Pastoral and Homiletic Review, 73
Paulists, 62
Peace Corps, 85
Pelagianism, 158, 164
Pennsylvania, 117, 149
Peoria, Illinois, 37
Philadelphia, 56, 69, 116, 148
Philippines, 69
Pittsburgh Platform, 101
Pluralism, 225, 247, 251, 257, 265
Poland, 95
Populists, 67
Presbyterians, 31, 126, 129, 131, 134, 135, 137, 139–152, 159, 184, 239, 258, 262
Protestantism, viii, 4, 6, 18, 24, 26, 28, 31–35, 37, 38, 48, 49, 51, 55, 78, 83, 85–87, 99, 116–153, 156, 169, 178, 183, 185, 242, 254, 256, 264, 269, 271, 282
Province of New York, Roman Catholic Church, 66
Public schools, viii, 8, 9, 22–26, 28–32, 34–43
Puerto Rico, 86
Puritanism, viii, 6, 140, 143, 144, 156, 159, 184

Readers's Digest, 77
Reconstructionist movement in Judaism, 111, 112
Reform movement in Judaism, 100–107, 111
Reformation, 185, 199, 247
Reformed Dutch, 141, 150
Rerum Novarum, 70
Review of Politics, 73
Revivalism, 196, 239
Rhode Island, 117
Roman Catholic Church, 4, 5, 24, 26, 27, 32–38, 45–93, 99, 158, 176, 179, 213, 231, 242, 247, 254, 256, 258, 264
Roman empire, 17, 248, 258
Rome, 15, 56, 57, 64, 65, 71–73, 88
Russia, 99

Sacred Congregation of Propaganda, 35, 53, 56, 57
Saint Bernard's Seminary, Rochester, New York, 68
Saint Charles Seminary, Philadelphia, 68

295